Participatory Action Research

SUNY Series, Teacher Preparation and Development
Alan R. Tom, Editor

PARTICIPATORY ACTION RESEARCH

International Contexts and Consequences

EDITED BY

Robin McTaggart

State University of New York Press

© 1997 State University of New York

For information, address State University of New York
Press, State University Plaza, Albany, N.Y., 12246

Production by Diane Ganeles
Marketing by Hannah J. Hazen

Library of Congress Cataloging-in-Publication Data

Participatory action research : international contexts and
    consequences / Robin McTaggart, editor.
        p.   cm. — (SUNY series, teacher preparation and development)
    Includes bibliographical references (p.   ) and index.
    ISBN 0-7914-3533-4 (HC : alk. paper). — ISBN 0-7914-3534-2 (PB :
alk. paper)
    1. Action research in education—Cross-cultural studies.
I. McTaggart, Robin. II. Series: SUNY series in teacher preparation
and development.
LB1028.24.P36 1997
370'.72—dc21   96-52807
                                                                    CIP

10 9 8 7 6 5 4 3 2 1

Contents

Acknowledgments

This book has been gestating for a long time. Some authors were extremely patient as the collection slowly took shape. Others struggled to produce texts under physically difficult circumstances, without the technology that now characterizes text production in more advantaged institutional settings. Text production itself is a preoccupation of some forms of institutional life that reward publication. So, while reading the insightful words of several of the contributors, remember that requests for documentation sometimes are an imposition on those people who spend their lives working closely with the most disenfranchised members of the world community.

The English language is not the first language of several of the contributors. This is another of the unfortunate impositions monolingual people such as myself make on friends and colleagues. I am grateful to these contributors for their tolerance and trust that our editing has not detracted from their intended meanings.

Several colleagues also have been very helpful. As always, I thank Stephen Kemmis and Colin Henry for their years of collaboration on the ideas and practice of participatory action research. But I am also grateful for the particular examples set by Yoland Wadsworth, Marie Brennan, Lynton Brown, Ruth Hoadley, and Leon White.

I would also like to thank Andrea Dunn, Fran Dickson, and Renate Moles of Deakin University who helped with the typing, scanning, and translation of some texts from original (and not very compatible) computing systems.

CHAPTER 1

Reading the Collection

Robin McTaggart

Participatory action research might be described as a broad church, movement, or family of activities. Each term is appropriate in its own way. The word *church* probably connotes community, solidarity, and commitment; all are necessary to carry the arguments to confront the psychologizing and sociologizing of research and method and their engagement with social life. The term *church* also invokes questions of ethics, morality, values, and interest that attend the research act, which is important. Participatory action research is also a 'movement' for reasons foreshadowed: it expresses a recognition that all research methodologies are implicitly political in character, defining a relationship of advantage and power between the researcher and the researched. What counts as research is not merely a matter of elegant argument about methodology; social research is also about the politics of having arguments heard, a precursor to their being understood and accepted. Because participatory action researchers sought to redefine the often privileged relation of the researcher to the researched, the vindication of participatory action research methodology required more than the validity of arguments to achieve acceptance by the research establishments it confronted and by the people it claimed to support. Describing participatory action research as a 'family' was suggested to me by Susan Noffke, a historian and an action researcher from the United States, for the humanistic and political reasons the term evokes.

The term *participatory action research* describes what I see as a convergence of traditions in certain kinds of action research and participatory research. The addition of the term *participatory* to action research is now necessary to distinguish authentic action research from the miscellaneous array of research types that fall under the descriptor 'action research' when data bases are surveyed. Those data bases show that the term *action research* is used to describe almost every research effort and method under the sun that attempts to inform action in some way. This might perhaps exclude linguistic analyses of ancient Etruscan funeral orations, but it gives little guidance about what

1

action research means in the terms intended by its originators, for whom participation—people doing research for themselves—was a *sine qua non* of action research.

Perhaps it is less necessary to add the word *action* to participatory research, because both definitionally and practically participatory research usually has been oriented to actions that people might take themselves to improve the conditions of their lives. Nevertheless, there are many extremely weak versions of 'participation' in research efforts that claim the name. Inserting the term *action* is important to the extent that it reminds people that it is participants' own activities which are meant to be informed by the ongoing inquiry, not merely the future research directions of external researchers. For several reasons, including perhaps the somewhat ambiguous one of legitimation, there has been considerable willingness in the participatory research movement to recognize the commonality of interest between participatory researchers and action researchers.

The collection of essays presented in this book illustrates some of the commonalities and differences between the theories, practices, and forms of organization of participatory action research in different countries. When I asked authors to contribute, I was explicit about inviting them to tell their stories of action research in their own ways. I want also to be explicit here regarding how I asked authors to contribute to the collection, how I saw it shaping up, and, in keeping with the aspirations of action research itself, how I documented my own work while trying to ensure that contributors wrote in terms of their own experience, but with a collective as well as an individual purpose.

Inviting Participants

I circulated a paper with the title "Principles for Participatory Action Research" with the invitations to contribute so people knew my thoughts regarding participatory action research. An edited version of that paper is included as chapter 2. I said then:

> I send it not to *prescribe* the nature of participatory action research, but to let contributors know what I think, and to give all authors a common point of reference. . . But again, I do not want to steer too much what contributors think it important to say.

I explained that the purpose of the collection was to document the nature of participatory action research in a variety of historical, political, and cultural contexts. It was obviously possible to write a whole book about *each* of these three influences on participatory action research, so authors were invited to select key aspects and place appropriate emphasis on history, politics, and culture for their own cases.

The Suggested Thematic Guidelines

I knew that contributions would range across several different substantive fields of inquiry and endeavor, as well as across widely differing contexts, and that this would create an issue of the conceptual unity of the collection. I suggested guidelines that I thought were directed at achieving that unity without stifling the creative hand of the contributors. I thought it absolutely important that the guidelines were not slavishly followed, and said so. Some of my suggestions were simply practical precautions for clarity, but, largely, they expressed thematic concerns that papers might approach, perhaps even in quite oblique ways.

Substantive fields of inquiry. By this, I meant fields such as agriculture, education, social work, health, and so on. Authors were invited to refer to one or any combination of these fields, perhaps reflecting on why each field was chosen and why it became important in the development of thinking about participatory action research. The relationships between fields were potentially important. I suggested, for example, that the question Why is participatory action research more difficult to get started in schools than it is in social work programs? be posed.

Political aspects. I knew these might be thought about in several different ways, but that the nature and role of the state is likely to be important. For example, in Nicaragua, where the Sandinista government sponsored a massive literacy campaign using participatory action research methods, the minister responsible for community development summarized the government policy in these terms: "In Nicaragua, the state is the precious instrument of community." Such a policy is obviously compatible with the principles of participatory action research, but how does it contrast with state interventions which insist, for example, on standardization of social programs across communities? In Australian education, moves (or rhetoric) to reinstate the role of local communities in influencing the curriculum have been confronted with contradictory efforts by the state to closely monitor student, teacher, and school achievement.

I thought it important not to restrict political discussion to the role of the state; power is relevant in all relationships, language, and practices. It creates the structures by which 'fields' are formed, governed, and understood. How does the exercise of power (blatant or subtle, micro, meso, or macro, direct or hegemonic) affect the way participatory action research is received, practiced, and understood in the 'institutions' under consideration? What are the relationships between the traditional research community (or other kinds of institutions) and social movements? What is the relationship between the individual and the state, the researcher and the researched, the person and the culture? What is the standing of participatory action research and of 'emancipatory' and 'advocacy' research generally? How is the ordinary knowledge and practice of everyday life respected? In short, I thought it would help if contributors were able to think about the politics (and ideology) of the state, the disciplines (and their methodological preferences), other institutions, and the relationships of action researching groups and individuals with and within each of these.

Cultural aspects. I encouraged authors to consider these at different levels. How does participatory action research compare with people's 'ordinary' ways of doing things? Are institutions always hierarchical, and is participatory action research always oppositional? Do religious practices nurture an interest in self-reflection? Is reflection an individualistic, introspective activity, for example, or is reflection interpreted and practiced in ways oriented more toward collective action? Do people typically link their circumstances to historical and material analytical concepts such as class, race, and gender? Is this context cross-cultural, and are people coming to terms with ideas like 'colonization'? What role do the arts play in expressing the plight of oppressed people, in educating them, and in supporting (even creating) their moves to change their circumstances?

What is the nature of the culture of the institutions people work in or with? Are they bureaucratic? How do people cope with them? What is the status of people's knowledge (popular knowledge, craft knowledge) in different kinds of institutions? To whom do people regard themselves as attached, accountable? Are people (and institutions and groups) caring, competitive, or collaborative? What is the culture of the groups people work with? For example, are people mutually warm and respectful as a matter of course? Do people talk about power and its abuses in interpersonal as well as institutional relationships? Do work relationships spill over into social activities and commitments to the same kinds of social movements?

Of course, these were all *my* particular suggestions and questions, invented with very little, if any, knowledge of other people's concerns in the contexts in which they were working. But I thought authors would probably recognize some themes which they might agree were common to much of the debate about participatory action research. Nevertheless, if authors thought other themes were important, I invited them to identify and use them in their discussions.

Discourses, Practices and Power

In suggesting the aforementioned sections, I felt I had emphasized the development of 'thinking' about participatory action research, disclosing my own predilection (and failing) for thinking about discourses. I also drew authors' attention again to three important aspects: language use, ordinary activities, and the social relationships which contend with each other in the formation of individual identity, institutional cultures, and the culture of society more generally. I said all authors should consider the question: "What has *changed* as a result of the commitment to participatory action research in this context?"

I thought it important that the collection provide four things for its audience:

1. Access to the literature which informs particular kinds of participatory action research—thus influential theorists and practitioners and their key works are identified in their appropriate historical place.
2. Reference to the kind of literature which informed the political and cultural discussion engaged by influential participatory action researchers.
3. Access and reference, where possible, to examples of participatory action research in the context being discussed.
4. An educative vision for the future(s) of participatory action research— how to understand the influences documented so the theory and practice of participatory action research are wiser in the future.

What styles did I expect the authors would use? That depended somewhat upon the nature of their own experiences. All contributors are experienced participatory action researchers themselves and wrote in various ways from their own informed, personal perspectives. Some contributors have been key players in the development of participatory action research in their own contexts and wrote biographically and historically. More recent entrants to the field are prominent students, as well as practitioners, of action research and draw on that balance of experience.

Key Emergent Themes

In these texts, there are both common themes and themes which cause the stories and accounts to differ.

Common Themes

Participation. Every author assumes that participatory action research is research done by the people for themselves: "Learning to do it by doing it" in Paulo Freire's phrase. Authentic participation in research means sharing in the way research is conceptualized, practiced, and brought to bear on the life-world. It means ownership: responsible agency in the production of knowledge and the improvement of practice. Mere involvement implies none of this, and creates the risk of co-option and exploitation of people in the realization of the plans of others. This is common in community programs that are portrayed as participatory action research but that in reality are little more than manipulation in the oppressive and unreflective implementation of some institutional or government policy. People often are involved in research, but rarely are they participants who have real ownership of research theory and practice as they do here.

Tandon's reference to control over 'the whole process' means that even the research methodology itself may be reinterpreted and reconstituted by participants. The interpretations of participatory action research presented here express that commitment.

Reflection as collective critique. The participatory action research portrayed in this book anticipates collective reflection on practice, relationships with others, and the way in which forms of life are conceptualized. The ways in which experience is objectified and subjectivity is disciplined may vary, but there is a commitment to use examined experience of concrete practice to inform future action. Each author recognizes that participatory action research is a collective activity. Three key reasons are implicit. The interpretation of experience is more trustworthy if others help; trying to change things impacts on others, and their consent and help is needed; change is political and social life is manifold, not broken into bits that can be changed one at a time: Individuals cannot accomplish change of much note by themselves, and they cannot change anything unless they change themselves at the same time.

Communitarian politics. Participatory action research expresses an explicit politics. It is not simply about change, but about change of a particular kind. Each of the themes discussed previously indicates that this form of research aspires to communitarian and egalitarian politics: people working together toward rationality, justice, coherence, and satisfactoriness in workplaces and in other areas of people's lives. However, it is a serious confusion about the nature of participatory action research to think that it is something that only 'practitioners' do. Both the politics and epistemology of participatory action research require broad participation; it must not be confused with 'political activism' or 'oppositional politics' among the less powerful, the poor, or the disenfranchised. Participatory action research is an obligation undertaken by all people at all levels and in all kinds of institutions who seek to develop the quality of their work and the symmetry and reciprocity of their relationships with others.

Participatory action research is political because it is about people changing themselves and their circumstances and about informing this change as it happens, but it is no more political than any other kind of research. The difference is that the politics of other kinds of research are undeclared and submerged under the spurious guises of 'objectivity' (rather than disciplined subjectivity), 'detachment' (rather than expressing a defensible human interest), and 'value-free' (rather than expressive of particular values in concrete research situations).

Research. Participatory action research *is* research, not just political activism or oppositional politics. Sometimes people's efforts to objectify their own experiences lead them to try to regain control over their work and lives. This is sometimes interpreted as mere politics by critics, especially those who have an interest in other forms of social organization, other ways of producing knowledge about the world, and other ways of acting *in* and *on* the social world. It is true that participatory action research occurs sometimes in contexts where political activism and oppositional politics are in evidence, but it is important for everyone, critics and advocates alike, that these are not seen as the same thing. Critics typically show a profound ignorance of the extensive methodological literature of participatory action research and the convergence of old intellectual traditions and new forms of discourse that both vindicate and inform it: Aristotelian ethics, dialectical materialism, participatory research and action research themselves, phenomenology, ethnography, symbolic interactionism, several different feminisms, post-colonialism, and some forms of post-modernism. Explicitly and implicitly, these essays show unambiguously that participatory action research is about the conscientious objectification of concrete experience and change. Some critics of participatory action research may want to ask whether it is really research or not; that is a perfectly legitimate question. What cannot be denied is the legitimacy of the affirmative answer. The literature of participatory action research and of concrete practices demonstrably informed by participatory action research show that it produces new insights and understandings that meet defensible standards for knowledge claims.

Themes of Difference

Differences among the papers show that the ideas about participatory action research evolved, advanced, and receded as participatory action research was shaped and reshaped by its proponents in their own contexts in response to local historical circumstances.

Institutions. An interesting location of difference is the role played by 'institutions.' At first glance, work under the rubric of 'action research' roughly corresponds with formal institutions such as universities. Participatory research can similarly be seen to correspond with informal 'community' efforts at development and change. However, these correspondences are soon complicated. We find that the first versions of action research in Western cultures have their roots in community development programs, and though it is seldom acknowledged, in feminist approaches to community activism. In turn, some more recent versions of participatory research have their practitioners advocating support from the universities, seeking substantive support, methodological legitimation, and political vindication. Proponents of both family branches now seem to find strengths in one another's theory, forms of organization, and practice. Perhaps this merely evidences an emergent understanding of the nature of social change, prefigured in the literature of 'innovation' that interpreted social and educational reforms in the United States in the 1960s. That literature indicates that in 'loosely coupled' systems, any group of participants in an innovation can exercise a 'right of veto' of its diffusion. This effect can be achieved by active resistance by people, by renaming what they already do or, more usually, by simply continuing on as before as if nothing had changed.

Although we need a broader concept than 'innovation' to embrace our concerns here—perhaps 'social change' is a better concept—we now know how broadly based and understood change must be if it is to last. That is, coalitions that represent support in different ways and at many levels in communities and institutions (public and private) will be necessary to change conditions and supplant practices that maintain irrationality, injustice, and incoherent and unsatisfying forms of existence.

The state. Much of what has been said about institutions obviously applies to the state as well, since public institutions at least sometimes function instrumentally in realizing policies formulated by the state. But in the writings in this collection there is an ambivalence about the role of the state with respect to participatory action research. In some nations, communitarian political aspirations expressed by the state were important in creating conditions supportive of participatory action research; in other nations, the state merely co-opted the language for its own purposes and left aside the forms of practice, social relationships, and organization that constitute authentic participatory action research.

Ontology and epistemology. Despite the considerable commonality evident in aspiration and method expressed in this collection, the papers here are grounded in several different ways of understanding reality. Implicit, and sometimes explicit, appeal is made to Aristotelian ethics, critical social science, Deweyan philosophy, feminism, Buddhism, popular knowledge, and perhaps others I have missed. Of course, each of these approaches embodies and anticipates different ways of working and of articulating the rationale for educational and social work of many kinds. But it is obvious also that these authors do see themselves as sharing a common agenda. How is *any* commonality possible from such disparate sources? I think perhaps there are two fundamental ways of answering the question. The first takes into account the view of social change intimated above. The proliferation of discourses of participatory action research is in one sense strategic, simply reflecting the different social (and linguistic) contexts in which the struggle for rationality, justice, and coherent and satisfying forms of life is engaged. The obvious fact that different authors have a different sense of audience reflects in part their actual if not their preferred location in that complex of struggles. The second reason engages the substance of the first—in the concrete situation, people of many different persuasions can come to agreement about fundamental aspirations for humanity. People cannot always see the same light on the hill, nor seek to wander the same Utopia, but can recognize starving and abused children, exploited workers, and victimized women—and know with whom to work to improve things. It is their understandings and aspirations we must heed, engage, and support.

Submerged Themes

Culture. In spite of my initial encouragement that writers might attend to the influence of local culture on the nature of participatory action research theory and practice, this does not appear as a strong theme in any of these chapters. This is a puzzle. My first reaction was to think this was due to the nature of culture itself: It is in a sense just what Illinois professor Harry Broudy casually remarked, that culture is "what goes without saying." However, I fear this reaction is a little too easy here. I suspect cultural difference is less of an issue than the sociopolitical context—in the experience of these authors. Why have contributors not attended to 'culture' explicitly in their chapters? We may speculate on their reasons, and I found that in the surfeit of contributors' commentaries it was difficult to give an overview, especially regarding cultural contexts with which I was not familiar. For example, to write about 'Australian culture' is fraught with difficulty. Pluralizing to 'Australian culture*s*' helps, but not much.

Nevertheless, it is clear that some influences of culture (s) are relevant at institutional and societal levels. The diversity of writing genre in the collection shows the difference in institutional and community cultural contexts. I shall say a little more about that after I address some issues that emerge in conducting participatory action research in cross-cultural settings, issues that are somewhat latent in the collection.

My own experience in working cross-culturally, for example, with Aboriginal people is that it is difficult to comprehend how participatory action research is reinterpreted in another cultural context. We said what we thought it was, invited reinterpretation, expected some 'back translation,' but generally could not work out what the method really looked like in Yolngu Matha (the language of the people we worked with), or indeed in Aboriginal social practice. Our advocacies seemed consonant with the ways in which Aboriginal people work through issues and plans in their communities, but perhaps detailed understanding is just another colonialist aspiration. In general, I think this is also the case with interpretation into the Thai language, as the following anecdote indicates.

During 1991, Dr. Kowit Pravalpruk of the Department of Curriculum and Instruction Development of the Thailand Ministry of Education wrote to Deakin University Press requesting permission to translate into the Thai language *The action research planner*, developed by Stephen Kemmis, myself, and others (Kemmis and McTaggart 1988a, 1988b).

We were concerned about literal translation, knowing that the principles of action research might best be expressed in different ways in other languages and in different cultural contexts. Our concern was fed by the number of requests that arrived to reproduce the 'diagrams' of action research in *The planner*, which we feared had come to stand for the idea of action research at the expense of the principles and theory of its use explained in the text itself and in several other publications (Carr and Kemmis 1986; Kemmis and McTaggart 1998a, 1998b; McTaggart 1991a). We had long been concerned about the reduction of action research to its 'iconic simplicity' (McTaggart and Garbutcheon-Singh 1986) and had encouraged people to reinterpret action research in ways that took into account their own discoveries about action research practice and the institutional and social contexts in which it was being tried (McTaggart 1991b, 1991c, 1993).

We thought it might be helpful to the Thai translator, Dr. Sor Wasana Pravalpruk of Srinakharinwirot University, Bangkok, for us to conduct some action research workshops in Bangkok. But most especially we thought it essential to seek the help of Dr. Arphorn Chuaprapaisilp (see her paper in this collection) of Prince of Songkla University who had a rich experience of the practice of action research in Thailand. We did that, and after conducting a workshop at Srinakharinwirot University, Dr. Arphorn, Dr. Sor Wasana, and a professor of English from Srinakharinwirot were working on the first completed draft of the translation.

The conversation was mostly in Thai, but occasionally I was asked a question about *The planner*, often causing me to recognize that Stephen Kemmis and I could do a lot to improve the clarity of our writing. Of course, being monolingual in itself is something most of us would do well to feel quite ashamed about. Nevertheless, the laughter and warmth of the meeting put me at ease, despite my stomach upset from overindulgence the day before on a grand tour through Kanchanaburi province to celebrate the king's birthday with my hosts. One question I remember regarded the particular sense in which we were using the term *discourse*. I will not reiterate my answer, lest my ineptitude become too obvious. The conversation continued in Thai, and then Arphorn asked me another question, which seemed to invite an even more elaborate answer that I proceeded to give. As I was warming up, Arphorn politely beckoned me to stop. She said:

> There is no need to explain, Robin. The problem we have here is one you cannot help us with. We understand *perfectly* what the details of action research mean in English; what I am afraid we cannot do at the moment is to translate them into Thai.

Despite such difficulties, it is worth making some observations about culture that might serve to present a perspective on at least some of the papers. These observations are not argued here and may be too sweeping, but are proffered in the hope of provoking thought.

Perhaps some key questions concern what the papers might tell us about the *research* culture of social inquiry. The Austrian, Australian, British, U.S., and Spanish papers manifest highly institutionalized research cultures. A key divergence between the Austrian, Spanish, and Australian perspectives and the others may be the role that critical theory has played in intellectual life in the research establishment. The history of action research (McTaggart 1991b) in the United States shows that it was pushed aside by a dominant positivist research ideology. That was not so easy in Europe, where strong traditions of critique existed. In Britain, Aristotelian modes of thought find expression in a strong interpretivist tradition that has mitigated the 'can do' social engineering impetus of U.S. research culture. Skepticism (to put it rather gently) about German intellectual traditions in the United Kingdom made for a more practical and liberal humanist approach to social inquiry.

In the United States, the culture that spawned McCarthyism may have obliterated the broad left hegemony necessary to hold out the colonization of social inquiry by the natural scientific method. Of course, there was always some resistance, and recent expressions of this struggle include advocacies about the validity of narrative accounts of personal experience as a defensible knowledge form. The Schubert paper is one such expression, although note that its continuity is with the work of John Dewey. Critique in the European sense is less evident. Note also that these debates rage *in* the academy as well, expressing the powerful emergence of the politics of 'difference,' main currents in feminist post-structuralism and post-colonialism in particular. These debates have created space for narrative approaches to reporting educational experience, but their relationship with bodies of theory remain unclear and often unexpressed. Educators' stories and indeed their work itself are important and can be disciplined by critique, but there is a case yet to be made that they are always sufficiently disciplined to be regarded as research. What, for example, are the criteria or principles, however contestable they might be, against which explicit or implicit knowledge claims might be considered or assessed?

The impetus of Thai culture is expressed primarily in Arphorn Chuaprapaisilp's chapter through her reference to Buddhism. Her study is influenced by Western institutional culture in a rather direct way: she wrote in part for her dissertation committee. One effect of that is to require the author to exercise a strong hand in reporting. This institutional imperative exerts an effect on the paper, possibly making it seem less self-reflective, more individualistic, and less attentive to problematizing the relationship between researcher and researched than participatory action research reports are now expected to be. Perhaps the paper's style could be viewed from another perspective. The often reported hierarchies in Thai (and indeed most Asian) institutions could influence action research practice because symmetry of power relations and reciprocity among participants is more difficult to achieve. However, the intensity of these hierarchies may be in the imaginings of the westerners who observe them, westerners who are all too oblivious to the silent hegemonies that discipline their own lives (such as the social rules that stop them from inviting their own vice-chancellors for a barbecue).

Papers describing participatory action research conducted in community rather than institutional contexts express something of the culture of oppositional work. There is delight that the academy is finally taking notice, an intimacy of relations at a personal level, and a concern to communicate. There also is a complexity of relations at the political level, and in the case of Venezuela and New Caledonia, an almost overwhelming concern with politics of organizations, nongovernment organizations, projects, and communities. This is not easily explained simply as the preoccupation of the authors. Rather, these things seem to me to be closely related. The working lives of participatory action researchers in developing countries are more personal and contingent upon the politics of relations among formal and informal groups. Perhaps what we see here is the limited reach of the nation state and the effects of the other institutions and activities which substitute for it. The detail provided indicates the importance of detail itself in these difficult situations. The culture of groups is both constituted by, and helps to constitute, the broader and tumultuous culture of the nation itself. There may be more detail in some chapters than some readers will relish, but the detail does not matter as much as knowing it is there.

Perhaps these rather speculative comments about culture are sufficient to orient readers to the difficulties of describing its influence. May I remind those who think I have gone too far in my attributions that that is the very problem I pointed out initially. One risks being provocative.

Method. This is not a book about the method or methodology of participatory action research. There are many such expositions as the bibliographies of the contributors show, but my introductory paper, which comprises the next chapter, is intended to indicate something of the methodological commitments of participatory action researchers. Contributors assumed that this paper would appear alongside theirs, and I believe these principles are widely accepted among participatory action researchers. Those seeking more technical accounts of method may be frustrated here. They may be even more frustrated by my further observation that authentic participation itself might almost be seen as *constituting* the method. Others are more wary and, for this reason, if not to assuage any of my own vestigial doubts, I should say something about the validation of knowledge claims in participatory action research. I expect that there will be different emphases among these validation approaches with the different contributions, but at the same time, I would not expect too much dissent from their underlying intent.

Validation in participatory action research is accomplished by a variety of methods, particularly those reported in methodological literature of interpretive inquiry and including the triangulation of observations and interpretations, by establishing credibility among participants and informants, by participant confirmation, by the deliberate establishment of an 'audit trail' of data and interpretations, and by testing the coherence of arguments being presented in a 'critical community' or a community of 'critical friends' whose commitment is to testing the arguments and evidence advanced in the account of the study. This is typically an extended process of iteration between the data, the literature which informs the study (substantively and methodologically), participants in the study, and critical friends and others who have an informed interest in the study. That is, validation is an explicit process of dialogue, it is not achieved by adherence to a fixed procedure. Validation in participatory action research can only be achieved if there are appropriate communicative structures in place throughout the research and action that allow participants to continue to associate and identify with the work of the collective project of change. I have identified elsewhere (McTaggart in press) some criteria for considering the validity of action research *reporting*, and although the papers in this collection are not all action reports as such, the following criteria are a useful point of reference to augment the methodological principles outlined in the next chapter. These criteria provide quite a stiff test, but do give a strong sense of the kinds of information gathered and the stance taken:

- explicit recognition that the account presented is just one among several defensible accounts that might be presented;
- presentation of, and attention to, the voices and views of participants, including their differences and agreements;
- careful attention to ensure that otherwise unheard voices (for example, disenfranchised groups) are given expression;
- explicit theoretical effort to comprehend the ways in which participants have come to describe their life-worlds, engage it with others, and enact their work practices, for example, through processes of deconstruction and ideology critique;
- demonstrated cognizance of the relevant substantive and methodological literature and the ways in which these frame both questions and practices;
- explicit iteration between the data, literature, and practical and interpretive activities of the researchers;
- questioning within the study about the ways in which both the research question and the methodology used are framed by the relationship between the researcher/author and his or her institutional obligations (for example, as a doctoral student); and
- deliberate attention to the planned (and incidental) reflexivity of the study, its catalytic effect on change and improvement, through intermediate reporting to its audiences, and through the relationship between the researcher (s) and others whose work is reported (or otherwise affected).

Although we add moral and ethical content here to the criteria by which research should be judged, it is important to remember that in conventional research literatures (and everyday usage) validity is a property of *inferences*, not of research or research design per se (House, Mathison, and McTaggart 1989). That is, validity is a property of the interpretations and conclusions which people make of information and the theoretical frameworks which guide its collection and use. In participatory action research, these are inferences which are drawn by others as well as the researcher, and the representation of any study typically should be quite rich with voices and observations to help readers come to their own conclusions or generate their own 'readings' (Lather 1993). By picking up some of the currents in the post-structuralist debates to affirm the possibility of multiple readings and the deliberate reflexivity of social inquiry, I argue along with Lather (1993) that there is a need to go beyond the views of validity expressed and implicit in the traditional conceptualizations of validity, for example, in Guba and Lincoln (1985), Yin (1989), and Wolcott (1992).

These commitments to validation might be used as point of reference in considering the papers. But do keep in mind that the notion of the surety of method is contested terrain in this literature.

The Papers

There are noticeable differences in the discursive genre of the papers in this collection. This is partly an accident of selection, itself a fortuitous accident of the acquaintances one makes (or acquaintances of acquaintances one discovers) in international participatory action research networks. However, the differences themselves are important signifiers. They reflect the nature of people's institutional and community affiliations, the diversity of audiences they anticipate, the linguistic communities they work in and, more generally, the breadth of activities identifiable as participatory action research. The order of papers is a bit intuitive. I have put first the papers which I think have more evident aspirations to inform a general 'theory of action research,' despite their obvious 'local' identifications. As I have already indicated, my own chapter, "Guiding Principles for Participatory Action Research," is included as a point of reference for readers as it was for those invited to contribute (see also McTaggart 1991a).

Herbert Altrichter and Peter Gstettner, once colleagues at the University of Klagenfurt, Austria, and now professors of the universities of Innsbruck and Klagenfurt, respectively, present a short history of action research in German language contexts. Altrichter writes as an experienced teacher educator with close knowledge of English and Australian participatory action research traditions. His interests include school development, educators' theories of action, and action research methodology, and he has published in both German and English in these areas. Gstettner comes to participatory action research with an interest in the history and psychology of childhood, and of direct relevance here, a perspective informed by ethnomethodology and issues to do with cross-cultural teaching and research, and problems faced by learners of ethnic and linguistic minorities. Theirs is a particularly salient history because it recovers the roots of the influential Lewinian conceptualization of action research in participatory community movements. Their critiques of action research theory and practice introduce some key issues evident in histories of action research (McTaggart 1991b; Noffke 1989, 1990): criticisms from reconstructed and unreconstructed positivists, issues about the methodology and its theoretical justification, issues about the relationship between researcher and researched (the problem of 'participation'), confusion with political activism, and internal disagreements about the appropriate nature of action research, and just how to establish action research practice.

The co-option of action research in an ideology of managerialism forms a key theme in Clem Adelman's chapter. With John Elliott, Adelman was initiator of the well-known Ford Teaching Project which remains one of the best exemplars of action research in education. Adelman is now a Professor in the

Faculty of Education and Community Studies in the University of Reading in England. Reaffirming the democratic and participatory impulse of action research, he presents an interesting account of the relationship between the assumptions of the British Humanities Curriculum Project and the action research of the Ford Teaching Project, still perhaps the most thoughtfully documented example of British action research. Interestingly, Adelman's analysis confirms a theme that underpins the whole collection: a need to converge the rather better-supported and researched individualistic versions of action research that characterize the staff development genre and democratic practices exemplified in the participatory research movement.

Orlando Fals Borda's life and career traverse a moral course that took him away from a prestigious position at the National University of Colombia to work for twenty years with peasants who were denied the agricultural land necessary for their survival. We can find no better expression of the failings of formal institutions to engage matters of social justice. For Fals Borda, participation in knowledge production is an essential concomitant of participation in the movement to achieve social justice, for people to become "free from blood and horror." For those who fear that participatory action research is part of some Marxist imperialistic plot to imbue people with a "science of the proletariat," he has this advice: Even if the fear was justified, people do not fall for it. Only through recovering their own histories, and indeed by reinterpreting their own versions of participatory action research, can people form an educational and political praxis that justifies their commitment. Although Fals Borda is modest about his achievements, attributing them to democratic methods of inquiry, ideas, and practices, it will help readers to know that he was again professor and emeritus professor of the National University of Colombia, was a member of the Colombian Constituent Assembly (parliament), worked on a new democratic Colombian constitution, and chaired two national commissions, one negotiating Colombian off-shore oil rights with Venezuela, the other designing land reform and electoral boundary reform for the whole country. A modest voice of the people has become an important voice of a nation, but Fals Borda would prefer to say that Colombians have demonstrated that a participatory action research movement can play a key part in transforming a nation.

The next paper was written by Anil Chaudhary who presently works at the Popular Education and Action Centre in New Delhi. When I first met him at the World Congress on Participatory Research in Managua Nicaragua in 1991, he was Joint Coordinator of the Society for Participatory Research in Asia. His paper is one of a pair sent to me by Suneeta Dhar. The second paper by Srilatha Batliwala and Sheela Patel of the Society for Promotion of Area Resource Centres (SPARC) in Bombay appears later in the collection and exemplifies some of the commitments of Chaudhary's short 'position' paper. I

have separated them in the collection because of the gentle organizing principle I have followed, but it also makes sense to read them together, because one
establishes principles and the other is a 'case' exemplifying them. Chaudhary
joins Rajesh Tandon in attempting to articulate an alternative and distinctive
epistemology for participatory research that gives due recognition to popular
knowledge, but with an eye to the international machinations of transnational
corporate capitalism, the World Bank, and the International Monetary Fund.

Shirley Grundy's historical account of Australian action research
reflects the intersection of state initiative and personal biography. Grundy was
a key advocate for participatory action research in Western Australia and
worked closely with Stephen Kemmis of the Deakin University Action
Research Group in the early 1980s. She is currently Associate Professor of
Education at Murdoch University in Western Australia and played a key role
in the National Innovative Links Project which sponsored close relations
between teacher educators, educational researchers, teachers, principals, and
consultants in the early 1990s. Her analysis of the different venues of advocacy for Australian action research shows a somewhat more communitarian
ideology permeated that work, strengthened over the decade or so of her
analysis. She describes the emergence of the debate about an appropriate epistemology for action research and an attendant concern for authentic collaboration and participation. This move explicitly contested the co-option of
action research as a technology of reform and gave Australian action research
a distinctive critical character informed by opposition to action research in the
United States, an empathy with the Aristotelian 'practical' tradition, and identification with German and Habermasian social science.

John Dinan and Yuraima Garcia describe the emergence and potential of
participatory action research in Venezuela as its economy and politics are
transformed before, during, and after an oil boom. Dinan graduated from the
London University Institute of Education, and has lived in South America
since 1972. At the time of writing, he was Projects Director and Consultant to
the Institute for Educational Consultancy (INDASE) in Caracas, Venezuela.
He is a founding member of the Centre for Experimentation in Life-Long
Learning (CEPAP) of the Simon Rodriguez University in Caracas, and also of
the Venezuelan Participatory Network. Garcia is a Venezuelan sociologist
with expertise in the planning, coordination, and research of rural development programs in Venezuela. This chapter documents a successful collaboration. The complexity of their analysis reflects another theme of the collection:
changing forms of social life involves a myriad of conditions, only some of
which nurture community initiatives. The number of organizations referred to
alone evidences that complexity. The issues identified for Venezuela by Dinan
and Garcia perhaps encapsulate key issues for the theory, organization, and
practice of participatory action research worldwide. They include:

- lack of communication among participatory action researchers, including the problem of too little documentation or reports being lost as 'fugitive' literature in mimeo and other less formal production (the informality of which has some advantages);
- weak reconciliation between theoretical and justificatory work and the studies of concrete cases;
- differences within the field which help to articulate and strengthen the justifications and strategies available to people, but which at the same time can weaken the reputation of participatory action research by detracting from its agreed fundamental commitments and principles and creating the appearance of confusion and disunity;
- difficulties for people with similar substantive concerns but different institutional affiliations to work together; and
- inadequate arrangements for work-site based education about the theory, organization, and practice of participatory action research among newcomers to the field and among experienced workers (in the field and in academe).

Maria Saez Brezmes is a science educator from the Department of Cellular Biology and Pharmacology at the University of Valladolid in Spain and consultant to OECD-CERI on science education. She has had close connections with the Centre for Applied Research in Education (CARE) at the University of East Anglia in England over the past decade because of her interests in qualitative methods and political analysis. She is a specialist in case study and democratic approaches to evaluation and a leading practitioner and theorist of evaluation in Spain. Her association with CARE and with John Elliott simulated her interest in participatory action research. She focuses on the decade of reform in Spain from the mid-1970s to the mid-1980s. An even more profound national political transformation provides the context of her analysis. The demise of a dictatorship, increasing economic and cultural contact with the European community, and the emergence of a decentralized democratic state composed of several 'autonomous communities' provided a context, at least in principle, nurturant of the fundamental aspirations of participatory action research. Efforts to sponsor action research in Spain raise important issues about the meaning of 'participation.' Teacher representation on innovation committees is not enough, and whole school change is apparently a precursor to individual teacher development. At another level, the traditional role of the universities in dominating and defining legitimate knowledge production remains an issue, as does the teaching profession's sense of itself as a legitimate career. Influenced by British action research especially but also by the German and Australian traditions, Spain provides an interesting site for studying the contestation between participatory action research and the vestiges of central curriculum and teacher control in the form of inspection and national assessment obligations.

Bill Schubert and Ann Lopez-Schubert of the University of Illinois in Chicago write about participatory action research from highly developed perspectives. He is Professor of Education and Chair of the Area of Curriculum, Instruction, and Evaluation. A former elementary school teacher, he has published widely on curriculum theory and history, the nature of educational inquiry, teacher and student lore, democratic involvement of teachers and learners in curriculum through action research, and the implicit curriculum assumptions in non-school learning environments. Ann Lopez-Schubert, also an academic, teaches in the elementary education program at the university and is herself a former elementary teacher and teacher of English as a Second Language in inner city schools in Chicago. Her publications include teaching and the arts, non-school learning, home education, curriculum theory and history, alternative paradigms of inquiry, and action research that involves teacher and learner collaboration. They present a view of action research which at first acquaintance seems much less methodological in its discursive form and much more firmly located in the day-to-day life of a working professional. There are dangers of misinterpretation here: action researchers are insistent upon regular and somewhat systematic collection, analysis, and interpretation of data. That is, action research does involve doing a little more than people ordinarily do, except perhaps the most conscientiously and explicitly self-reflective workers. These authors, too, reassert the links between democratic movements and the idea of participatory action research. But in the United States, perhaps even more so than elsewhere, the not-so-invisible hand of the marketplace confronts the Deweyian tradition of action research. Teachers feel themselves compulsorily deskilled as they are forced to respond to the reductions of the meaning of education implicit in transnational corporate capitalist ideology and its peculiarly U.S. expression, the corporate marketing of educational testing. Perhaps changing this is more than participatory action research can do alone, and it is worth remembering that all good things in the world are not participatory action research. But these authors inform and strengthen the view that, in the United States, participatory action research will play an essential role in the struggle for changing the fundamental practices of Westernism itself.

Jean Delion describes his work in agricultural extension in New Caledonia. Delion draws on his extensive experience in participatory action research in a variety of cross-cultural settings, especially in the South Pacific, but also in Southeast Asia and francophone Africa. He was born in Madagascar, but took out a PhD at Sorbonne University. I tracked him down first in Yaounde, Cameroon, but subsequently communicated with him in Bressuire, France and later in Vientiane, Laos. His work was drawn to my attention by Richard Morse, then Director of the East West Center in Hawaii, where he had done some writing on pedagogy and participation in rural development. His account revisits the issue of participation, drawing special attention to the way in which close association with disenfranchised people can be interpreted by those with power. The attribution of 'political activist' (and, therefore, undesirable person) can be made, conveniently, even if not justifiably, by those threatened by communities coming to understand their circumstances more clearly. There is no romanticism about indigenous people here either. While Delion draws our attention to the difficulties of making cross-cultural interpretations, he tells us often enough to suggest that participatory action research can sometimes be co-opted within oppressed groups to confirm existing advantages within those groups. He also points out the need for close personal contact between 'animateurs' and the communities they work with and for case studies using different kinds of media so others may learn not only how change can be effected, but that they can do it for themselves. Nevertheless, despite the density of the animateur network (one animateur for every 200 adults), he argues from this experience that broad forms of political and substantive support are necessary for successful participatory action research. This includes support located in the formal institutions of government and higher education—in other words, participation must be broadly understood and practiced, not quarantined as a modus operandi of oppositional community groups.

Nurse educator Arphorn Chuaprapaisilp provides her reinterpretation of participatory action research for staff development in her field at Prince of Songkla University, Thailand. Now Associate Dean for Research and Foreign Affairs, Dr. Chuaprapaisilp is a strong advocate for participatory action research in nurse education and community development in Thailand. She has recently collaborated with Anglia Polytechnic University Professor Richard Winter to develop a jointly recognized postgraduate certificate in action research. Here she draws upon her earlier work in participatory action research. Focusing especially on reflection on experience, she argues that very disciplined data collection is necessary for nurse educators to reform an old tradition in much professional education. This old tradition assumes that 'theory' is taught in class and is then tried out or, perhaps more accurately, 'applied' by students in practice. This tradition, of course, contrasts with the fundamental idea of participatory action research, which is about theorizing *in* and *from* practice.

Chuaprapaisilp's approach to participatory action research locates participants in the research act and is somewhat individualistic, reflecting perhaps the action learning and process management movement in adult education. While the paper does not focus on the politics of action research and perhaps tends to writing about the action research of others without problematizing the role of the academic researcher, at the same time, her informative reference to the deeply introspective teachings of Buddhism raises important questions about the trend in Western action research to be critical of 'individualism,' in this context at least.

When I asked Suneeta Dhar and Anil Chaudhary (whom I met at the Third World Encounter on Participatory Research in Nicaragua in 1989) for examples of PRIA's principles in action, it was the Society for Promotion of Area Resource Centres (SPARC) paper by Srilatha Batliwala and Sheela Patel that they recommended. The recommendation came for good reason. The Society for Promotion of Area Resource Centres (SPARC) was formed in 1984 and has an exemplary record of participatory research practice. It is a non-governmental organization which works in alliance with other organizations it has helped form, such as the National Slum Dwellers' Federation and Mahila Milan (Women Together) to find workable solutions for communities of pavement dwellers. Along with its partner organizations, SPARC has shown that pavement-dwellers have the ability not only to save for their houses (as demonstrated by the Mahila Milan savings scheme) but also to make judicious decisions about the design and other aspects of their shelter. SPARC also assists communities and their federation to undertake research, education and training. Batliwala and Patel provide a concrete example of the PRIA epistemology in action. Some might say the example lacks the dynamism expected of participatory action research—in a technical interpretation of Lewinian terms, was this just one cycle or perhaps just an initial reconnaissance? Of course, the questions are misplaced. What is important is seizing the opportunity, however limited, and *creating* the possibility that people now understand what participation might mean. Chances are it will be much more difficult to work with them in nonparticipatory ways again. This is not merely disseminating the idea and practice of research done in a participatory way, it is innoculation against alternatives, the beginning of substantive knowledge about how to proceed when opportunities to do research of any kind can be forged into concrete progress. Before his engagement with ideas of reform, Chaudhary said that to him, "the world looked like hell." This case shows that participatory action research can make the world not only look less hellish, but actually less like hell for disenfranchised people.

Themes, Issues, and a Fundamental Purpose

The literatures of participatory action research and qualitative research generally bristle with issues about the ownership of social inquiry and its role in social amelioration. This collection aims to address some of these issues by bringing together the experience of people with somewhat different backgrounds, but with shared interest in, and concern for, participatory action research. There are two key strands to that interest and concern. First, a methodological strand, which comes from an interest among academics to forge common cause with educators working to improve education and the ways in which it is understood, and by the perceived need for legitimating action research in the academy (and other institutions). Second, the communitarian strand which stems from recognizing action research in various community development programs. It is my hope that this collection brings these strands together to inform that shared interest and concern and to formulate a new generation of issues for all people who wish to practice participatory action research (and, of course, to articulate theory about it at the same time). I think all contributors would agree with Kemmis (1992, xxxiii) that we need to work practically and theoretically to help people analyze their suffering (Fay 1975, 1988), articulate the conditions that disfigure their lives (Hall 1986), and use these processes of enlightenment to help develop social movements that can change the conditions of social life which maintain irrationality, injustice, and incoherent and unsatisfying forms of existence.

References

Carr, W., and S. Kemmis. 1986. *Becoming critical: Education, knowledge, and action research.* London: Falmer Press.

Fay, B. 1975. *Social theory and political practice.* London: George Allen & Unwin.

————. 1988. *Critical social science.* Ithaca, NY: Cornell University Press.

Guba, E., and Y. S. Lincoln. 1985. *Naturalistic inquiry.* Beverly Hills, CA: Sage.

Hall, S. 1986. On postmodernism and articulation: An interview [by Lawrence Grossberg]. *Journal of communication inquiry* 10(2):40–56.

House, E. R., S. Mathison, and R. McTaggart. 1989. Validity and teacher inference. *Educational researcher* 18(7):11–15, 26.

Kemmis, S. 1992. Practica de la teoria critica ensenanza: Experiencias. Lectures given (in English) at an international symposium, March, University of Valladolid, Spain.

Kemmis, S., and R. McTaggart (eds.). 1988a. *The action research planner.* 3rd ed., substantially revd. Geelong, Vic.: Deakin University Press.

————. 1988b. *Como planificar: La investigacion-accion.* Barcelona: Laertes.

Lather, P. 1993. Fertile obsession: Validity after post-structuralism. *Sociological Quarterly* 34(4):673–93.

McTaggart, R. (in press). Revitalizing management as a scientific activity. *Management learning.*

———. 1991a. Principles for participatory action research. *Adult Education Quarterly* 41(3):168–87.

———. 1991b. *Action research: A short modern history.* Geelong, Vic.: Deakin University Press.

———. 1991c. Western institutional impediments to Aboriginal education. *Journal of curriculum studies* 23(4):297–325.

———. 1993. Dilemmas in cross-cultural action research. In *Health research: Political, ethical and methodological issues*, eds. D. Colquhoun and A. Kellehear, 65–96. London: Chapman & Hall.

McTaggart, R., and M. Garbutcheon-Singh. 1986. New directions in action research. *Curriculum perspectives* 6(2):42–6.

Noffke, S. E. 1989. The social context of action research: A comparative and historical analysis. Paper presented at the Annual Meeting of the American Educational Research Association, March, San Francisco (ERIC ED 308756).

———. 1990. Action research: A multidimensional analysis. Ph.D. thesis, University of Wisconsin, Madison.

Tandon, R. 1988. Social transformation and participatory research. *Convergence* 21(2/3):5–14.

Wolcott, H. F. 1992. On seeking and rejecting validity in qualitative research. In *Qualitative inquiry in education: The continuing debate*, eds. E. W. Eisner and A. Peshkin. New York: Teachers College.

Yin, R. K. 1989. *Case study research: Design and methods.* Newbury Park, CA: Sage.

CHAPTER 2

Guiding Principles for Participatory Action Research

Robin McTaggart

The Value of Principles

It is easy to become bedazzled with the bright light of a pristine set of 'principles.' All too often they can be used to take the high moral ground and judge out of context the quality of people's work. A preoccupation with 'principle' has also been criticized as a masculinist failing that distracts attention from authentic caring about the lives of people (Noddings 1984). In its worst form, obsession with principle, or at least the determined application of one set of principles when others are demonstrably relevant, becomes manifest as the immorality which is embodied in all kinds of fundamentalism—religious, political, or scientific (sometimes known as positivism).

Nevertheless, I want to propose in this paper[1] a theory of participatory action research in the form of a set of principles defining what participatory action research is and what it is not. I do this for two reasons. First, such principles are an effective way of distilling knowledge accumulated from the experience of participatory action research. In this sense, principles are descriptive as well as prescriptive (but only as a thesis about participatory action research to be tested in future practice). Second, the principles should perform an educative function. There is a sense in which participatory action researchers must reinvent the wheel as part of the commitment to owning the practice of research as well as the social practice the research informs and is informed by. But this does not preclude the common sense of trying to learn something from the experiences of others. When trying to decide on concrete action in a particular situation, it helps to know how others fared in similar or somewhat related circumstances. In this respect, descriptive accounts of concrete cases can be useful to make extrapolations to different cases (Cronbach 1982; House, Mathison, and McTaggart 1989; Stake 1978). At the same time, general principles can provide useful guidance to assess the appropriateness and validity of examples and formulate plans for concrete action.

When contemplating work which claims to be participatory action research, it is important to keep in mind three general questions: How is *this* example participatory action research? What does this example tell us about the criteria we might use to judge claims that an endeavor is participatory action research (to test our theory of what participatory action research is)? And, most important of all, what contribution has this example made to the improvement of the understanding, practice, and social situation of participants and others in the context described (acknowledging that all good things in our experience are not necessarily participatory action research)? If we decide that something *is* an example of participatory action research, we are suggesting that it is likely to have improved the lives of those who have participated. If we decide to the contrary, we are questioning whether the activity has done as much as it might have (without necessarily condemning it, for it might have accomplished something). In emphasizing the issue of how an example might have been *better* participatory action research, the strategy becomes less judgmental and more oriented to future action.

To address these questions we need not only identify good examples of participatory action research, but propose some criteria or characteristics which can be used to consider what is and what is not participatory action research. Of course, judging whether activities are examples of participatory action research would be a pointless exercise if strong arguments for participatory action research did not exist. These arguments do exist and in reality demonstrate the convergence of several distinguished intellectual traditions (Carr and Kemmis 1986; Kemmis and McTaggart 1988a; McTaggart 1990; Tandon 1988). But even that convergence is an understatement, because the modern conception of participatory action research is a convergence and coalescence of theoretical *and* practical traditions in many fields—agriculture, social work, education, health, obstetrics, housing, and community development, to identify just some examples. This convergence is sometimes attributed to the revitalization of communitarian politics, and that is relevant, but by no means the sole cause, nor even the most important cause. There is an important substantive reason as well. In all of these fields, it has been demonstrated time and time again that the *application* of the researches of others (especially positivist research, which blithely claims or assumes universal applicability) in new social, cultural, and economic contexts is unlikely to work. People must conduct substantive research themselves on the practices that affect their own lives.

Because of the diversity of fields in which participatory action research has been developed as a way of improving and informing social, economic, and cultural practice, it is perhaps understandable that the idea can mean quite different and sometimes contradictory things to different people. Despite some considerable emergent agreement about what participatory action research is, any literature search using the descriptors 'participatory research,' 'action research,' or ' participatory action research' will still identify a confusing and meaningless diversity of approaches to research. It is impossible to discover from such a sample just what participatory action research is. This is because the term is often misused, sometimes because of lack of understanding and sometimes to represent research deliberately as inspired by communitarian values when it is not.

The Basic Idea of Participatory Action Research

Some confusion arises because of differing views about distinctions that might be made between participatory action research and concepts such as 'participatory development' and 'political activism.' It is important to recognize that the term *research* carries with it some important connotations: intensive study of a situation and the production of knowledge in some form or another, including important ideas like informed practice. In due course, the nature of the research aspect of action research will be explained in more detail. Nowadays, it is not so necessary to argue from first principles the validity of practitioners' knowledge; a considerable literature in the philosophy of social science already has accomplished that. That literature also has some important implications for the appropriate definition and practice of participation, and the meaning of participation is another area of confusion to which we will return.

At one level of analysis, the idea of participatory action research is straightforward enough. Social psychologist Kurt Lewin (1946, 1952), inventor of the term *action research* in English usage, described action research as proceeding in a spiral of steps, each of which is composed of planning, acting, observing and evaluating the result of the action. In practice, the process begins with a general idea that some kind of improvement or change is desirable. In deciding just where to begin in making improvements, a group identifies an area where members perceive a cluster of problems of mutual concern and consequence. The group decides to work together on a 'thematic concern' (Kemmis and McTaggart 1988a).

The cyclic nature of the Lewinian approach recognizes the need for action plans to be flexible and responsive. Lewin recognized that, given the complexity of real social situations, in practice it is never possible to anticipate everything that needs to be done. Lewin's deliberate overlapping of action and reflection was designed to allow changes in plans for action as people learned from their own experience. Put simply, action research is the way in which groups of people can organize the conditions under which they can learn from their own experience and make this experience accessible to others. Two of the ideas that were crucial in Lewin's work were group decision and commitment to improvement. A distinctive feature of action research is that those affected by planned changes have the primary responsibility for deciding on courses of critically informed action that seem likely to lead to improvement and for evaluating the results of strategies tried out in practice (Henry and Kemmis 1986; Kemmis and McTaggart 1988b). However, the Lewinian conceptualization had some limitations. Lewin did not spell out the nature of action research in much detail. But it seems from his writings that his interest in the theory of group dynamics overshadowed what we would now see as fundamental to participatory action research, the commitment that all participants actually do research for themselves. At least in the literature of the time, we do not see participatory action researchers from the communities Lewin worked with on race relations and community housing articulating their own theories for improved race relations and community development.

Participatory action research is in principle a group activity. But in situations where people with different power, status, influence, and facility with language come together to work on a thematic concern, the idea of participation becomes problematic. A disturbing confusion about the nature of participatory action research arises because of the corruption of the meaning of the term *participation*.

Thinking About "Participation"

The first step in analyzing this confusion is straightforward. It involves making the distinction between 'participation' and 'involvement,' which is made clear in standard English dictionaries:

> *participate*, v. i. Have share, take part, (*in* thing, *with* person); have something *of* (*his poems participate in the nature of satire*); so partici*pant* . . .
>
> *involve*, v. t. *1*. Wrap (thing *in* another); wind spirally. *2*. Entangle (person, thing, *in* difficulties, mystery, etc.); implicate (person *in* charge, crime, etc.); include (*in*), imply, entail. *3*. (in *p. p.*) Concerned (*in*), in question; complicated in thought or form (*volvere volut-* roll). (*Concise Oxford Dictionary* 1976, 804, 570)

Authentic participation in research means sharing in the way research is conceptualized, practiced, and brought to bear on the life-world. It means ownership, that is, responsible agency in the production of knowledge and improvement of practice. Mere involvement implies none of this and creates the risk of co-option and exploitation of people in the realization of the plans of others. This is common in community programs that are portrayed as participatory action but in reality are little more than the oppressive and unreflective implementation of some institutional policy. People often are involved in research, but rarely are they participants with real ownership of research theory and practice.

Rajesh Tandon (1988) has identified several determinants of authentic participation in research:

- people's role in setting the agenda of the inquiry;
- people's participation in the data collection and analysis; and
- people's control over the use of outcomes and the whole process. (Tandon 1988, 13)

Tandon's reference to control over 'the whole process' means even the research methodology itself may be reinterpreted and reconstituted by participants. This can be extremely important in the cross-cultural contexts where participatory action research is often practiced. Not to recognize the inevitability of this is to engage in cultural imperialism. Why should indigenous people engage in *our* brand of participatory action research? Elaborated upon next is a more detailed expression of the idea of participatory action research, an idea that presses the point that the real test is that people are actually conducting the research for themselves and reflecting on its nature.

The Idea of Research on Practice By Participants

To develop this point it helps to analyze the idea of participatory action research a little further. We use the term *participatory action research* to differentiate it from other kinds of research that typically involve researchers from the academy doing research *on* people, making the people objects of the research. Research on people can be either empirical-analytic or interpretive, and as Habermas (1972, 1974) has argued, because neither of these approaches to research has an explicit politics, both empirical-analytic and interpretive research express an interest which is not emancipatory. The knowledge produced from such research can be used in coercive kinds of ways, but somewhat contradictorily can create the *illusion* of participation. People can be required to work out ways of implementing policy developed on the basis of knowledge produced by research *on* them rather than *by* them. This is *not* participatory action research but the co-option of people into the research, development, and dissemination approach invented by a coalition of policy makers and social scientists whose primary interest is in maintaining control.

Participatory action research engages people from the academy and workplace in an entirely different relationship. For simplicity, I will use the terms *academic* and *worker* to label the two groups of people typically engaged in participatory action research, although it is obvious that both terms are too narrow for the diversity of agencies and people who collaborate in participatory action research projects. I make the distinction because it helps to show the common task of participatory action researchers, as well as the distinctive tasks they may play in their own institutional and cultural contexts. It also is appropriate to add a word of caution: the distinction between academics and workers must not be taken to imply a distinction between 'theoreticians' and 'practitioners' as if theory resided in one place and its implementation in another. Such a view is the antithesis of the commitment of participatory action research that seeks the development of theoretically informed practice for all parties involved.

Academics and workers in participatory action research are joined by a thematic concern, that is, a commitment to inform and improve a particular practice. This practice is not a narrowly conceived technical activity, but in MacIntyre's terms is

> any coherent and complex form of socially established co-operative activity through which goods internal to that activity are realised, in the course of trying to achieve those standards of excellence which are appropriate to, and partially definitive of, that form of activity, with the result that human powers to achieve excellence, and human conceptions of the goods and ends involved, are systematically extended. (MacIntyre 1981, 175)

This means that throwing a football with skill is not an example of a practice, but the game of football is. Bricklaying and turnip planting are not practices, but architecture and farming are. In a similar vein, explaining how to design an essay is not a practice, but education is. MacIntyre distinguished practices from institutions:

> Practices must not be confused with institutions. Chess, physics, and medicine are practices; chess clubs, laboratories, universities, and hospitals are institutions. Institutions are characteristically and necessarily concerned with . . . external goods. They are involved in acquiring money and other material goods; they are structured in terms of power and status, and they distribute money, power, and status as rewards. (MacIntyre 1981, 181)

MacIntyre went on to explain that institutions not only sustain themselves but also the practices they were designed to sustain. He cautioned that institutions and practices characteristically form a single causal order in which the ideals and creativity of the practice are made vulnerable to the acquisitiveness of the institution. The collaborative work necessary for maintaining and developing the practice is jeopardized by the competitiveness of the institution.

This broad view of practice and the location of practices in historically formed institutions[2] enables us to identify both the common and distinct contributions participatory action researchers must make from their different institutional and cultural contexts. Academics and workers may join forces to improve the theory and practice of education, social welfare, agriculture, and health but with the focus typically in the workers' own work contexts.

Principles

Identification of the Individual and Collective Project

The common project of participatory action research has several aspects. Every participant, academic, and worker must undertake:

- to improve his or her own work and the way it is understood (theorized);
- to collaborate with others engaged in the project (academics and workers) to help them improve their work; and
- to collaborate with others in their own separate (academic and worker) institutional and cultural contexts to create the possibility of more broadly informing (and theorizing) the common project, as well as to create the material and political conditions necessary to sustain the common project and its work.

That is, participatory action research is concerned simultaneously with changing individuals, on the one hand, and, on the other, the culture of the groups, institutions, and societies to which they belong. But it is important to emphasize that these changes are not impositions: individuals and groups agree to work together to change themselves, individually and collectively. Their interests are joined by an agreed 'thematic concern.'

Changing and Studying Discourse, Practice and Social Organization (the Distribution of Power)

MacIntyre's work also leads us to consider the tension created by the institutionalization of practice and the formation of institutional culture. The culture of any group can be defined in terms of the characteristic substance and forms of the *language and discourses*, *activities and practices*, and *social relationships and organization* that constitute the interactions of the group (Kemmis and McTaggart 1988a).[3]

- The individual is a bearer of language, but 'comes to' language, as it were, finding it preformed as an aspect of the culture of a group or society; language 'contains' expressive and communicative potential, and the way we use language can only be changed by also changing social 'agreements' about how language is used, that is, patterns of language use that are a first aspect of the culture of the group.

- The individual is an actor, but his or her acts are framed and understood in a social context of interaction; changing social action usually requires also changing the ways others interact with us, that is, patterns of interaction that are a second aspect of the culture of the group.
- Individuals define themselves partly through their relationships with others, but the nature and significance of these social relationships should be understood against the fabric of social relationships that characterize wider groups, institutions, and societies; changing social relationships usually requires that others also change their perspectives on the ways we relate to them and how our relationships with them fit into the broader fabric of relationships which structure society, that is, patterns of relationships that are a third aspect of the culture of a group.

Institutionalisation and contestation. We can see from this analysis that both *individual identity* and *institutional culture* (and the forms of work made possible) come about through complex, mutually formative, dialectical interactions. The *institutionalization* of particular kinds of educational work, for example, occurs through *contestation*. Some activities are chosen and reshaped ahead of others through an essentially political process. Clearly the development of educational work cannot be achieved by looking at 'teaching' practice alone. Particular forms of words are selected and invented to form the *discourse* of the school or college; particular kinds of activities are selected and constructed to form the *practice* of the school or college; and particular kinds of social relationships are selected and constituted to form the *organization* of the school or college. It is relatively easy to see that there can be enormous disjunctions between the social medium of ordinary community life and the institutional form of the school or college, especially where domination by bureaucratic edict has characterized the outcome of contestation. And as I have suggested above, the resultant disjunctions may not only be destructive for the culture necessary for educational work, but also for the individual. Similar considerations apply for other kinds of endeavor in the social sphere.

Seeking out contradictions. The development of educational and social work can be enhanced through the identification of contradictions that arise across and within registers within the social medium, within the institutional forms, and through the dialectical process of institutionalization and contestation. It is possible, for example, for language which is appropriate for the description of educational ideas to be lost in the forms of discourse in the school, or to be incompatible with the particular ways in which school life is organized. All of these interactions must be examined carefully to reveal new possibilities for educational action and to change or subvert conditions or ways of describing situations that confound the reconstruction of effective praxis (critically informed, committed work).

Changing the culture of working groups, institutions, and society. In participatory action research, the culture of three kinds of groups is subject to influence: the culture of the group of academics and its extension into the academic workplace; the culture of the collaborative participatory action research group itself; and the culture of the workers' workplace and its extension into the community. Unfortunately, there is still a reasonable expectation that academics will be imperialistic in their relationships with workers because of the ways in which academics typically come to participation, because of their command of particular specialized discourses, and, perhaps, because of the deference and uncertainty of workers who have been forced concretely and hegemonically to adjust to being told what to do.

Confronting the subtlety of power. To counter this expectation of the academic role, considerable energy must be directed at ensuring reciprocity and symmetry of relations in the participatory action research group, and at maintaining community control of the project (and its staff). The group must ultimately engage an ideology critique to ensure its work is not misdirected and its understandings not distorted by deference to illegitimate authority. When status and power differentials exist among participants, these must be suspended to allow collective work to begin, but combatted in the course of that work. To claim to be participatory action research, any activity must attend to these criteria ahead of all others. And it is in this context that the substantive knowledge of the academy can be most useful to help people see what they have intuitively understood, that their own subjectivity is likely to be gendered (Eisenstein 1984; Hollway 1984), colonialized, and nationalized (Chatterjee 1986), westernized (Lanhupuy 1987) and supplanted by the mass enculturation of the capitalist impulse (Aronowitz 1977; Aronowitz and Giroux 1985). That is, the work of ideology critique can be expected to involve 'decolonizing the mind' in a number of dimensions (Ngugi wa Thiong'o 1986).[4]

Expanding participation and the scope of the work. Participatory action research recognizes that people are social beings, and members of several different groups: active participants in the living, local, and concrete process of constructing and reconstructing the language, activities, and relationships that constitute and reconstitute the culture of their groups. To change the culture of their groups (let alone of whole institutions or society, more broadly), people must change themselves, with others, through changing the substance, forms, and patterns of language, activities, and social relationships that characterize groups and the interactions of their members. In participatory action research, they do this collectively and collaboratively and deliberately set aside time to reflect on these matters as a basis for conscious individual and group decision. Participatory action research is therefore contingent upon authentic participation: it is research through which people work toward the improvement of their own practices (and only secondarily the improvement of other people's practices). Through dialogue among participants, regular checks are made to ensure that the agenda of the least powerful become an important focus of the group's work.

Social improvement through participatory action research entails explicit analysis and exploratory change both on the side of the individual and on the side of the culture of the groups (and, more broadly, the society) in which people constitute their forms of life. Changing a whole society and culture is, on the face of it, beyond the reach of individuals; in participatory action research, groups work together to change their language, modes of action, and social relationships, thus, in their own ways, prefigure, foreshadow and provoke changes in the broader fabric of interactions that characterize our society and culture. In other words, participatory action research has individual and collective and local and extended aspects: individual action researchers change themselves, support others in their own efforts to change, and together work to change institutions and society. Through critiques of these efforts to change, in the slogan made famous by the environmental movement, participatory action researchers "think globally, act locally."

Getting Started Quickly

Starting small: planning, acting, observing, reflecting. Participatory action research starts small and develops through the self-reflective spiral: a spiral of cycles of planning, acting, (implementing plans), observing (systematically), reflecting, and then replanning, further implementation, observing, and reflecting again. The collective plays an important role in deciding where the group and individuals may exert their efforts most effectively. In turn, the collective reflects on observations made about action taken so far and uses this reflective activity to inform decisions about future action steps taken by the group and by individuals. In this way, the public and personal spheres of thought and action complement each other.

Being explicit about collecting data. One good way to begin a participatory action research project is to collect some initial data in an area of general interest (a reconnaissance), then to reflect and make a plan for changed action. Another way to begin is to make an exploratory change, collect data of what happens, reflect, and then build more refined plans for action. In both cases, issues and understandings on the one hand and the practices themselves on the other develop and evolve through the participatory action research process, but only when the Lewinian self-reflective spiral is thoughtfully and systematically followed in processes of group critique. Gradually, as the scope of the work increases, the group may expand its membership. It may act on broader fronts and develop its use of social theory, but control still rests with workers.

Doing It Yourself and Gaining Momentum

As Rajesh Tandon (1988) has cogently argued, knowledge production in participatory action research places an emphasis on workers developing their own understandings. Arguing for prison reform, Michel Foucault (1981) argued in the same way:

> If prisons and punitive mechanisms are to be transformed, it won't be because a plan of reform has found its way into the heads of the social workers; it will be when those who have to do with that penal reality, all those people have come into collision with each other and with themselves, run into dead-ends, problems and impossibilities, been through conflicts and confrontations; when critique has been played out in the real, not when reformers have realised their ideals. (Foucault 1981, 13)

In considering the political role of analyzing the realities of total institutional life, Foucault was equally explicit about whose work the critique was to inform:

> Critique does not have to be the premise of a deduction which concludes: this is then what needs to be done. It should be an instrument for those who fight, those who refuse and resist what is. Its use should be in processes of conflict and confrontation, essays in refusal.

Unifying the Intellectual and Practical Project

Self-critical community. Participatory action research establishes self-critical communities of people participating and collaborating in all phases of the research process: the planning, action, observation, and reflection. It aims to build communities of people committed to enlightening themselves about the relationship between circumstance, action, and consequence in their own situation, emancipating themselves from the institutional and personal constraints that limit their power to live their own legitimate educational and social values. It involves a systematic learning process in which people act deliberately, although remain open to surprises and responsive to opportunities. But participatory research is not just learning; it has knowledge production and action aspects as well as constituting new ways of relating to each other to make the work of reform possible. It is a process of using 'critical intelligence' to inform action and developing it so social action becomes the praxis through which people may consistently live their social values.

Theorizing practice. Accordingly, participatory action research involves people in theorizing about their practices, that is, being inquisitive about circumstances, action, and consequences and coming to understand the relationships between circumstance, actions, and consequences in their own lives. The theories that participatory action researchers develop may be expressed initially in the form of rationales for practices. They may develop these rationales by treating them as if they were no more than rationalizations, even though they may be our best current theories of how and why our social (and educational) work is as it is. They subject these initial rationales to critical scrutiny through the participatory action research process.

Producing knowledge. Of course, the work of the action research group will result in many shared understandings, and the work of academics in the group will reflexively inform their relationships with the institutions from which they come. That is, knowledge production is of three general kinds: knowledge developed by workers; knowledge shared by the group; and knowledge developed by academics. These forms of knowledge are intimately related, but it is the first category of knowledge, the knowledge of the workers, which is the primary focus. And this focus is achieved by directing energies to improvements from the *workers'* perspective. This focus may be informed by a critique developed from an understanding of social theory, but the practical decisions about what counts as a sustainable move toward improvement must always belong to the workers:

Engaging the Politics of Research and Action

Arranging for support. As will now be obvious, participatory action research is a political process because it involves people making changes together that also will affect others. For this reason, participatory action research sometimes creates resistance to change, both in the participants themselves and in others. Participatory action research involves people in making critical analyses of the situations (projects, programs, systems) in which they work: these situations are structured institutionally. The pattern of resistance a participatory action researcher meets in changing his or her own practices is a pattern of conflicts between the new practices and the accepted practices of the institution (accepted practices of communication, decision making, and educational work). By making a critical analysis of the institution, the participatory action researcher can understand how resistances are rooted in conflicts among competing kinds of practices, competing views of social (and educational) positions and values, and competing views of social organization and decision making. This critical understanding will help the participatory action researcher to act politically toward overcoming resistances, for example, by involving others collaboratively in the research process, inviting others to explore their practices, or by working in the wider institutional context toward more rational understandings, more just processes of decision making, and more fulfilling forms of social work for all involved.

Recognizing the need for evidence. Partly because it is an explicitly political activity as well as being a species of research, participatory action research requires that people put their practices, ideas, and assumptions about institutions to the test by gathering compelling evidence that could convince them that their previous practices, ideas, and assumptions were wrong or wrongheaded. It is open-minded about what counts as evidence (or data): it involves not only keeping records that describe what is happening as accurately as possible (given the particular questions being investigated and the real-life circumstances of collecting the data), but also collecting and analyzing each researcher's own judgments, reactions, and impressions about what is going on.

Methodological Resources

Engaging subjectivity and meaning. Especially in their early engagement with existing discourses, practices, and social relationships, participatory action researchers draw on the research methods of phenomenology, ethnography, and case study (Stake 1978), seeking an understanding of the case within which they are working. Participatory action researchers all seek understanding of people's subjective experience of their institutional situation and at the same time try to give working accounts of the contexts in which meanings are constituted. They also use the views of others to engage their own experience and to discipline their own subjective interpretations.

Information is collected in the usual naturalistic research ways, for example, participant observation, interview, the compilation of field notes, logs, document analysis, and the like. Validation is achieved by a variety of methods, including triangulation of observations and interpretations, participant confirmation, and testing the coherence of arguments being presented. Participatory action research involves participants in a process of objectification of their own experience, for example, by keeping a personal journal in which participants record their progress and reflections about two parallel sets of learnings: their learnings about the practices they are studying (how the practices—individual and collective—are developing) and their learnings about the process (the practice) of studying them (how the action research project is going). As confidence and theoretical understanding develop, participatory action researchers begin to engage the ways in which understandings are shaped (and distorted) by power relations. Academic participants (or others) may bring social theory to the group's attention, but the way in which this is done must scrupulously avoid academic imperialism (Fay 1987).

It is important to recognize that the interpretive aspect of participatory action research is not an end in itself. Its primary purpose is to make action taken by individuals and the collective in the situation better informed and more prudent. However, one of the products of an action research project may be a case study, constructed by participants, of their efforts to change over a period of time.

Creating the object and subject. The importance of documentation is another reason participatory action research starts small, by working through changes that even a single person can try and toward extensive changes, even to critiques of ideas or institutions, which in turn might lead to more general reforms of projects, programs, or system-wide policies and practices. Participants should be able to present evidence of how they started to work on articulating the thematic concern which would hold their group together and how they established authentically shared agreement in the group that the thematic concern was a basis for collaborative action. It starts with small cycles of planning, acting, observing, and reflecting which can help to define issues, ideas, and assumptions more clearly so that those involved can define more powerful questions for themselves as their work progresses. Long cycles of activity (like changing annual examinations) simply stifle momentum. Small groups of collaborators at the start help people get to know each other and make the objectification of experience less painful and daunting than it sometimes can be. Of course, widening the community of participating action researchers so it gradually includes more and more of those involved and affected by the practices in question becomes necessary and possible as participants increase their understanding of themselves, the direction of their work, and other changes which must be made to allow continued articulation of the theory and practice of their educational ideas and values.

Articulating biography (individual identity) and making history (group culture). For substantive and political reasons, participatory action researchers must create a record of their own progress as producers rather than receivers of history. Participatory action research allows and requires participants to build records of their improvements: (1) records of their changing activities and practices; (2) records of the changes in the language and discourse in which they describe, explain, and justify their practices; (3) records of the changes in the social relationships and forms of organization which characterize and constrain their practices; and (4) records of the development of their expertise in the conduct of action research. Participants must be able to demonstrate evidence of a group climate where people expect and gather evidence to support each other's claims. They must show respect for the value of rigorously gathered and analyzed evidence and be able to show and defend evidence to convince others.

Creating the Theory of the Work

Participatory action research allows and requires participants to give a reasoned justification of their social (and educational) work to others because they can show how the evidence they have gathered and the critical reflection they have done have helped them to create a developed, tested, and critically examined rationale for what they are doing. Having developed such a rationale, they may legitimately ask others to justify their own practices in terms of their own theories and the evidence of their own critical self-reflection.

Five Things Participatory Action Research is Not

1. Participatory action research is *not* the usual thing social practitioners (academics and workers) ordinarily do when they think about their work. It is more systematic and collaborative in collecting evidence on which to base rigorous group reflection, and in planning change.
2. Participatory action research is *not* simply problem solving. It involves problem posing, not just problem solving. It does not start from a view of 'problems' as pathologies. It sees values and plans problematized by work in the real world and by the study of the culture and nature of work by people themselves. It is motivated by a quest to improve and understand the world by changing it and learning how to improve it from the effects of the changes made.
3. Participatory action research is *not* research done on other people. It is research by particular people on their own work, to help them improve what they do, including how they work with and for others. Participatory action research is research that treats people as autonomous, responsible agents who participate actively in making their own histories and conditions of life, able to be more effective in making their histories and conditions of life by knowing what they are doing, and collaboratively potent in the construction of their collective history and conditions of life. It does not treat people as objects for research, but encourages people to work together as knowing subjects and agents of change and improvement.

4. Participatory action research is *not* a 'method' or 'technique' for policy implementation. It does not accept truths created outside that community or truths created by researchers working inside the community who treat the community as an object for research. Participatory action researchers may accept propositions from outside as worthy of testing, or they may elect to study their own situation from first principles, as it were, to develop their own understandings of what is happening as a guide to action.

5. Participatory action research is *not* 'the scientific method' applied to social (educational, agricultural) work. There is not just one view of the scientific method, there are many. Participatory action research is not just about testing hypotheses or using data to come to conclusions. It adopts a view of social science that is distinct from a view based on the natural sciences (in which the objects of research may legitimately be treated as 'things'). Participatory action research also concerns the 'subject' (the researcher) himself or herself. Its view is distinct from the methods of the historical sciences, because action research is concerned with changing situations, not just interpreting them. Participatory action research is systematically evolving, a living process changing both the researcher and the situations in which he or she acts; neither the natural sciences nor the historical sciences have this double aim (the living dialectic of researcher and researched [Carr and Kemmis 1986]).

These principles can be used as a guide to deciding whether accounts of research are genuine examples of participatory action research and, more importantly, as a guide to planning how participatory research practice might be improved. The principles are not absolute criteria but a product of the work of a group of participatory action researchers, that is, a theory of participatory action research. Any study claiming to be participatory action research might present evidence that these general principles have been observed or even why the principles themselves must be changed to take into account new evidence. That is, it is essential that the principles are not applied imperialistically because that would conflict with the fundamental idea of action research, which indicates that principles such as these are problematized by practice.

Concluding Comment

In his closing remarks at the Participatory Research Conference held in Calgary, Canada, in July 1989, Colombian researcher Orlando Fals Borda defused concerns that some studies reported at the conference and in the literature were not authentic participatory research by suggesting that people would learn from their mistakes. That is true, but only if people are prompted and supported to reflect critically on their work. We could even say participatory action research only exists because some enlightened practitioners of social inquiry have developed the science of learning from their own mistakes and from the mistakes of others. Mao Zedong once asserted, "The important thing is to be good at learning," while noting that it was unrealistic to expect even his best generals to have victories all of the time.

Unfortunately, we all learn too slowly, partly because we have become imbued with a Western consciousness that devalues and distrusts collective and critical self-reflection as a source of legitimate understanding. We all need all of the help, substantive and social, we can get. I hope, therefore, that there is some virtue in proposing principles such as those I have articulated here. I hope such a declaration helps us not only learn from our own mistakes and successes, but also to avoid the mistakes and emulate the successes of others, and to do so more quickly and painlessly. That hope embodies the aspiration that people will also help us by pointing out how these particular principles seem to be wrongheaded (or confirmed) and need to be amended and extended on the basis of their own particular experience of participatory action research.

Notes

1. This paper is a slightly edited version of the paper sent to contributors. Of course, action research debates have moved on since then, but my views of the fundamentals of action research have not changed a great deal. For more recent commentary on some of these matters, see McTaggart (1996, 1994, and 1991).

2. There is a sense in which institutions as we know them are social practices too. One of their obvious failings stems from the fact that they are practices created by people other than those who have to work in them, hence the constraint on the substantive efforts of workers in the institution. Partly because they are made by others, institutions are disabling as well as enabling (in particular predetermined directions, which is often tantamount to saying the same thing).

3. I owe much of the conceptual furniture of this work to my collaboration over several years with Stephen Kemmis and Colin Henry and other members of the Deakin University Action Group.

4. In the Nicaraguan context, Lankshear (1986) made a similar point about participatory action research in the literacy process known as *Alfabetizacion*:

Both prior to the overthrow of Somoza in 1979 and subsequently, this deliberate fusion of literacy teaching with an explicit ideological position has had a dual aspect. In some cases, for example, with illiterates who had actively joined the revolutionary forces, the literacy process combined teaching the skills of reading and writing with helping 'pupils' to analyse and understand more clearly something they had already intuitively grasped: namely, that oppression, poverty, disease, and ignorance were not aspects of a 'natural' or 'given' reality, but, rather, consequences of how Nicaraguan society operated under Somoza, and that a new social order could be built once the old had been overthrown (Lankshear 1986).

References

Aronowitz, S. 1977. Mass culture and the eclipse of reason: The implications for pedagogy. *Teachers college record* 38(8):768–74.

Aronowitz, S., and H. A. Giroux. 1985. *Education under siege: The conservative, liberal, and radical debate over schooling.* South Hadley, Mass.: Bergin & Garvey.

Carr, W., and S. Kemmis. 1986. *Becoming critical: Education, knowledge, and action research.* London: Falmer.

Chatterjee, P. 1986. *Nationalist thought and the colonial world.* London: Zed.

Concise Oxford Dictionary. 1976. 6th ed. London: Oxford University Press.

Cronbach, L. J. 1982. *Designing evaluations of educational and social programs.* San Francisco: Jossey-Bass.

Eisenstein, H. 1984. *Contemporary feminist theory.* Sydney: Allen & Unwin.

Fay, B. 1987. *Critical social science.* Ithaca, NY: Cornell University Press.

Foucault, M. 1981. Questions of method: An interview with Michel Foucault. *Ideology and consciousness* 8:3–14.

Habermas, J. 1972. *Knowledge and human interest.* Trans. J. J. Shapiro. London: Heinemann.

————. 1974. *Theory and practice.* Trans. J. Viertel. London: Heinemann.

Henry, C., and S. Kemmis. 1986. A point-by-point guide to action research. *The Australian Administrator* 6(4):1–4.

Hollway, W. 1984. Gender difference and the production of subjectivity. In *Changing the subject: Psychology, social regulation, and subjectivity*, eds. J. Henriques, W. Hollway, C. Urwin, C. Venn, and V. Walkerdine, 227–63. London: Methuen.

House, E. R., S. Mathison, and R. McTaggart. 1989. Validity and teacher inference. *Educational researcher* 18(7):11–15, 26.

Kemmis, S., and R. McTaggart (eds.). 1988a. *The action research planner*. 3rd ed. Geelong, Vic.: Deakin University Press.

———. 1988b. *The action research reader*. 3rd ed. Geelong, Vic.: Deakin University Press.

Lanhupuy, W. 1987. Balanda education: A mixed blessing for Aborigines. *The Aboriginal child at school* 15(3):31–6.

Lankshear, C. 1986. Dawn of the people: The right to literacy in Nicaragua. *Discourse* 7(1):31–45.

Lewin, K. 1946. Action research and minority problems. *Journal of social issues* 2:34–46.

———. 1952. Group decision and social change. In *Readings in social psychology*, eds. G. E. Swanson, T. M. Newcomb, and E. L. Hartley, 459–73. New York: Henry Holt.

MacIntyre, A. 1981. *After virtue: A study of moral theory*. London: Duckworth.

McTaggart, R. (1996). Issues for participatory action researchers. In *New directions in action research*, ed. O. Zuber-Skerritt, 243–55. London: Falmer Press.

———. 1990. *Action research: A short modern history*. Geelong, Vic.: Deakin University Press.

———. 1991. Action research: Issues for the next decade. *Curriculum perspectives* 11(4):43–65.

———. 1994. Participatory action research: Issues in theory and practice. *Educational action research* 2(3):313–37.

Ngugi wa Thiong'o. 1986. *Decolonizing the mind: The politics of language in African literature*. London: James Currey.

Noddings, N. 1984. *Caring: A feminine approach to ethics and moral education*. Berkeley: University of California Press.

Stake, R. E. 1978. The case study method in social enquiry. *Educational researcher* 7:5–8.

Tandon, R. 1988. Social transformation and participatory research. *Convergence* 21(2/3):5–14.

CHAPTER 3

Action Research:
A Closed Chapter in the
History of German Social Science?

Herbert Altrichter and Peter Gstettner

The idea of this paper is to provide a historical overview of the development of action research, its theories and practices in German-speaking countries. In doing so, we also attempted to analyze what the main topics and biases, as well as what the specific ideological, cultural, and political contexts were that might have contributed to the shape and course this research tradition eventually took.

The information in this paper comes from three sources. First, both of the authors have gained personal experience as action researchers. Peter Gstettner was one of the researchers working on the establishment of the earlier German action research tradition, discussed later in this chapter. Herbert Altrichter is currently engaged in the 'second wave' action research projects, also discussed later. Second, we draw upon an analysis of relevant literature. Since the German language will not be familiar to most readers, we cannot relate as much of the original thoughts of German action researchers in their original words as we would have wished. The list of references should give a preliminary orientation for readers who wish to do further research; more comprehensive bibliographies may be found in Kordes (1984), Merz (1985), Gunz (1986), and Nonne (1989). Third, we sent letters with three sets of questions relating to the topics of this article to sixty-one researchers in Germany, Austria, and Switzerland who have had an influential position in the German action research debate. Without any reminders, we received twenty-two responses. We used these answers as a first round in critiquing and complementing our own personal interpretation of the development of German action research.[1]

When we use the term *German-speaking countries* we ask you to keep in mind that the Federal Republic of Germany, Austria, and the German-speaking parts of Switzerland—in terms of the scientific community, its fashions, and careers—make up a fairly coherent region in the geography of academic learning and research. This is not true to the same degree for the school systems and the educational policies which, due to changing governments and different bureaucratic traditions, are not always analogous, although it is fair to say that in most educational matters these three countries are more similar to each other than they are, for example, to England or France.

A Movement For a New Social Science in a New Society?

> Empirical social research is an occult science. . . . [Its] methodological doctrine is only productive as long as it is unknown to the great majority of the population. If all potential test persons were informed about its techniques, they would be no longer applicable. Then, social research would be dependent on the test person's voluntary and reasonable co-operation in the research process. Thus, differences of knowledge and orientation competency which are produced by the social system are conditions of applicability of this methodological doctrine. (Fuchs 1970–71, 1)[2]

> Once the narrow positivistic interpretation of the social scientific concept of 'experience' is broken—which was achieved in the *Positivismusstreit* [that is, controversy on positivism in German social science, see Adorno et al. 1969; authors]—it seems quite possible to count means of political and social practice as research techniques and everyday communication processes as social research. . . . Through their claim to be able to integrate political learning and political action, increase of information and change of the field of action more or less without any friction in their own action, the West-German student movement and its successors contributed to opening the door to hitherto unusual procedures of research and action (Fuchs 1970–71, 13).

These are some extracts from what is considered *the* seminal paper for the German action research movement. Although Fuchs' article was not the first one that used the term *action research* (Bittner and Flitner 1969, 65; Haag and Pongratz 1970) it was the one that seemed to have set the tone for the coming debate and introduced the main arguments that had to be worked through by German action researchers: It starts from a *critique of traditional social research,* its reification of persons, its 'occult techniques,' and its lack of both practical influence and social theory. It aligns itself with the *student movement* and its will and practices to develop a socially responsible society. One of its ideological resources was the then newly thriving *critical theory* from which it took the latest developed version of the concept of emancipation.

At the same time, even Fuchs' early paper contained a slight critique of the dominant critical theorists in that it claimed that they concentrated on ideology critique, different—namely critical—formation of concepts, open consideration of political interests during problem definition and publication of results, however, not on the level of research procedures and techniques. Critical social scientists have hitherto rarely realized that the interaction of the researcher with the research object has itself a political dimension, that it can be understood and systematically pursued as political practice (Fuchs 1970–71, 1; see also Radtke 1975, 12).

Actually, Habermas (1969, 235) had said:

> . . . my criticism is not against the research practice of a strict empirical science, . . . my criticism is exclusively leveled at the positivistic interpretation of such research processes. The false consciousness of a correct practice has a retroactive effect on this practice.

The new breed of action researchers, however, was rather critical of concepts developed as a consequence of these sentences which, in their view, just amounted to the formula "traditional research in a framework of critical interpretation." *The research process itself had to be different, not only its interpretation.* Thus, it does not come as a surprise that Habermas (e.g., 1971, 18) distanced himself from action research.

> The fashionable demands for a type of *action research* which combines investigation with political enlightenment fail to notice the fact also valid for the social sciences that an uncontrolled change of the field is incompatible with concurrent collection of data in the field.

We shall return to this criticism later, but first let us work more systematically through the relevant arguments of the German action research debate and its context.

Born Out of Protest

The idea of 'action research' has been discussed in the German social science since the mid-1960s under a variety of terms such as *Handlungsforschung, Aktionsforschung* (both terms translate as action research), *aktivierende Sozialforschung* (activating social research), *handlungsorientierte Forschung* (action-oriented research), *betroffenenorientierte Forschung* (research oriented to the people concerned), *eingreifende Praxisforschung* (interventive practice-research), and so on. Even this variation of terminology indicates that there were profound uncertainties in the beginning as to whether this new community of researchers should be built on quasi-buried traditions of social research or seen as an alternative to all existing approaches and create its own new standards. In any case, there was a consensus that action research could not yet be pinned down to strictly delineated obligatory canons of method and that in fact openness (even when giving the research process characteristics of uncertainty) and theoretical and practical flexibility were its essential features (Gstettner 1977, 261; Knetsch 1979, 132).

At the beginning of the German action research debate, there were some attempts to establish relationships between home-grown action research projects and theoretical arguments in other countries or to distinguish them from such traditions (e.g., Haag et al. 1972; Moser 1978; Rathmayr and Wagner 1976). One reference point was to Lewin's field theory and its practical transformations into group dynamics and action research. Petzold (1980) and Gunz (1986) argued that not Lewin but J. L. Moreno should be seen as the founder of action research. J. L. Moreno, physician, social philosopher, poet and inventor of concepts, such as sociometry, psychodrama, sociodrama, role play, etc., might also have been the first to use such terms as *interaction research* and *action research* and to insist on principles like field-based research, participant observation, participation of lay people concerned in the research, and improvement of social situations as an aim of research. As early as 1913, he thought of group participants in development initiatives as co-researchers (e.g., in the work with prostitutes in the Vienna suburb of Spittelberg). Lewin and Moreno knew each other; researchers like Lippitt, Benne, and Bradford studied with both of them (Gunz 1986, 29). Nonne (1989, 156), however, argued that Moreno's *direct* influence on action research was small, although some of his ideas and research strategies—as impulses and models—might have *indirectly* influenced the development of the concept pushed forward by Lewin and his students. Gunz (1986, 34) saw Lewin and Moreno in polarity and, maybe, complementarity: "Moreno, the committed actionist filled with intuition and charisma, and Lewin, the reserved social researcher of traditional style interested in logics and precision but on the brink of a paradigm change." Gunz (1986, 35) also pointed to the irony that the German 'renaissance of action research' implicitly tended to the Moreno line of thinking, although references were almost exclusively made to Lewin.

Anglo-American developments in the action research field were referred to from time to time, although rarely in more than accidental descriptive remarks in legitimatory interest. This means German action research developed relatively independently as a specific 'oppositional' alternative to the dominant practice of research. Thus, this kind of action research cannot look back on a long tradition and even its short history, which is closely related to the birth of the student movement in 1968, is still largely in the dark.

Political Ambitions—Societal Causes

In 1968, the restoration phase of the German postwar society, the so-called *Wirtschaftswunder* (economic miracle), ran into a sudden eruption of opposing ideas from the younger generation. Profound skepticism of cumulative growth and exponential progress was spreading. The growth society's immanent destructive potentials seemed to devalue its material wealth. At first, the psycho-social costs inherent in this process and, later, on its global ecological costs, became topical. Uncertainty grew in the education field regarding whether the large-scale reform projects typical of the social-liberal climate of the late 1960s and beginning 1970s (such as curriculum reform, comprehensive schools) were actually to be realized or were bogged down in the technocracy and bureaucracy of big administrative mechanisms: high-pitched expectations of compensatory education and higher qualifications of the (educationally) underprivileged did not come true for the time being.

The urge for quick equalization of opportunities, the 'revolutionary impatience' of the youth, and the spontaneous and 'unprocessed' breaking up of frustrated social expectations took shape as protest reactions, which were reflected in increased aggressiveness in schools, in learners' loss of motivation, in refusal to study, and in rebellion against the authority of university teachers. Parallel to the rebellion at the production sites of scientific knowledge, a potential for unrest developed in the factories. As in Italy but not as frequently, unauthorized strikes in industry were called in Germany and attempts were made to connect the workers' industrial action and the 'anti-authoritarian' demands of the youth movement.

Protest also was launched against the mainly positivistic social sciences, which did not bring as much emancipation and participation as had been hoped for in the general belief in progress. In the field of education, this stock-taking has to be modified slightly: a long-standing hermeneutic tradition was still dominant at German universities and was just in the process of being severely challenged by more modern empirical approaches; one argument, among others, was that hermeneutic educational science was merely contemplative and not a practical force for the improvement of education. Thus, action research was seen by some researchers from the traditional-hermeneutical camp as offering points of departure for overcoming alleged or real shortcomings in traditional hermeneutical education, whereas others introduced action research as an attack on two fronts against impractical hermeneutics caught in old-fashioned ideologies and against a new wave of social technologists propagating seemingly more modern concepts which, upon closer examination, turned out to reiterate ideologies of dependence and oppression in a slicker outfit.

When in 1945 a certain perverted 'natural scientific understanding' had seemed to be discredited once and forever, a lot of hope was invested in the modern social sciences for providing new and rational instruments for the planning and control of the democratic society. The traditional capitalistic ideology of growth and progress, however, was vigorously eroded by the 1968 problematizations and, thus, trust in social scientific competencies for planning and action collapsed.

The 'scientization of all areas of living' in consequence of the scientific-technical revolution had frequently produced processes that turned out to be basically counterproductive for the development of enlightened and democratic societies, for example, loss of competencies, dequalification, alienation, isolation, and other phenomena that aided and abetted a pauperization of everyday life. These developments obviously contradicted the accumulation of 'cultural capital' in the monopolies and centers of knowledge production (e.g., in the Ordinarien[3] universities and large state research institutions). The old social fault lines were reappearing, such as the separation of manual and brain work, theory and practice, academic knowledge and everyday experience, objective results and subjective insights, expert and lay competency, and the researcher and the researched.

This social situation was one reason for the call for a type of social research that did not derive its understanding primarily from collaboration with and legitimation of the existing political system, but rather saw its role as oppositional, as an attempt to help the underprivileged and powerless in the articulation of their interests (Gstettner and Seidl 1975, 120) to reintegrate processes of knowledge production and use into everyday worlds and submit them to the shared control of everyone concerned. Thereby, the course was set theoretically and with respect to research strategy, making obsolete the existing methods of behavioral observation, survey research, attitude measurement, psychological tests, and so on (Fuchs 1970–71).

Epistemological Premises and Strategic Starting Points

The most important theoretical work to develop the concept of action research took place from 1975 to 1985. The new scientific community had constituted itself in 1974 during the first Wiesbaden symposium on action research. Afterwards, action research was a prominent theme at several conferences of German learned societies, until 1986, when participants discussed the question Can action research still be saved? during the annual conference of the *Deutsche Gesellschaft für Erziehungswissenschaften* (and one respondent's impression was that the climate was an "unlucky mixture of apologies and (self)-funeral orations"; Lt. 22). As far as we understand the publication market, the last attempt to integrate action research practice with adequate theory work dates from this as well (Staufer and Stickelmann 1984; Wedekind 1986). Later publications are clearly signalling the effort to view *Aktionsforschung* as one qualitative method, among others, and to establish relationships between action research and procedures of hermeneutical interpretation (Heinze 1987; Braun 1987).

German action research broke the methodological conventions of traditional research practice in several ways. It did not choose its 'subject' according to theory-immanent criteria, and it did not recruit its 'objects' according to criteria of statistical representation, but assessed its practice in terms of whether or not it theoretically and strategically succeeded in reaching human beings (also including researchers themselves) who were alienated, externally directed, and stereotypically thinking and acting in the capitalistic environment, that is, by including them in a process of socially relevant communication and self-reflection on the scene of action. Thus, action research aimed typically for the everyday processes of raising political consciousness and, eventually, for the formation of a social movement as a basis for individuals gaining more influence over their own everyday practice through conscious participation in learning, work, leisure time, family, and so forth.

Action research criticized the dominant approach in disciplines such as education, psychology, and sociology and was multiplying a bad social reality since it was imitating and stabilizing a constitutive moment of social reality by strictly separating the roles of 'researcher' and 'test persons': the researcher controls the conditions for relevant behavior, test persons are kept in relative ignorance and must orient themselves to an externally set context.

Dialectical-materialistic researchers (Holzkamp 1972) asserted an anthropological argument: the individual must not be trapped in the vicious circle of alienation of theory (insight) from practice (action) through research itself. If wrong consciousness and wrong practice in living feed on each other, social science must further both insight into these relationships and the means of liberation from them. This impetus coincided with an interactionist-phenomenological interpretation of dialectical social models, since the potential for enlightenment (Heinze et al. 1975, 23) is definitely inherent in this research tradition. From management theory, social psychology, and group dynamics, every form of hierarchical-unilinear information flow and anti-emancipatory structures of order and obedience was called into question (Mertens 1975). Additional theoretical reinforcement was provided by social philosophy approaches, which developed a concept of intersubjective understanding on the basis of a *herrschaftsfreier Diskurs* (discourse free from all constraints of domination), which was seen as the central medium for the societal liberation of the individual from internal and external colonization (Habermas 1971, 1981).

Action Premises and Action Fields

Around the key date of 1968, it was mainly the young and nonestablished researchers who pushed forward the protest against the methodological

conventions of positivistic social research and the tradition of the hierarchi-
cal-authoritarian, predemocratic organization of science that had been cultivated in the universities. It was they who set up the first action research projects between 1969 and 1971: the project "Osdorfer Born," which combined
social care in a Hamburg suburb and project work by university students, was
started in 1969 (Haag et al. 1972, 205). The project "Maerkisches Viertel" in
a newly built satellite suburb of Berlin also was oriented toward social pedagogy and commenced in 1970. In 1971, a team of social researchers at Wiesbaden (FRG) set up action research in schools (cf Heinze et al. 1975). The
"Marburger Grundschulprojekt" (Marburg Primary School Project, discussed
later) also had recruited its research team by 1971.

It is not surprising that the initial action research projects were located
in those fields in which the structures of authority and hegemony of the classical German self-image of 'Bildung' (that is, 'education,' in a very German
sense) had been restabilized after 1945. A survey of the first practical projects
may substantiate this claim, which included projects in the following fields:
in the education of teachers and social science students, which was bogged in
the swamps of the theory-practice divide into which universities had maneu-
vered themselves by intellectualizing the everyday life of education; in classrooms and schools, where lack of curricular participation for the persons concerned and lack of democracy in the learning environment were the main
targets of attack; in the leisure time outside of schools, which was regarded
either as completely externally directed or as a field of socialization neglected
by economic progress; in the field of the so-called social fringe groups and
their existence in 'total institutions' (such as reformatories, prisons, psychi-
atric institutions, etc.), which were seen as repressive and identity-destructive
mechanisms built to keep society clear of rebel and deviant groups and to
readapt them to the normality of industrial society; in the more or less handicapped and deformed world of 'problem' groups (old and sick people, alco-
holics, drug addicts, immigrants, etc.); and in social work, aiming to help self-
determination and the discovery of identity in the family, workplace, suburb,
or block of flats.

In these fields, action research tried to find its position under the following premises:

1. Action research intends an improvement of the 'Lebenswelt' ('world of
   everyday life') and these innovations are to be negotiated and pursued in
   a conscious and planned way. This implies that form and content of
   change are to be subjected to discursive legitimation. No matter how
   small the willingness for discourse and how restricted the potential for
   verbal expression may be, research must start from the existing communicative competencies and develop them within a communication climate
   free from all constraints of domination in the direction of shared and con-

sensual orientations for action. It was a political premise in which the people concerned were engaged in each of these discourses out of an interest in a "substantial democratization of social circumstances" (Moser 1978, 105).

2. Action research finds its basis in the constitution of social groups which themselves design possible changes in a justified way because of their experience of being concerned with precarious circumstances of life. Thus, action research may be seen as a "specific science of the subject" (Holzkamp 1977, 64) in which practical activity and theoretical consideration mean "experiential dimensions of equal right" (Knetsch 1979, 132) for all participants and add up to a "unity of research and development" (Schneider 1980, 197).

3. Within this process, action research has to prove itself as a self-reflective practice of research in which the 'theoreticians' also know what they are doing and why they are doing it (Gstettner 1979). Social scientists are involved in this process by virtue of their acting and theorizing, for example, by helping to identify new possibilities and barriers, disturbances and deficits which prevent individuals and society from broadening their competencies of action and speech and from transforming their world of everyday living.

The Marburg Primary School Project (MPSP)

In the following section, one of the big action research projects is outlined to provide an idea of the practice of German action research. Although it was not exemplary in the sense that all or most German action research endeavors followed similar lines, the debate that arose around it might be called 'exemplary,' as we try to argue later in this chapter.

The Project

The MPSP was one of the big action research projects in the school sector and was funded by the Volkswagenwerk Foundation, one of the most prestigious German sponsors providing industrial money for scientific research. For nearly a decade, the project was an influential model for innovative school development, practice-oriented curriculum research, and action-oriented educational science (cf Klafki et al. 1982).

The core of its practice-oriented curriculum development, which took place in various forms of cooperation, consultation, and support between researchers and teachers, was comprised of the following guiding ideas derived from the democratic principle "advancement of individual competency for self-determination and social competency of critique and participation" (Klafki 1973, 495):

- self-determination: students were to be increasingly enabled to steer their learning processes themselves; and
- social learning: students were to be enabled to learn in cooperative groups and to reflect on the interaction processes.

These ideas also were to be realized in a product-oriented manner. That is, there was an attempt to have new pedagogical concepts and, consequently, new curricular material developed by schools, to test their feasibility in practice and to explore their potential for transfer to other schools. Alongside the development, adaptation, and evaluation of classroom concepts and curricular units there was a cluster of additional project objectives (Klafki 1973, 494), including: development of forms of cooperation in teams of researchers and teachers, eventually aimed at the teachers' emancipation from the researchers' support; development of forms of self-evaluation, aimed at enabling teachers to monitor whether their actual behavior and objectives conformed to plans and aspirations; and development of forms of cooperation with parents and the wider public and of forms of influencing opinion leaders and schools, through in-service work to enhance the understanding and acceptance of innovative school change, both inside and outside the project schools, and to reassess conventional attitudes toward learning and education.

From the start, there was controversy among members of the research team regarding the relative importance and feasibility of traditional methods for evaluating school innovation. A way out was finally attempted by using the concept of a multi-method system. That is, on the one hand, the project was striving for results collected and analyzed according to traditional standards (such as a questionnaire for parents, standardized competency tests, IQ tests); on the other hand, it also was interested in qualitative data and procedures that conformed to the processual, flexible, and interactive character of an action research project.

The specific role definitions (of 'theory' and 'practice,' 'research' and 'action') were found to be highly relevant for all research problems and their pragmatic solutions. The way in which they were negotiated and in which definitions were 'routinized' and sometimes processually modified was crucial. Programmatically, the researchers claimed that researchers and practitioners must not be "locked into different roles on principle" (Klafki 1973, 504) and that processually occurring dominance always called for enlightenment and transparency: "It remains crucial that in action research there are no research secrets and that research procedures must not be used *against* the practitioners' will" (Klafki 1973, 505; emphasis in the original).

For the actual research practice, a "pragmatic-flexible task differentiation" (Klafki 1973, 506) with different responsibilities in different phases was to account for "different professional socialization and different pressure to act in the practical field.'" Thereby, a core element of action research is alluded to, namely the question of the interactive strategies by which the representatives of 'theory' and 'practice' mutually convey their competences and wishes for change (Gstettner 1976). It is one of the questions seen as crucial for the methodological image of action research and is dealt with in the controversy between Radtke and Klafki on the MPSP.

The Radtke-Klafki Controversy

Radtke (1975) was critical of researchers, like Klafki (1973), using positivistically contaminated methods hoping to be able to cleanse them afterwards in the framework of ideology-critical interpretation (thereby reiterating Fuchs' initial argument; see the beginning of this chapter). He illustrated three examples from Klafki's project that showed that the choice of methods prevents the accomplishment of the declared set of emancipatory aims.

1. Division of roles: What Klafki described as "pragmatic-flexible task differentiation" was, in Radtke's (1975, 19) eyes, a division of labor that left "the well-known role distribution of researcher and 'research object' untouched, at most modified by carving the full process into feed-back steps which are easier to survey." As usual, the researchers retreated to process the data; the most decisive learning processes took place within their group, with only the results being presented to the teachers. Also, the selection of the collaborating schools and teachers took place according to demographic variables instead of relying on criteria, such as "pressure of problems, awareness of problems, and problem solving initiatives" (Radtke 1975, 18), which were more relevant for a shared learning process. Radtke (1975, 18) emphasized the necessity for an initial project phase to "constitute a balanced dialogue on needs, interests, and aims"; however, he was aware of the central problem "that the people concerned are severely handicapped in terms of the competency to articulate their 'true' needs."

2. Division of research and action: Radtke argued that the use of an individualistic competitive performance test in the MPSP contradicted the educational aim of 'group work.' Actually, the test was used, however, in a "not too rigid way." This amounted to a 'problematic compromise' in which both action research's strict acceptance of the subjectivity of the persons concerned and the claim of traditional methods for objectivity are lost (Radtke 1975, 21). Furthermore, the results just depicted a status quo, thus were of little use for defining how to proceed to a modification of the teaching procedure.

3. Product orientation: Klafki (1973, 498) aimed for the "subsequent 'transfer'" and adaptation of the project results and experiences by other schools, thus, for a "generalization of research results in some sense or another." Radtke (1975, 23) questioned

> how results which would have remained without value for the people concerned without the respective learning process might be 'transferred' . . . The validity of a curriculum unit is precisely founded on this reflection process of all the people concerned. The only extra-insight for the researchers were experiences in organising and managing these reflection processes which are transferable in that they can be inserted in the organisation and management of further reflection processes.

Rather than for products, action research processes should opt for experiences and competency.

Klafki's reply (1975) was forceful. First, his research strategy was not rightly described as a basically positivistic investigation interpreted in a framework of ideology-critique; rather, he aimed for "the consistent development of the immanent interrelationship of hermeneutics, empirical research, and ideology-critique' (Klafki 1975, 28). Both emancipatory and practical aims required a sufficient measure of aim-related objectivity, methodological precision, and distance of the observer, that is, some distancing from the immediacy of the action context, because there is no other way for the people concerned . . . to achieve a higher or more differentiated level of reflection and action . . . for the sake of the emancipatory development of the people concerned is neither possible nor necessary to unify 'research' and 'change' *permanently* . . . ; rather they must be dialectically interrelated, for example as feed-back processes . . . (Klafki 1975, 31).

Once more, Klafki seemed to refer to the Habermasian figure of the sub/super/ordination of different knowledge-constitutive interests: emancipatory interpretation can overturn technical procedure (which had been criticized by the young breed of German action researchers, discussed earlier).

Second, (Klafki 1975, 29) questioned whether all traditional research methods were unavoidably impregnated by technological interests, however, conceded that a more subtle question has not been sufficiently considered so far: "In what way do research methods determine or constitute their objects and potential ways of knowing?"

As to Radtke's three criticisms, Klafki argued:

1. To overcome the division of roles is difficult under the conditions of a project that cannot give more time for research and reflection to the teachers involved. "But even under considerably better conditions it might be an illusion to think that working up all problems and tasks popping up in an action research project might be accomplished under participation of *all* persons concerned in joint co-operation." (Klafki 1975, 35)
2. The 'competency testing' example was not typical for the project and, thus, had been wrongly generalized. However, even competency testing

results might be useful to convince some groups of parents that project schools achieved the same results as 'normal schools' with regard to traditional criteria, even if these criteria were irrelevant for the project (Klafki 1975, 32).

3. Teachers themselves want some 'objectivizations' occasionally in their process of self-reflection, as a sign of their increasing professionalism, a justification for their workload, and a means for comparing experiences with other teachers (Klafki 1975, 37). Why should only researchers and not teachers gain 'transferable extra-insights'? To Klafki, this amounts to a "boundless 'subjectivisation' of knowledge and experience . . . an emphatic *Verabsolutierung* [i.e. making absolute; authors] of the immediacy of experience and its supposed mirroring in reflection."

Thus, in Klafki's eyes, Radtke's paper presents an "indefensible [in terms of a philosophy of science], practically unrealizable, eventually abstract program of a total alternative to all research hitherto . . ." (Klafki 1975, 38).

Criticisms and Decline

Weaknesses and Reasons for the Decline of the German Action Research Movement

There was a boom in publications on action research between 1972 and 1982. Nonne (1989, 140) counted more than 400 papers and books in this period. Since the early 1980s, however, the term *action research* has become less fashionable in German academia. In 1990, virtually every respondent in our postal inquiry agreed that the concept—at least in the way it had been introduced in the beginning of the 1970s—had disappeared from the German social science debate. In the following paragraphs, we try to provide a summary of what have been considered weaknesses of this concept and a personal assessment as to which of these weaknesses might have contributed to the decline of action research after a rather short period in which it flourished.

Criticism from the traditional-empirical approach. In the climate of reform, there initially had been broad interest in a research approach that claimed to push forward research-based changes. Evidence for this appears in the proceedings of the conferences of the German Society for Educational Research (e.g., Rolff 1971). However, a stiffening of different camps was soon occurring again. There was criticism from some followers of the traditional-empirical approach. The harshest assault came from Lukesch and Zecha (1978, 40), who criticized that the basic terms and methods of action research remained unclarified and that its objectives were characterised by "vague terms, unclarified preconditions, and contradictions." Their impression was that otherwise disunited German action researchers merely agreed in their 'socio-political orientation' and concluded that *Handlungsforschung* cannot be considered a new research strategy but rather a more or less disguised method of politico-pedagogical manipulation. Although not every criticism was so crude, there obviously had been deep reservation from the leading figures of the (then in Germany also comparatively new) traditional-empirical approach, which did not help obtain research grants for major projects.

However, skepticism also was voiced in the action researchers' own ranks (Seidl & Seidl 1977; Horn 1979). In fact, publication and analyses of failed projects or conflicts within projects were epistemologically adequate to the action research strategy (Nonne 1989,143), however, they were then a relative novelty which seemed to have unpreparedly struck competitive academia. One respondent told us: "In those days, I considered these publications correct in principle and courageous. However, they unleashed malicious echoes rather than stimulating imitation" (Lt. 22).

Methodological weaknesses. In fact, the developing concept of German 'action research' seems to have been stricken by some methodological weaknesses. At the starting point of action research, there was criticism of the procedures of traditional social research, which even today seems to be quite to the point. "But from this criticism no direct path—in terms of methods or research policy—leads to action research. This criticism makes the 'different behavior' of action research clear but it cannot *found* action research" (Rammstedt 1979, 41). There have been attempts to establish a methodological discussion and provide a foundation for the approach (cf, for example, Moser 1978), however, the proponents of the action research debate obviously did not succeed in progressing from criticism of other approaches to establishing a passably coherent constructive methodological discourse. As one of our respondents wrote: "There were too many conceptual innovations—subjected to only cursory analysis and then quickly claimed as a 'common good.' This might have contributed to rendering narrow empirical approaches obsolete rather than establishing methodical and argumentative figures genuinely of one's own" (Lt. 4).

Symptoms of this might also be seen in the Radtke-Klafki debate: for example, Radtke is, on the one hand, critical of traditional empirical 'objectivity' but uses, on the other hand, a fairly traditional conception of 'objectivity via rigidity of procedures' (Radtke 1975, 21) to make his criticisms. Klafki, in his concentration on the over-arching process of ideology-critique, leaves the empirical phase untouched and, thus, implicitly asserts methodological arguments which are, as we see today more clearly, desperately in need of development.

Theoretical deficiencies. Some of our respondents claimed that within the entire socio-critical vein the formulation of social theory or the discussion of what established social theory had to offer had been neglected. Basic concepts, such as the role of the university and (social and natural) sciences in a changing society (Lt. 6), or the underlying theory-of-action (Lt. 16/21; Rammstedt 1979) had not been satisfactorily clarified.

Relationship Between the Researcher and the Researched

The latter issue might have contributed to problems and frictions in the relationship between the researcher and the persons being researched. Action researchers start with the basic tenet of suspending the distinction between socially responsible researchers and the former research objects. The aspiration was to establish a symmetrical dialogue and a really cooperative research between professional researchers and the people concerned. In practice, however, a rather unilinear role differentiation took place: researchers were methodologically and procedurally more experienced, more eloquent as to the socio-political aims and, in addition, confronted with expectations of support. "It was mostly the researchers who initiated projects, took charge of them, and, in contradiction to their official aims, produced new dependencies" (Moser 1989, 7). Instead of mutual learning, the emphasis was mostly on "change on the part of those being researched" (Heinze 1986, 8). However, there were also reports and analyses of role conflicts within action research teams (Gstettner 1976). Retrospectively, many respondents indicate that the ideas relating to the identification of roles of researcher and persons being researched were too simplistic and optimistic. A shared political aim was assumed but actually rarely existed within the project teams (Lt. 15). The different interests of researchers and persons concerned were not sufficiently clarified and, thus, remained unbalanced with the result that the researchers' interests (for example, in development of substantive theory and unsettling of petrified everyday views) were often dominant (Lt. 1, 3, 8; Moser 1989, 8). This even lead to the leftist critique that action research was just a new wave of "correction and patronizing" of teachers by researchers, this done "under the mask of cooperation" (Wünsche 1979, 23).

Theory-practice relationship. What superficially looks like a clash between aspiration and performance might be more deeply rooted in a clash between contradictory or, at least, insufficiently harmonized aspirations; or, to put it in another way, rooted in too simplistic a concept of the theory-practice relationship. Basically, the following assumptions seem to have been preeminent:

- Action research wanted to make theory practical in order to improve practice. Theory and practice as 'products' (that is, knowledge) were more important than processual views (for example, 'theory' as a process of dealing with problems).
- To achieve the improvement of practice, the main point was to critique everyday knowledge theoretically. The transformation of the 'improved consciousness' into a 'new practice' was a more minor point.
- The abstract concepts of 'theory' and 'practice' were often too easily personalized in the sense that professional researchers stood for 'theory' and practitioners for 'practice.' Thus, a hierarchy was established which made learning in the other direction more difficult, for example, the development of the researchers' theory and practice through theoretical and practical critique by practitioners.

Looking back, an action researcher says: "I think at the beginning we operated very much as 'true believers in science' in spite of all our criticism of established normal science" (Lt.16/21). The heightened dignity of 'theory,' at least, of one's own specific theory, remained surprisingly unchallenged. The innovation strategy basically consisted in 'rationalization of the world,' even if it appeared in a revolutionary vocabulary. This belief in the rational powers of one's own theory seems to have made action researchers rather sure of their own interpretations and political aims in communication with persons who were subjects of the research but at the same time rather naive as to the opportunities to convince societal powers by rational argument (Lt. 16/21). Thus, building relationships with societal powers and finding allies in the educational and scientific systems seem to have been badly neglected (Lt. 10, 17, 16/21).

Habermas (1971, 37) distinguished three functions in the mediation of theory and practice that have to be assessed against different criteria: First, there is the development of critical theorems that have to bear examination by symmetrical 'theoretical discourses.' Second, there is the problem of "organizing enlightenment processes, in which such theorems are applied and tested in a unique way as to their potential for triggering reflection processes in specific target groups" (Habermas 1971, 37). Since processes of enlightenment (like processes of therapy) are initially asymmetrical by definition, they can only be organized

> (in order to avoid exploitation of delusion) under the precondition that those who are doing active enlightening work bind themselves to safeguards [e.g., as psychoanalysts do in their professional ethics; authors] and secure some room for manoeuvre in communication according to the model of therapeutic 'discourses.' (Habermas 1971, 39).

Third, there is the area of political struggle in which strategic and tactical questions are relevant but reflexive theories cannot be applied without contradiction (Habermas 1971, 43). Retrospectively, it seems that German action researchers were sometimes oscillating between these different levels: although there was much rhetoric of establishing 'symmetrical discourses' between researchers and participants, it was frequently interspersed with the vocabulary of 'enlightenment' which sometimes seems to have turned—in the face of practical and communicative problems—into strategic action.

In a recent overview, Susan Noffke (1989) claimed that the history of action research is characterized by a *tension between democracy and social engineering*, which continues to be worked out in changing configurations in the practice of action research. We suggest as an explanation that through their belief in the powers of their theory, German action researchers were not in a position to accept the 'social engineering' element in their own work, thus could not sufficiently take safeguards against secret imbalances in their relationships with the persons concerned. Accordingly, one of the most prominent German action researchers tells us retrospectively of his disenchantment:

> Also action research has lost its naive confidence in the 'great story' of emancipation since it caught itself exercising dominance. In any case, it cannot take for granted any longer the ability to act more or less automatically and directly—in the service of social progress (whatever its definition may be). What is left is the attempt to express enlightenment and reflexion in the diverse moves of different language games or different cycles of action and research again and again—within a more or less disillusioned informational society (in the sense of Lyotard), which cannot believe any longer in the big designs of the past which were meant to found meaning and interpretation. (Moser 1989, 8)

Political changes. One must also see that German action researchers had very little time to elaborate their research program. Lakatos (1974, 173) argued that young research programs must be given some protected time to develop their methodology and supporting theories of which older programs can more freely dispose. Certainly action research was not given this protected time and that might have had political reasons in a double sense: First, action research that promoted progressive educational and socio-political aims was too leftist for some (Lt. 3). Its pronounced activism and admitted partiality was a scientific flaw for some and a political provocation for others (Geissler and Hege 1985, 26; Lt. 20). On the other hand, one must see that just about the time action research was in the position to build up a critical discourse and practical projects, profound political changes occurred. The student movement which had been the ideological background of many action researchers dissolved into rival factions and the period of educational reform which had produced high expectations for new comprehensive schools, more education for everybody, and more democracy in education turned into a period of 'roll back' of reforms in the wake of the oil crisis (Lt. 1, 2, 4, 6, 8, 16/21). Thus, action research was deprived of its most important power bases within a comparatively short time, and it had to pay dearly for neglecting to find other allies in society, such as in the progressive parts of the educational administration or the university system. This, however, had always been difficult because, as in the student movement, there had not been too much hope in the evolution of existing institutions. Thus, the defeat of the student movement's revolutionary option left action researchers without strategy.

Factionalism. We said earlier that action researchers did not succeed in establishing a passably coherent theoretical and methodological discourse. Time might have been one factor but there seems to have been a second one. Reading the Radtke-Klafki controversy today, one feels Radtke had identified some really critical issues for the development of action research that could have served as a starting point for a fruitful theoretical debate. On the other hand, one also feels he had presented many of these issues in a brisk language of solutions that was too bold with respect to substantive matters and clearly offended his counterpart. In some sense, just like the student movement, German action researchers lost too much energy in factionalism and invested too little energy in finding allies (Lt. 3, 11, 16/21). Additionally, there were very few international contacts: too little attention was paid to developments in the action research strategy in English-speaking countries after Lewin (Cremer et al. 1977, 171; for exceptions see Moser and Ornauer 1978; Sitte and Scholz 1976). However, German action researchers did some work in developing countries (Lt. 3, 4). Contacts with other research programs, which could have been potential allies, such as critical theory or qualitative research, were not cultivated until later, when action research was in the process of fading away (Zedler and Moser 1983).

Practical deficiencies. In spite of the incoherence of the action research debate (or maybe because of it), there was much more emphasis on theoretical debate and the formulation of 'right' objectives, concepts, and strategies than on practicing the preached things in concrete projects. There was certainly impressive research and development work done, however, on the whole, many projects were too poorly finance and of too short a duration to have a chance of achieving the expectations which had been raised by the criticism of established research and educational institutions (Lt. 1,3, 8). Kreissl and Wolffersdorf-Ehlert (1985, 102) claimed that in the middle of the 1970s there was a boom of interest in practice-oriented research, which led to an inverse theory-practice proportion: "The fewer the action research projects which were realized in practice, the more the number of publications *on* action research written at academic desks increased—increased in number,

process of contrasting both sides could learn something about themselves. To conclude, we want to propose at least some hypotheses for further discussion.

Aristotelian vs. Platonian Science

When John Elliott explained the origins of action research, he did not merely go back to Lewin but some steps further

> Long ago, Aristotle, in his 'Ethics,' outlined a form of Practical Philosophy or Moral Science, which involved systematic reflection by social practitioners as the best means of realising practical values in action. Aristotle called this form of reflection 'Practical Deliberation.' He argued that through deliberative reflection the practitioner not only clarifies the wise course of action in the situation, but deepens his understanding of the values they should realise . . . Concepts of values cannot be grasped in abstract terms. They are embodied in the concrete actions practitioners select to realise their values. Therefore, moral concepts can only be developed by reflecting about their instances in action. (CARE/UEA 1989, 5)

If it is permissible to divide the stream of occidental thought into two parts, it seems strikingly clear that German action researchers are swimming in the Platonian creek while English action researchers are in the Aristotelian one: German action researchers would not have felt inclined to see their activities situated in the moral rather than the theoretical camp. They were keen on theories and systematic thought and wanted to get their objectives and ideas right *before* they were realized in practice. On the other hand, English action researchers seem to have more entelechistic confidence in processes, dynamics, evolution, and hypotheses, even if they are wrong. They also are interested in the clarification of aims or values, although they tend to see that as a task which has to be solved in practice again and again. The knowledge from which action research starts is personally constructed local knowledge underlying the practitioners' action, instead of general knowledge generated in some discourse of social science.

In accordance with this distinction, English action researchers started their project work in a rather pragmatic vein, based on their background experiences in curriculum research and some concise formulations by Lawrence Stenhouse. Their practice, however, helped them win allies in the teaching force and in local administration. "Action research was perceived as providing an understandable and workable approach to the improvement of practice through critical self-reflection" (Carr and Kemmis 1986, 167). Attempts to formulate a more comprehensive theoretical justification of their work were of later date (Elliott 1985b; Carr & Kemmis 1986) and could build on pragmatic successes. In German action research, it seems to have been just the other way around. The starting point was theoretical critique, and the struggles that were fought at first were theoretical ones concerning the right way of doing research.

Two Meanings of Cooperation

In German action research, 'cooperation' or 'collaboration' between practitioners and academics meant that both parties worked within the same project in hopefully symmetrical relationships, more or less on the same task; concepts like 'pragmatic-flexible task differentiation' (Klafki 1973, 506) only indicate that the "normal thing" was to work on the same task. This is profoundly different in English action research: Stenhouse (1985, 57) emphasized that educational professionals cannot cede their responsibility for the educational process to external agencies, be it academic research or political power. Consequently, *the practitioners are the action researchers* and not the external academics collaborating with them. An ethical code has to ensure that the teachers' action research is not hijacked by external agents. Since the outsiders also are engaged in an educational practice, Elliott (1985a) required external academics to do *second order action research* into their own educational practice of providing a framework conducive to the teachers' reflection and action. Action research is understood as research *in* education and not as research *on* education (Elliott 1985a) and, consequently, the educational theories of academic action researchers[5] do not tend to focus directly on classrooms but rather resemble self-reflections by professional teacher educators and organizers of curriculum projects, as has been lucidly exposed by Skilbeck's (1983, 12) obituary for Stenhouse. In the English tradition, more than by German action researchers, it seems to have been accepted that teachers and academics work on different levels, however, within one educational system that they are contributing to through their own practice. Thus, a rather clean-cut, easily visible separation between roles and responsibilities is achieved, which might provide a better chance of avoiding role conflicts and "correction and patronizing under the mask of cooperation" (see Wünsche 1979, 23); it is interesting to note that some German action researchers are now suggesting similar strategies (Moser 1989; Lt. 16/21).

Administrative Cultures

English schools were traditionally seen not as a state responsibility but as a local service within a county. Curriculum was the single school's responsibility. Until recently, the school system was founded on a partnership between the central ministry, the local education authorities, and the teaching force; quality was supposed to be ensured mainly by the professionalism of teachers, inspectors, and administrators (Maw 1987, 3). Decentralist systems usually are more pluralistic (in the sense that there are more chances for outsiders to have influence), need more small-scale initiatives, and are based on local negotiation, which are all features that might be conducive to the establishment of action research. The German and Austrian education systems, on the other hand, are more centralist. Centralism is not conducive to small-scale incremental innovation; an innovation has to be a big design suited to more or less all schools, thus, "you have to get it right before you try." The 'radicalism' of German action researchers who considered most institutions desperately in need of being radically changed is strangely fitting to their vernacular administrative culture, as is the pragmatism and incrementalism of English action researchers fitting to theirs.

Professionalism of Teachers

Our impression is that English action researchers show more confidence in the powers of teachers for self-support and constructive development, whereas German action researchers tend to see teachers as rather doubtful collaborators whose everyday knowledge might be contaminated by false consciousness. We do not think English action researchers are just optimistic or more naive people (although there might be a dash of Aristotelian naivety); rather, we assume there is a more concrete basis for their beliefs. English teachers seem to have acquired professionality by making curricula for their school, negotiating within the school and community, formulating their educational views in interviews for promotion, and attending in-service courses that had some relevancy for promotion and sometimes provided them with additional diplomas and degrees. In Germany or Austria, teachers more resemble civil servants who are fairly strictly built into a bureaucracy without too much chance and zest for initiative, further development, and promotion.

The English 'liberal educational establishment' of teachers, inspectors, and educationally aware administrators was an obvious ally of action researchers who wanted to provide more say in educational development to practitioners and who provided them with an additional strategy to justify their claims. On the other hand, thanks to a comparatively unprofessional teaching force and educational administration, there were not so many progressively minded allies available for German action researchers, which explains why they were rather skeptical about the possibility of evolution of both practitioners' everyday knowledge and existing institutions, thus opted for 'reeducation' of teachers and profound changes of structures.

Downfall, Renaissance, Change, or What Else?

Having described 'new beginnings' of action research in a specific field, namely teacher research in Austrian schools, there remains the question: How do we generally assess the state of action research in German-speaking countries and its opportunities for development? This question seems particularly relevant considering the current social changes in Europe, such as the opening up of the former East Bloc countries, the unification of the two German states, the revival of old nationalisms, migration, European isolation, and new racism. The answer will necessarily be speculative, since it is simply not yet observable if there are substantial changes in the 'order book' of established social research (as Giesen and Leggewie 1991 think), or if researchers themselves are tending to a 'paradigm shift.' Although it is difficult to imagine that social science does not reflect these changes at all, it is still possible that it will continue with business as usual. But what will happen to action research?

First, we think that the time of the great controversies between abstract theories and methodologies seems to be over. Thus, the wave of publications, which was based upon intensive academic skirmishes on concepts and ideologies, has died down. Learned struggles such as the *Positivismusstreit* in German sociology, the recent debate of historians on the modern history of the Nazi Reich, the controversy between bourgeois psychology and its critical counterpart of historical-materialistic alignment, and so on have usually left heaps of books on the academic battlefield that do not seem to be in any sound relationship to their influence on research practice, but rather helped provide an intellectual means of mutually immunizing the respective methodological procedures. With the benefit of hindsight, one sees a lot of sham fights; whether action researchers voluntarily participated in them or were forcibly dragged into them is difficult to assess retrospectively. However it may be, German action researchers have spent much more energy in the closed circles of academic seminars than would be permissible by their own standards.

Second, if our analysis is correct, then action research—understood as a social-critical, subject-oriented, emancipatory research strategy—has neither dissolved without any trace nor camouflaged itself so perfectly that it is invisible to the searching eye of the sociology of science. Action research now almost naturally finds a fixed place within the repertoire of modern social research as might be gathered by the respective chapters in recent encyclopedias, handbooks, and textbooks on methods. Action research approaches (although not always using this name) may be found in project cooperation between politically committed researchers and self-critical practitioners. As well, the fields of application have partly changed in this second generation of action researchers; they now read, for example, as drug scene, migrant camp, women's shelter, child protection center, anti-racism office, skin head and neo-Nazi scene, and so on more often than as playground, kindergarten, school, youth club, and spare time club. Today, this work is increasingly taking place outside universities and in collaboration with nongovernmental organizations. At the same time, at some universities, in paraprofessional training institutions, adult and continuing education, the educational work of unions, and so on, action research approaches have become such essential and integral elements of project-oriented studies that the term itself has become virtually invisible.

Third, in its new beginnings and continuation (in some fields), action research seems to have become tactically wiser and more pragmatic in its claims. Thus, proponents no longer exhaust and wear themselves out fighting against the 'monuments' of traditional science concepts to arrive at an alternative as 'pure' as possible. Rather, there is more unself-conscious experimentation with modes of theory-practice-linkages, partly inspired by the Anglo-Saxon tradition. Thereby, German action research can move beyond its merely legitimatory references to non-German traditions and bring its empirical, theoretical, and practical experiences into a qualitatively new relationship with action research approaches of different provenance.

Finally, for all of that, we conclude that the methodological mainstream of academic social research—neither under stable social circumstances and economic prosperity, nor in times of quick and radical change, unsimultaneousness and economic crises—has not been able and will not be able to satisfy urgent societal demands for social research relevant to practice. Action research still seems to be a possible answer to the contemporary challenges. Some respondents even think an action research boom is still to come, because the planning competency of the state and the steering knowledge provided by traditional social science are in the process of reaching their limits. In a situation of increasing social dynamics that are constantly producing *neue Unuebersichtlichkeit*[6] through the changing politics of power, economic, technological, cultural mixings, and shiftings, even the most elaborate simulations and multivariate methods cannot guarantee that politics and research actually grasp relevant social reality. Additionally, it is possible that the 'objects of research' will continue to evade the political and scientific grasp, be it in a vague protest against 'those at the top' or out of alienation from the 'sorcerers of social science' (Andreski 1977), or be it in conscious opposition to the preparation for total availability of internal and external nature, subjectivity, and the everyday world. If this is so, then action research—for all of its pragmatic reason and science-political tactics—will not be able to avoid writing its own *radical* program (in the sense of touching the roots of its self-understanding) so as not to lose touch with the social basis of its practice. Otherwise, there will be nothing but helplessness and frustration, even for the most committed action researcher when rational discourse is refused, and no interest at all for social science as it is occurring in parts of the 'alternative scene' (Gerwin 1982). So far, action research, like no research strategy before, has attempted to scientifically elaborate and reflexively balance the relationship of interest and commission, commitment and distance, and emancipation and utilizability. Whether it can continue to do so under the changing and brutal-izing social conditions and mega-trends, such as nuclear threat, ecological cat-astrophes, biotechnology, and so on will soon be seen.

Notes

We extend our thanks to those Austrian, German, and Swiss researchers who invested much of their time in answering our postal survey. We also are very grateful to Bridget Somekh, Robin McTaggart, and Peter Posch for their advice concerning the language and content of this paper.

1. Reference to these letters is indicated by "Lt." plus the number of the letter; for example, "Lt. 3" refers to a statement given in letter 3.

2. All quotations from German sources have been translated by the authors.

3. 'Ordinarius' is the Latin-derived term for high-status full professors at Ger-man universities. The 'Ordinarius' in his gown was the symbol of a traditional acade-mic system (and, maybe even more broadly, the nearest symbol for the well woven nets of traditional political power) which the student movement was fighting against.

4. Parts of the argument are included in publications in English language (see Altrichter 1986; 1990b).

5. Although most of them had been practically teaching before which, by the way, might be an additional reason for their relatively high confidence in teachers' pro-fessionalism.

6. A term coined recently by Habermas derived from 'new situations difficult to survey' but, of course, presented as an abstract noun.

References

Adorno T. W. et al. 1969. *Der positivismusstreit in der deutschen Soziologie.* Neuwiedl Berlin: Luchterhand.

Altrichter, H. 1986. Visiting two worlds: An excursion into the methodological jungle including an optional evening's entertainment at the Rigour Club. *Cam-bridge journal of education* 16(2):131–43.

———. 1988. Enquiry-based learning in initial teacher education. In *The enquiring teacher,* eds. J. Nias, and S. Groundwater-Smith, 121–34. London: Falmer.

———. 1990a. *Ist das noch Wissenschaft? Darstellung und wissenschafstheoretische diskussion einer von lehrern betriebenen Aknonsforschung.* Munich: Profil.

————. 1990b. Do we need an alternative methodology for doing alternative research? In *Action research for change and development*, ed. O. Zuber-Skerritt, 103–18. Brisbane: CALT/Griffith University.

————. 1991. *Quality features in an action research strategy.* OECD/CERI 'Environment and school initiatives,' Series No. 12. Vienna: ARGE Umwelterziehung.

Altrichter, H., S. Kemmis, R. McTaggart, and O. Zuber-Skerritt. 1990. Defining, confining, or refining action research? In *Action research for change and development*, ed. O. Zuber-Skerritt, 13–20. Brisbane: CALT/Griffith University.

Altrichter, H., and P. Posch. 1989. Does the 'grounded theory' approach offer a guiding paradigm for teacher research? *Cambridge journal of education* 19(1):21–31.

————. 1990. *Lehrer erforschen ihren Unterricht.* Bad Heilbrunn: Klinkhardt.

Altrichter, H., Wilhelmer, H., Sorger, H., and Morocutti I. (eds.). 1989. *Schule gestalten: Lehrer als Forscher.* Klagenfurt: Hermagoras.

Andreski, S. 1977. *Die hexenmeister der sozialwissenschaften.* Munich: dtv.

Argyris, C. 1972. Unerwartete folgen 'strenger' forschung. *Gruppendynamik* 3(1):522.

Auernheimer, G. 1976. Protestbewegung gegen die herkömmliche 'Wissenschaftspraxis.' *Zeitschrift für Pädagogik* 22(3):377–86.

Berger, H. 1974. *Untersuchungsmethode und soziale wirklichkeit.* Frankfurt/M: Suhrkamp.

Bittner, G., and A. Flitner. 1969. Aufgaben und methodik sozialpädagogischer untersuchungen. *Zeitschrift für Pädagogik* 15(1):63–74.

Blankertz, H., and A. Gruschka. 1975. Handlungsforschung. Rückfall in die empiriefeindlichkeit oder neue erfahrungsdimension? *Zeitschrift fdr Pädagogik* 21(5):677–86.

Braun, K. H. 1987. Was kann die padagogische handlungsforschung von den diskussionen um die 'objeknve Herrneneutik' lernen? In *Neue bildung-Neue schule*, eds. K. H. Braun and D. Wunder, 66–86. Weinheim/Basel: Beltz.

Brugelmann, H. 1972. Offene curricula. *Zeitschrift für Pädagogik* 18:95–118.

CARE/UEA 1989. *Coming to terms with research.* Norwich: University of East Anglia.

Carr, W., and S. Kemmis. 1986. *Becoming critical. Education, knowledge, and action research.* London: Falmer.

Cremer, C., H. Haft, and W. Klehm. 1977. Entwicklungslinien von action-research. In *Handlungsorientierte schulforschungsprojekte*, eds. U. Hameyer and H. Haft, 171–98. Weinheim: Beltz.

Eichner, K., and P. Schmidt. 1974. Aktionsforschung—eine neue methode? *Soziale Welt* 25(2):145–168.

Elliott, J. 1984. Improving the quality of teaching through action research. *Forum* 26(3):74–7.

———. 1985a. Facilitating educational action-research: Some dilemmas. In *Field methods in the study of education*, ed. R. Burgess. London: Falmer.

———. 1985b. Educational action-research. In *World yearbook of education 1985: Research, policy and practice*, eds. J. Nisbet et al., 231–50. London: Kogan Page.

Elliott, J., and C. Adelman, C. (n.d.). *Classroom action research.* Cambridge: Ford Teaching Project, Institute of Education.

Felberbauer, M., I. Jung, and J. Juna. 1987–88. Collaborative inquiry and school improvement. *PI-Mitteilungen* 10:9–13.

Fuchs, W. 1970–71. Empirischer sozialforschung als politische aktion. *Soziale Welt* 21/22(1):1–17.

Geissler, K. A., and M. Hege. 1985. Verlorene hoffnungen—Gewonnene einsichten. zum verhaltnis von politik und beratung, *Supervisio*, 8:25–36.

Gerwin, J. 1982. Integration von konfliktpotentialen oder artikulation von widerstand? *Psychologie und Gesellschaftskritik* 6(1):51–61.

Giesen, B., and C. Leggewie (eds.). 1991. *Experiment vereinigung. ein sozialer groB-versuch.* Berlin: Rotbuch.

Gstettner, P. 1976. Handlungsforschung unter dem anspruch diskursiver verstandigung analyse einiger kommunikationsprobleme. *Zeitschrift für Pädagogik* 22(3):321–33.

———. 1977. Zum innovationsanspruch von handlungsforschung. In *Handlungsorientierte schulforschung*, eds. U. Hameyer and H. Haft, 253–68. Weinheim/Basel: Beltz.

———. 1979. Distanz und verweigerung. In *Aktionsforschung balanceakt ohne netz?*, ed. K. Horn, 163–205. Frankfurt/M: Syndikat.

Gstettner, P., and P. Seidl. 1975. *Sozialwissenschaft und bildungsreform.* Koln: Kiepenheuer & Witsch.

Gunz, J. 1986. *Handlungsforschung. Vom wandel der distanzierten zur engagierten sozialforschung.* Vienna: Braumüller.

Haag, F., H. Krüger, W. Schwärzel, and J. Wildt (eds.). 1972. *Aknonsforschung. Forschungsstrategien, forschungsfelder und forschungsplane.* Munich: Juventa.

Haag, F., and L. Pongratz. 1970. Forschungsstrategien für sozialtherapeutische anstalten, *Kriminologische journal* 2(1):10–14.

Habermas, J. 1969. Gegen einen positivistisch halbierten rationalismus. In *Der posinvismusstreit in der deutschen soziologie*, eds. T. W. Adorno et al., 235–66). Neuwied: Luchterhan.

———. 1971. *Theorie und praxis*. Frankfurt/M: Suhrkamp.

———. 1981. Theorie des Kommunikativen Handelns, 2 vols. Frankfurt: Suhrkamp.

Heinze, T. 1986. *Rekonstruktion und intervention*. Paper presented at the conference Alternative forschungsmethoden. Vienna: IFF.

———. 1987. *Qualitative ozialforschung*. Opladen: Westdeutscher Verlag.

Heinze, T., E. Müller, B. Stickelmann, and J. Zinnecker. 1975. *Handlungsforschung im padagogischen Feld*. Munich: Juventa.

Holzkamp, K. 1972. *Kritische Psychologie*. Frankfurt/M: Fischer.

———. 1977. Kann es im rahmen der marxistischen theorie eine kritische psychologie geben? In *Kritische psychologie*, vol. 1., eds. K. H. Braun and K. Holzkamp, 44–75. Köln: Pahl-Rugenstein.

Horn, K. (ed.) 1979. *Aknonsforschung—Balanceakt ohne Netz?* Frankfurt/M.: Syndikat.

Klafki, W. 1973. Handlungsforschung im schulfeld. *Zeitschrift für Pädagogik* 19(4):487–516.

———. 1975. Replik auf Frank~laf radtkeskKritik am verstandnis der aktionsforschung im marburger grundschulprojekt, *Beitrage zur Bildungstechnologie* 1:26–38.

Klafki, W. et al. 1982. *Schulnahe curriculutnentwicklung und handlungsforschung*. Weinheim/Basel: Beltz.

Knetsch, H. 1979. Handlungsforschung = forsches handeln? In *Venusfliegenfalle. sozialarbeit—Geometrisierung der nachstenliebe*, M. Winter, A. Vogel, N. Ochmann, E. V. Kardorff, and H. Knetsch, 127–34. Frankfurt Syndikat.

Kordes, H. 1984. Padagogische aktionsforschung. In *Methoden der erziehungs und bildungsforschung*, Enzyklopadie Erziehungswissenschaft, vol. 2., eds. H. Haft and H. Kordes, 185–219. Stuttgart: Klett-Cotta.

Kreissl, R., and Ch. Wolffersdorf-Ehlert. 1985. Selbstbetroffenheit mit summa cum laude? *Soziale Welt, Sonderband* 3:91–110.

Kroath, F. 1989. How do teachers change their practical theories? *Cambridge journal of education* 19(1):59–69.

————. 1991. *Der Lehrer als Forscher*. Munich: Profil.

Lakatos, I. 1974. Falsifikation und die methodologie wissenschaf~icher forschungsprogramme. In *Kritik und Erkenntnisfortschritt*. eds. I. Lakatos and A. Musgrave, 89–189. Braunschweig: Vieweg.

Lukesch, H., and G. Zecha. 1978. Neue handlungsforschung? Programm und praxis gesellschaftskritischer sozialforschung. *Soziale Welt* 29(1):26–43.

Maw, J. 1987. *The current context for evaluation in Britain: Centralization and control*. Mimeo. London: Institute of Education.

Mertens, W. 1975. *Sozialpsychologie des Experiments*. Hamburg: Hoffmann and Kampe.

Merz, G. 1985. *Konturen einer neuen Aktionsforschung*. Frankfurt/M.: Lang.

Mollenhauer, K., and C. Rittelmeyer. 1975. 'Empirisch-analytische wissenschaft' versus 'Padagogische Handlungsforschung': Aine irrefuhrende alternative. *Zeitschrif fur Pädagogik* 21(5):687–93.

Moser, H. 1978; *Aknonsforschung als kntische theorie der sozialwissenschaften*. 1st ed. 1975. Munich: Kosel.

————. 1989, Aktionsforschung. In *Worterbuch der Soziologie*, 9. Stuttgart: Enke.

Moser, H., and H. Ornauer. 1978. Internationale aspekte der aknon~orsch~ng. Munich: Kosel.

Noffke, S. E. 1989. *The social context of action research: A comparative and historical analysis*. Paper presented at the AERA conference: San Francisco.

Nonne, F. 1989. *Annautoritarer Denksnl, kritische Wissenschaft und Aktionsforschung*, Ph.D. thesis, Bielefeld University.

OECD/CERI 1991. *Environmental schools and active learning*. Paris: OECD/CERI.

Petzold, H. 1980. Moreno—nicht Lewin—der Begriinder der Aktionsforschung. *Gruppendynarnik* 11(2):142–66.

Pongratz, L, and F. Haag. 1971. Sozialer lernproze von straftatern in einer ubergangsanstalt des Hamburger strafvolllzugs, *Kriminologische Journal 3*, 3/4:239–47.

Posch, P. 1986. University support for independent learning: A new development in the in-service education of teachers. *Cambridge journal of education* 16(1):46–57.

————. 1990. Educational dimensions of environmental school initiatives. *Australian journal of environmental education* 6:79–91.

————. 1991. *Networking in environmental education*. Paper presented at the international conference "Handling complexity in environmental education": Manchester.

Radtke, F.O. 1975. Wider ein restringiertes verstandnis von Aktionsforschung—Bemerkungen zu klafkis schilderung des 'Marburger Grundschulprojekts.' *Beitrage zur Bildungstechnologie* 1:11–25.

Rammstedt, O. 1979. Überlegungen zum historischen Stellenwert von Aktionsforschung. In *Aktionsforschung: Balanceakt ohne netz?*, ed. K. Horn, 41–53. Frankfurt: Syndicat.

Rathmayr, B. 1976. Ein neues Selbstverstandnis der Aktionsforschung? *Zeitschrift fur Pädagogik* 22(3):369–76.

Rathmayr, B., and I. Wagner. 1976. *Wissenschaft als Innovationshilfe*. Vienna: Jugend and Volk.

Rolff, H. G. 1971. Perspektiven einer projektorientierten und kooperativen Gesamtschulplanung. Zeitschrift für Pädagogik, 9:125–40.

Schneider, U. 1980. *Sozialwissenschaftliche methodenkrise und handlungsforschung*. Frankfurt: Campus.

Schratz, M. 1990. Researching while teaching: A collaborative action research model to improve college teaching. *Journal on excellence in college teaching* 1:98–108.

Seidl, H., and P. Seidl (eds.). 1977. *Bildungsforschung für eine demokratische Schule*. Vienna: Jugend and Volk.

Sitte, K., and G. Scholz. 1976. Ford T: Modell gelungener Zusammenarbeit. *betrifft: erziehung,* 27–30.

Skilbeck, M. 1983. Lawrence Stenhouse: research methodology. *British education research journal* 9(1):1120.

Staufer, J., and B. Stickelmann. 1984. *Klient Schule?* Reinheim: Jugend & Politik.

Stenhouse, L. 1975. *An introduction to curriculum research and development*. London: Heinemann.

————. 1985. *Research as a basis for teaching*. eds. J. Rudduck and D. Hopkins. London: Heinemann.

Treiber, B., and N. Groeben. 1981. Handlungsforchung und epistemisches subjektmodell. *Zeitschrift für sozializationsforschung und erziehungssoziologie* 1:117–38.

Wallmann, H., W. Seilerbeck-Tschida, and H. Kaufmann. 1987. *Padagogisches Kommunikationszentrum* St. Andra—Langeck. Mimeo. Eisenstadt: PI Burgenland.

Wedekind, E. 1986. *Beziehungsarbeit*. Frankfurt/M.: Brandes & Apsel.

Wellenreuther, M. 1976. Handlungsforschung als naiver Empirismus? *Zeitschrift fur Pädagogik* 22(3):343–56.

Wünsche, K. 1979. Aufforderung an die Lehrer: Macht Eure eigene Unterrichtswissenschaft. paed.ema (1), 22–6.

Zedler, P., and H. Moser (eds.). 1983. *Aspekte einer qualitanven Sozialforschung*. Opladen: Westdeutscher Verlag.

CHAPTER 4

Action Research: The Problem of Participation

Clem Adelman

In the late 1930s, Kurt Lewin and his students conducted quasi-experimental tests in factory and neighborhood settings to demonstrate, respectively, the greater gains in productivity and in law and order through democratic participation rather than autocratic coercion. Lewin not only showed that there was an effective alternative to Taylor's 'scientific management' but through his action research provided the details of how to develop social relationships of groups and between groups to sustain communication and cooperation. To achieve such conditions and relationships required forms of leadership quite different from those purveyed by the literal followers of Taylor and the misinterpretation of Tyler, which led to a link with Watsonian behaviorism, thus 'behavioral objectives.'

One of the best-known summaries of the forms of leadership is by two of Lewin's former students, Cartwright and Zander (1953). Action research was the means of systematic inquiry for all participants in the quest for greater effectiveness through democratic participation.

I begin by considering the 1960s revival of action research in the United Kingdom before going into some detail about the pioneering work of Lewin. I then compare the Ford Teaching Project's achievements against the principles of democratic action research, outlined by Lewin. Last, I evaluate some recent U.K. developments which use action research as their means to educational development.

Action Research in the 1960s

During the 1960s, U.K. and U.S. social policy provided exceptionally large budgets for intervention programs in education, health, and housing. These programs were intended to raise the life chances, achievement, and expectations of the poor, otherwise the 'disadvantaged' (Coates and Silburn

1970). At that time, sociologists and psychometricians were confident enough in their knowledge of learning, social change, and organization to eagerly suggest and participate in social engineering and re-education programs. The details of this history can be found in Silver and Silver (1991). Suffice it to say here that the pioneering work of Tyler in the assessment of learning and the work of Lewin in the principles of cooperative action research became urgently relevant and available through their respective former students Benjamin Bloom and Martin Deutsch. In education, these interventions were termed *compensatory* or *enrichment*. Although they were prone to justified criticisms then and subsequently (for instance, Bernstein 1970; Baratz and Baratz 1970), at least those initiatives went beyond the previously dominant determinist notions that the poor could do little for themselves or were to be blamed for their faults and even made to feel guilty for what was ascribed as their inadequacies.

British educationalists, Her Majesty's Inspectors (HMIs), senior civil servants, and politicians made many study visits to the United States during the decade. Some were seeking methodologies for systematic social development and a new means for evaluating the impact of public policy expenditure. Under the banner of social action experiments, the government funded the Educational Priority Area (EPA) and Community Development Projects (CDP) in England and Wales (Halsey 1972; Midwinter 1972, 1975). Social reform was to be constructed rationally, using information that arose from the dialogue between social science researchers and policy makers. For the most part, neither the EPA or CDP projects were proceeded by cooperative action research.

By the time the EPA project had begun in 1968, action research as a means to cohesive social development had lost its coherence in the United States. Instead of empowering ordinary people in their own communities, action research had been incorporated as part of the armory of managerial development for 'corporate excellence' (Blake and Mouton 1968). Lewin's ideas were so thoroughly digested and reformed as axioms, rather than critically assimilated for further testing, that there is no former or present reference to his work in that and many other similar volumes. Lewin's work on the understanding of intergroup conflict by means of the community self-study was said by Rowan (1974) to be defunct, while Sanford (1970) claimed that action research was never accepted as bona fide research in the United States.

It never really got off the ground; it was never widely influential in psychology or social science. By the time the federal funding agencies were set up after the Second World War, action research was already condemned to a sort of orphan's role in social science, for the separation of science and practice was now institutionalized, and it has been basic to the federal bureaucracies ever since. This truth was obscured for a time by the fact that old-timers in action research were still able to get their projects funded, even after younger researchers had discovered to their sorrow that action research proposals per se received a cool reception from the funding agencies and were, indeed, likely to win for their authors the reputation of being 'confused.'

Kurt Lewin

Action research gives credence to the development of powers of reflective thought, discussion, decision, and action by ordinary people participating in collective research on 'private troubles' (Wright Mills 1959) which they have in common. That was how Kurt Lewin (1890–1947), whose first ideas on what he called 'action research' were espoused around 1934 (Marrow 1969), came to describe its characteristics after a series of practical experiences in the early 1940s. "No action without research; no research without action," Lewin concluded.

Lewin had fled Berlin in 1933, assuming a temporary position in the home economics department at Cornell University, then moving to the psychology department at the University of Iowa. His initial attempt to establish a program of action research was to propose a Psychological Institute of the Hebrew University to seek "the wisest solutions and the best practical administrative alternatives" (Marrow 1969, 81) to develop better communities by helping the new immigrants to Palestine adjust and thrive in their new environment. His efforts in this regard did not come to fruition, notwithstanding that his sponsors included Eleanor Roosevelt, John Dewey, Edward Thorndike, Frank Boas, and other outstanding American academics and philanthropists.[1]

The immediate concern of Jewish philanthropy was to help Jews escape from Nazi-occupied Europe. Ideas like the Psychological Institute were given little priority at that time; sufficient funding was not forthcoming. However, opportunities to explore the possibilities of community action research did arise subsequently in the United States.

While at the University of Iowa, Lewin was invited to work as a consultant to the Harwood factory in Virginia; Marrow was the managing director. The newly opened factory was finding it difficult to recruit skilled workers. Three hundred unskilled trainees, mainly local women, had been employed. There was considerable prejudice amongst the predominantly female managers, who took the view that the trainees would not be able to do the tasks fast enough or up to the same standards. After twelve weeks of training, the new employees produced only half as much as apprentices who were doing similar tasks in northern U.S. factories. In addition, morale within the factory was low.

Lewin and his principal co-worker, Alec Barvelas, took charge of the new workforce and divided it into two groups. The first group received direct training, given didactically, with little opportunity to raise questions. The second group was encouraged to discuss and decide on the division of tasks and comment on the training they were given. Over several months, the productivity of the second group was consistently higher than that of the first. The staff of the second group learned the tasks faster and their morale remained high, whereas in the first group morale remained low. This initial field experiment seemed to vindicate Lewin's observations and beliefs in democratic rather than autocratic workplaces. The problem of social relationships and efficiency in industry had been troubling Lewin since the early 1920s, marked by a critical paper on Taylorism (Lewin 1920). The influence of Lewin's work on industrial relations has been enormous throughout the world, as several of those interviewed by Marrow for the biographical volume attested. It was part of Lewin's insight that he could take contentious social issues and refute the taken-for-granted, often pessimistic assumptions about human nature, and replace them with what has become a new 'common sense.'

Action research for Lewin was exemplified by the discussion of problems and followed by group decisions on how to proceed. Action research must include the active participation by those who have to carry out the work in the exploration of problems that they identify and anticipate. After investigation of these problems, the group makes decisions, monitoring and noting the consequences. Regular reviews of progress follow. The group then decides when a particular plan or strategy has been exhausted and fulfilled, then brings to these discussions newly perceived problems.

The experiment at the Harwood plant was inspired by the earlier work on the relationships between autocracy and democracy in the workplace, conducted by Lewin's students, Lippitt and White (Lewin, Lippitt and White 1939). However, it was not until just after Lewin's death in 1947 that the opportunity arose at the Harwood plant for what seems the definitive action research on the efficacy of democratic group decision making in industry.

I quote from Marrow:

French, aided by Lester Coch, the personnel manager, was able to carry out the experiment as planned. The investigation called for introducing the required changes in jobs in three different ways, each involving a different degree of employee collaboration in working out details of the proposed new job assignments.

The first group did not participate in any way: the workers were told of the changes in their jobs, and the production department explained the new piece [wage] rate. The second group was asked to appoint representatives to meet with management to consider methods, piece rates and other problems created by the job changes. The third group consisted of every member of the unit—not just the representatives. They met with management, took an active part in detailed discussions about all aspects of the change, made a number of recommendations and even helped plan the most efficient methods for doing the new job.

The differences in outcome of the three procedures were clear-cut and dramatic. Average production in the nonparticipation group dropped 20 percent immediately and did not regain the pre-change level. Nine percent of the group quit. Morale fell sharply, as evidenced by marked hostility toward the supervisor, by slowdowns, by complaints to the union and by other instances of aggressive behavior.

The group which participated through representatives required two weeks to recover its pre-change output. Their attitude was cooperative and none of the members of the group quit their jobs.

The consequences in the total-participation group were in sharp contrast to those in the non-participating group. It regained the pre-change output after only two days and then climbed steadily until it reached a level about 14 percent above the earlier average. No one quit; all members of the group worked well with their supervisors and there were no signs of aggression.

French concluded that 'the experiment showed that the rate of recovery is directly proportional to the amount of participation and that the rates of turnover and aggression are inversely proportional to the amount of participation.' (Marrow 1969)

Lewin had said that the constancy of the level of production at Harwood or at any similar plant could be viewed as a quasi-stationary process in which two types of forces are in gear: those component forces pushing production in a downward direction and those pushing production up. The difference in the strength of these forces makes the difference of the production level between the participating and nonparticipating group.

To those expecting accounts of action research to emulate a case study, this exemplifier of Lewin's work does not leave the interpretation to the reader. Indeed, Lewin and his collegues framed their interpretations in the form of scientific axioms. Although Lewin's understanding of science was strongly informed by his professor, Ernst Cassirer, the onus on empirically testable propositions as the vindication of expenditure on research, whatever the paradigm, was strongly evident in his and his colleagues' reports and in their valuing of 'experimental' action research above the three other approaches they identified (discussed later). This does not detract from Lewin's principles and procedures for cooperative action research as a means of inquiry specially suited to democratic participation. However, Lewin's ideas on democratic participation in the workplace did not include any critique of the wider society, particularly the range of economic relations between worker and employer, capital and labor. Indeed, a fair observation would be that although Lewin and his co-workers demonstrated the efficacy of action research for improving productivity, they did not develop conceptual structures which took explicit account of the power bases that define social roles and strongly influence the process of any change in the modes of production. In the context of industrial management, the criticisms by Landsberger (1958) are precise and pertinent; equally astonishing is the freedom from attack enjoyed so far by the followers of Lewin and the group dynamics approach. Coch and French's action research, "Overcoming resistance to change," is far more blatant in accepting management's goal of effficiency and the desirability of manipulating workers than any study ever undertaken by a follower of the late Elton Mayo.

In the context of progressive education, as espoused by John Dewey and George Counts, Lewin had developed the methods and principles to enable the school to act as the agency of democratic change within its community. Lewin and Dewey met and corresponded briefly on a few occasions. I have yet to locate any record of Lewin knowing about the contemporaneous work of Ralph Tyler at Ohio University during the eight-year study (1932–40). However, the resemblance between action research and the 'service' studies by groups of teachers into their own practices that Tyler developed is uncannily close (Madaus and Stufflebeam 1989). Tyler had studied Dewey, and they were subsequently colleagues at Chicago University. Myles Horton (Kohl and Kohl 1990), a major figure in education for adult empowerment, corresponded with Lewin and Dewey but did not, at that time, know Tyler. Horton contended that action research was too esoteric for working people.

Argyris, Putnam, and McLain Smith (1985), evaluate the contributions of Lewin and Dewey to the founding of what they term *action science*. In the quotations that follow, it is worth noting that the radical ideas of Lewin and Dewey remained largely untried until the late 1960s.

Action science is an outgrowth of the traditions of John Dewey and Kurt Lewin. Dewey was eloquent in his criticism of the traditional separation of knowledge and action, and he articulated a theory of inquiry that was a model both for scientific method and social practice. He hoped the extension of experimental inquiry to social practice would lead to an integration of science and practice. He based this hope on the observation that "science in becoming experimental has itself become a mode of directed practical doing."

This observation, that experimentation in science is but a special case of human beings testing their conceptions in action, is at the core of the pragmatist epistemology. For the most part, however, the modern social sciences have appropriated the model of the natural sciences in ways that have maintained the separation of science and practice that Dewey deplored. Mainstream social science is related to social practice in much the same way that the natural sciences are related to engineering. This contrasts sharply with Dewey's vision of using scientific methods in social practice.

One tradition that has pursued the integration of science and practice is that exemplified by Lewin, a pioneer in group dynamics and action research. Lewin is considered the founder of the cognitive tradition within social psychology in the United States. Citing the classic Lewinian studies of democratic and authoritarian group climates, Festinger suggests it is because Lewin showed how complex social phenomena could be studied experimentally that many regard him as the founder of modern experimental social psychology. This is not to say, however, that each of the many research programs that can trace their core ideas to some aspect of Lewin's work also are consistent with action science. We consider Lewin himself to have been an action scientist.

But since his time there has been a tendency to divorce his contributions to science from his contributions to practice. Research in social psychology has relied on experimental methods for testing hypothesized relationships among a few variables, and it has become distant from practice. Practitioners in the applied behavioral sciences, with some exceptions, have focused on helping clients and have given little attention to testing scientific generalizations.

The Lewinian tradition of action science, in contrast, is that of scholar-practitioners in group dynamics and organizational science who have sought to integrate science and practice. Members of this tradition have emphasized the continuities between the activities of science and the activities of learning in the action context, the mutually reinforcing values of science, democracy, and education, and the benefits of combining science and social practice.

Whatever the details of these important histories, the 'American dream' of diversity and equal opportunity for all was considered in need of protection from the influence of the rising totalitarian regimes of Europe. All means of research and development were encouraged from the 1930s to the 1960s to foster the 'democratic' rather than the 'autocratic' mentality in the home, school, and workplace. That is a long and, in the main, yet-to-be-told story of conflicting interests, finite resources, and crumbling theories.

Lewin and his workers classified their work into four types of action research:

1. *Diagnostic* action research, designed to produce a needed plan of action. The change agents would intervene in an already existing situation (for example, a race riot or an anti-Semitic vandalism), diagnose the problem, and recommend remedial measures. Unless the proposed cures were feasible, effective, and acceptable to the people involved, however, this design of action was often wasted.

2. *Participant* action research, in which it was assumed that the residents of the affected community who were to help effect a cure must be involved in the research process from the beginning. They would thereby realize more keenly the need for the particular steps finally decided upon; at the same time, their 'ego investment' would support the remedial program. This type of action research—an example would be a community of self-survey—seemed to be most effective for a limited range of problems. It was useful in disclosing particular and local facts (not general principles) that could provide examples for other communities.

3. *Empirical* action research, primarily a matter of record keeping and accumulating experiences in day-to-day work, ideally with a succession of similar groups, such as boys' clubs. An inherent weakness in this procedure was that conclusions were drawn from experience with a single group, or with several groups differing in numerous ways, without test controls. Despite this handicap, empirical action research could lead to the gradual development of generally valid principles as clinical medicine had already demonstrated.

4. *Experimental* action research, which called for a controlled study of the relative effectiveness of various techniques in nearly identical social situations. Of all of the varieties of action research, the experimental had the greatest potential for the advancement of scientific knowledge. Under favorable circumstances, it could definitively test specific hypotheses. It was, however, the most difficult form of action research to carry out successfully (Marrow 1969, 198).

Given Lewin's emphasis on participation, we might expect this classification to provide emphasis to processes more than outcomes. As it is expressed, the classification is consistent with Lewin's search for axiomatic empirical relationships. An argument for emphasis on process rather than outcomes in participatory research may be found in Adelman and Fletcher (1982).

By the time Lewin had established, in 1945, the Center for Group Dynamics Institute at the Massachusetts Institute of Technology, his colleagues included former students from Iowa, Festinger, and Cartwright. The chief methodological approach was to develop group experiments, especially experiments of change to be carried out in the laboratory or field. The Center was to concern itself not only with the gathering of data but with theorizing, which Lewin hoped would steadily keep ahead of the data gathering. Lewin would wait until he perceived the critical conditions for a field experiment pertained before engaging in that work. He wanted his 'experiments' to be naturalistic yet interventive. The fundamental tenet was studying things by changing them, in natural situations.

Lewin could not rest on his successes but was in constant pursuit of further funds for contracts and funding for research staff. Lewin had reluctantly acknowledged (pace Sanford) that action research was an onerous and risky business and that sponsorship for action research was difficult to find. Eric Trist asked Lewin to act as consultant to a new Institute for the Study of Human Relations in London, founded in part to develop the discoveries about group conflict and cohesion, leadership, and influence for change made during the Second World War by U.K. and North American researchers in close cooperation. Lewin and Trist saw the parallels in their ideas, but to Lewin's regret he could not accept the offer. Instead, one of his postdoctoral students, Eliot Jacques, established the Tavistock Institute.

When Lewin died of heart failure in 1947, the Center for Group Dynamics, under the direction of Lewin's close associate Ronald Lippitt (formerly a Director of Research with the American Boy Scouts), moved to Michigan University at Ann Arbor. Lippitt's previous work in collaboration with Lewin included the establishment, in 1945, of the National Training Laboratories in Connecticut, which focused particularly on sensitivity training to combat racial and religious prejudice and racism. The Training Laboratories drew upon the work of the Commission on Community Interrelations established, in 1944, through Lewin's persistence, with sponsorship from the American Jewish Congress.

The pioneering action research of Lewin and his associates showed that through discussion, decision, action, evaluation, and revision in participatory democratic research, work became meaningful and alienation was reduced. Although power relations became more equitable in the workplace, this reconstructionist research made little difference to the ownership of capital. Lewin and Dewey had similar ideas on participatory democratic workplaces and schools, but the institutionalization of these relationships had only been possible in parts of nations where wealth was more evenly distributed, such as Norway (Wirth 1983). This has become known as the 'quality of life' approach.

Action Research in the United Kingdom

Next I will consider the Educational Priority Area (EPA) (1968–72), Humanities Curriculum (1967–72), and Ford Teaching Projects (1972–74) in light of Lewin's definitive pioneering action research.

Educational Priority Area Project 1968–72

In the EPA work, which comprised five regional projects, the problems to be explored in the United Kingdom were, in most cases, already designated by the central team (Smith 1987). Furthermore, discussions among those who would be the participating workers tended to be restricted to whether they were amenable to the project's ideas and how they would accomplish the methods of data collection. The participants did have a strong say in the group decisions on implementation, and in all this they were studied by researchers rather than keeping their own records. The exceptions to this generalizaton included the Red House project and those in Liverpool (Midwinter 1972) and Deptford (Silver and Silver 1991). Information from the projects was received by Halsey, who then edited the material, putting a social science gloss and systemization over what he saw as highly contentious and "untidy," both in process and outcome. Whereas Lewin saw different ways of reporting action research work as a commitment to informing the lives of the participants, Halsey's reference group was other social scientists and policy makers.

Humanities Curriculum Project (HCP)

The Humanities Curriculum Project (Stenhouse 1980) engaged participating teachers in the discussion of issues they identified from classroom practice: the problems of implementing a humanities curriculum which was itself based on pupil discussion, with the teacher acting as a provider of resources and procedural chairperson. Although the project was successful in many ways, teachers did not have the opportunity, as recognized at the time, to make group decisions about change, implement these, and evaluate the process and outcome. However, the process of introduction of the HCP strategies was evaluated under the rubric of innovation by the HCP evaluation team, led by Barry MacDonald and Rob Walker (MacDonald and Walker 1976).

John Elliott had been a member of the HCP curriculum team, and in his subsequent draft proposal to the Ford Foundation in 1971 he highlighted the need to follow through the problems of innovation and the realizing of pedagogies of inquiry and discovery in classrooms. The approach proposed was that of action research. Elliott was quite clear about the need to engage teachers in active participation and discussion, but less clear about whether decisions regarding further developments should be followed through by individuals or groups. It is worth a reminder that Lewin insisted that action research was a group commitment. As well as focusing on inquiry and discovery methods, at the outset, Elliott suggested some of the problems in curriculum areas and the methods by which these would be researched.

The EPA project was not 'action research' in Lewin's definitive terms. In what respect was the Ford Teaching project similar to Lewin's model?

Ford Teaching Project (Ford T)

I joined the Ford Teaching Project central team in March 1972. Rob Walker and I had been working at the Center for Science Education, Chelsea

College, on a Social Science Research Council project. We found a few people who shared our developing ideas about school and curriculum change.
One of those people was Barry Macdonald, whom I had heard on an Open
University broadcast talking about the problems of evaluation. I wrote to
MacDonald and invited him to visit Walker and myself to see samples of our
work before contracts concluded. In his reply, he asked if he could bring his
colleague John Elliott. Subsequently, Elliott sent me a copy of his draft proposal to the Ford Foundation. The draft contended that although stimulating
and challenging curriculum materials had been devised, no such major change
had been achieved in teachers' pedagogic practices. The curriculum may have
been designed to foster inquiry through independent reasoning, but teachers
were not articulating the means to communicate these desired processes to
students. There was an alarming gap between the aspirations of education policy makers, with their expenditure on curriculum development, and the slow
change in relationships, social and knowledge, in classroooms. What Elliott
proposed from his work with the HCP was a project to enable teachers,
through collaborative action research on their own teaching, to make plain the
impediments to pedagogic change. The Humanities Curriculum Project had
begun this line of teacher-based inquiry and the long-term observations by
Walker and myself had raised similar questions, but neither of us had the
devotion to teachers' theorizing and research as in what became known as the
Ford Teaching Project.

In spring 1972, Elliott was engaged in identifying East Anglian schools
where teachers were interested in the problems of implementing inquiry and
discovery teaching. He had hoped to raise between twenty-four to thirty-two
teachers from eight schools with not less than three from each school, three
being the lower limit of what could be considered a group. Initially, Elliott
contacted the local authority advisory services, who suggested Elliott contact
the head teachers directly. Elliott found the responses were of three types:
acknowledgment of interest in the project problem and a suggestion of names
of one or more teachers within the school, sometimes including themselves;
an invitation to visit the school to talk with staff; and the occasional rebuff in
the form of lack of interest in the project problem or lack of time to take on
additional activities. The means of seeking teachers for the project may have
given head teachers too much discretion over who might participate.

Elliott embarked on an intensive series of visits to about twenty schools
and eventually enlisted forty teachers across twelve schools. In at least two of
these schools only one teacher was involved, but as part of the plan was to
have regular regional meetings as well as meetings of the whole project, the
single teachers would not feel they were working outside of a group. Elliott
also tried to negotiate time out from teaching duties for participation in the
project and managed to get a range from zero to two hours per week, this

being within the jurisdiction of the head teacher. Three head teachers participated as members of school teams.

The draft proposal I had seen in November 1971 drew much of its material from the experience of the Humanities Curriculum Project, but the proposal that went to the Ford Foundation provided a fuller description of the
intended approach for the new project. Action research was to be a main
methodology and Ford T was the first school-based action research since
Corey (1953) who had been an associate of former students of Lewin, Bennis
and Chin.

Elliott intended to give every Ford T participant a copy of his long,
albeit accomplished, review of the literature and research on inquiry and discovery teaching. I told him this was liable to preempt a lot of the issues that
would be raised by teachers' own research. Elliott's research procedures, carried over from HCP, were dialectical. He would propose something and
expect the listener to suggest criticism, contraries, or agreement. I suggested
the project discover what the teachers understood by their own practice. To
provide what would be interpreted as authoritative suggestions of the range of
their practice would be to preempt the teachers' own efforts to give accounts
of what they did. No one method was adequate for covering the layers and
perspectives. Yet for several months Elliott was insistent on using video
recordings as the means of keeping records of teachers' classroom practices
and I, admittedly with equal confidence, wanted to use a means of recording
by synchronizing tape with photographic slides, leaving 'gaps' and being
more selective in the visual documentation. When this was played back, the
teacher was almost obliged to fill in the absent information to describe what
had happened between one slide and another. This was what I understood we
wanted at the beginning of the project: teachers giving accounts of their own
practice in as full and reliable a way as possible.

I found then and subsequently (Adelman et al. 1983) that the most difficult phase of action research were the preliminaries. To move from felt
'troubles' and 'anxieties' to a statement of an *issue*, teachers have to engage
in persistent reflexive thought about their own and other's practices; at which
point, often with help from the 'change agent,' appropriate methods for investigation of an issue can be suggested and constructed by participants. It is at
this point that the action research process begins to become within the grasp
of the participant researcher. However, prior to the clarification, there is a
period of between one week to three or four months of awkward speech
around anecdotes and images, trying to locate key actions and acceptable terminology.

I found that participants' attempts to record accounts of their thoughts
were valuable in the process of reflective participant research. The problem
of initial incoherence had nothing to do with the literacy or intelligence of

the Ford T teachers or subsequently of other teachers. It seemed to have more to do with the gap between the ability of most people to perform appropriate actions in an accomplished way and their ability to provide descriptions of their own performances. This is a well-known problem in psycholinguistics and ethnography, and it is also central to the work of Donald Schon (1983).[2]

In the literature on educational action research, however, this vital phase has been given far less attention than it deserves. The issue is often presented as easily arrived at when the reality is quite contrary. When we asked groups of Ford T teachers to decide on which issue to explore in their research, there were various forms of consternation such as, "we thought you would tell us what we would research." Subsequent to initial discussions about what was meant among the teachers about inquiry and discovery teaching, two of the forty teachers said they could no longer be involved in the project because they no longer had the aspiration to teach in that way.

After the first conference, the teachers had agreed that the formulation of hypotheses for testing would be the first task. The central team waited for six weeks for a call from one of the schools to assist, either by observation or discussion of formulation of propositions about their teaching or any other facilitation. Inquiries were met with "Everything's fine. We'll let you know when we need you." At this point, the central team formulated a list of areas in which propositions might arise and sent this list around the schools. This intervention had the required effect in that some teachers began formulating propositions and testing them. The central team was called in by the teachers to assist.

One of the most consistent requests was for the central team to interview pupils. Teachers who tried this found they were not getting honest replies. The central team member would act as an interlocutor between pupil and teacher and, in addition, having observed the lesson, as an interlocutor during observations on the effects both intended and unintended of the teacher's actions and responses to the pupil's responses. The pupil's responses to particular parts of the lesson to the teacher's justification of his or her actions and an account of their intended effects, along with the central team members' witnessing of the event, formed a complex of three accounts, which I termed triangulation, after Cicourel (1973).[3]

This active focusing of effort onto a visible, explicit problem in its context helped focus teachers in their research into their own and others' pedagogies. Their discussions with colleagues at the school and regional level were often based on reports about their research on their own teaching. These reports were a required part of the project membership. Circulation of such reports to the more isolated teachers enabled the research into propositions to be shared.

Although teachers entered the project voluntarily and were supposed to be aspiring to inquiry and discovery pedagogies, four teachers withdrew soon after the commencement of the project. Having received the first documents from the central team, they realized that the inquiry and discovery pedagogies were not possible to implement in their schools. One teacher withdrew because the school was oriented to preparing children to pass formal examinations; another thought what he was doing was not inquiry and discovery pedagogy but some form of guided instruction. A few teachers voiced strong skepticism about the aims of the project in its initial formulation. However, these skeptical teachers remained within the project and were extremely valuable as critics, contributing a considerable number of documents about their research. They became committed to the project's aims, while reserving a detachment from drawing any firm conclusions.

The teachers who had the most difficulty in facing feedback from pupils, documents written by the project teachers, or discussions were those whose personal identity was inextricably bound with particular views of the professional role of a teacher. These teachers underwent considerable stress, reported nightmares and insomnia, and required extra support from the central team. They stayed within the project and wrote documents but developed much more slowly than did the teachers who could reflect on their own practices more readily.

Elliott and I suggested the teachers go through stages of self-monitoring of their practices, from awareness of the effects of their teaching practices, both intended and unintended, to a systematic practice of self-monitoring. Only one of the teachers in the project did not modify his self-monitoring practices or accounts in any marked way. This was the teacher who, prior to the project, was already self-monitoring and capably and effectively practicing a diverse range of pedagogies. However, this teacher said the project assisted him in that he came to articulate his pedagogic practices in a more consistent and precise way.

While the teachers were researching their own teaching, Elliott and I interviewed, observed, recorded, and discussed problems the teachers were having doing research. We wrote numerous reports initially lettered A to J (Adams 1980) about our overall understanding of the problems teachers' research was raising, both substantively, with regard to inquiry and discovery teaching, and methodologically, with regard to teachers' research on their own practice (see, for instance, Elliot and Adelman 1975). These papers, the reports by the teachers, and recordings of their classroom teaching were presented for discussion at regional and whole project meetings. By this means, the terminology, concepts, interpretations, and theoretical structures for understanding pedagogy were given further clarification by refutation, substitution, refinement, and, to some extent, immediate acceptance.

From the outset, Elliot and I encouraged the teachers to think of the data as their own rather than some sacrosanct information pillaged by professional researchers. To encourage this equity, teachers' reports were professionally typed and presented in the same format as those of the central team. Indeed, after about a year of the project, some groups of teachers were taking the initiative, making demands on the central team and their secretary in connection with facilitating and presenting the results of the teachers' research. This sense of teacher autonomy was concordant with the principles of inquiry (rather than discovery) pedagogy and grew more extensive with the teachers' growing confidence in understanding their own practice. Although Elliot and I proposed overviews of developments in the project, it was the teachers who sought their application and provided any validation.

By the middle of the project, only about twenty-five of the original forty teachers were full participants in the process of research on their own teaching. Although six teachers left the project quite early on, some lingered but did not contribute. Those who did not participate fully in the project did not seem to develop their understanding of their own practices by reading the documents that were distributed to all members of the project.

Two of the teachers, having been quiescent throughout most of the project, suddenly began to take a very active part. These two had entered the project quite skeptical about the value of inquiry and discovery pedagogy; they preferred individualized instruction to describe their pedagogy. Both worked in schools that emphasized the development of basic skills. They were critical of the beliefs about inquiry and discovery pedagogy that some teachers on the project took for granted. As the project collected and disseminated information, these two teachers located substantive issues with which to relate both to the other teachers and to test their own skepticisms. Participation in discussion, expression of beliefs that had formerly been tacit assumptions, allowed teachers to discuss the most sensitive and formerly rather secret aspects of their own classroom. Teachers in the project gradually became frank with each other. They unlocked their classroom experiences and shared them with their peers.

Primary teachers discussed live issues with secondary teachers, instead of merely reacting unreflectively to each other's stereotyped typifications, as they had in the initial stages of the project. The tendency was for the primary teacher to express strong commitment to the child as an individual, seeing the secondary teacher as being committed to the subject discipline, and vice versa. These honest discussions were vital to the consolidation of the project and undermined one of the project's main propositions: that the problems of inquiry teaching were common to all teachers.

The Project schedule and the extent of its fulfilment. Document D (revised) set out the schedule, tasks, procedures, and methods with respect to the project's work. Only by the fourth term had the teachers caught up with this schedule. Elliott and I were able to envisage developments well ahead of the teachers' research. As the central team, we took it as our task to theorize and plan ahead for the whole project; although our time and resources were stretched, they were considerably more than those available to teachers to keep up the envisaged schedules. Nevertheless, the teachers could see how the project was developing overall but, unlike many so-called collaborative projects, they were not forced to pace their work according to the exigencies of the researchers' contract. A circulated description of research methods, which a few teachers were beginning to employ and develop in the first term, was well-received by the teachers generally and prepared the way for Document G, "Teachers' actions and their effects on pupils" (September 1973). Document G was an important landmark, as it provided well-defined propositions that the teachers could monitor in the classroom. We had hoped that the contents of the document would be generated by the teachers themselves, but very few teachers diligently followed through the tasks set out in Document D. No one could prescribe levels of commitment; the project was voluntary and there were numerous unanticipated calls on teachers' time.

The self-monitoring stage, when teachers formulated and tested their own hypotheses, was reached by the majority toward the end of the project. The central team was constantly having to find ways of accelerating progress toward self-monitoring (hence Document G). Coordinators did not present, in any consistent way, a report after each term, as originally agreed upon in Document D. If they did, it was only a perfunctory statement.

The coordinator. The central team had expected school meetings to be situations for open discussion, but although useful in the initial stages of the project—for instance, to clarify school policy in relation to work on initial tasks, or to clarify terminology—the regional meetings proved more fruitful in the long term with respect to classroom analysis. Here the status and identity of the teachers within their own schools was in abeyance as they talked with teachers from other schools. In this context, the participants were aware that those from other schools were feeling the vulnerability of threats to their personal and professional identities. This engendered sensitivity and respect which contrasted with the over-familiarity and 'ribbing' within the schools where biographies weighed heavily against the acknowledgment of fresh thinking and even insight by immediate colleagues. The regional meeting became more productive after the basic research methods, aims, and structure of the project were determined with the teachers involved.

The important role of coordinator within the school was conferred by the head on one of the teachers at the commencement of the project. Some heads appointed themselves coordinator, while others appointed coordinators and teams and then showed little further interest until, in several cases, perhaps at times when they strongly disagreed with certain documents from the project. In the experience of the project, the head either:

- took the coordinator's role, monitoring the project's development in relation to their own policy (two cases);
- appointed a coordinator and had a continuing interest (six cases); or
- appointed a coordinator and had no further substantial interest (four cases).

One of the heads who appointed himself coordinator used his rank to further his own opinions rather than acting as a mediator between the project and the rest of the school team. In fact, as the project continued, this head's interest in organizational policies clashed with the project. Three members of his team were effectively insulated from easy access, in spite of two of them having a strong interest in the project. This head broke the agreement of participation that was outlined in an early document to the schools. As time was largely given voluntarily to the project, any further load on the teachers tended to detract from their participation in the project. In this case, such detraction was attributed to the head teacher who, with project participation as an excuse, required teachers to organize a resource center to be used by all of the pupils in the school.

Another primary school head held strong opinions, did a lot of teaching, and encouraged colleagues to sustain involvement. Although many of his views clashed with other teachers on the project, he was respected for his commitment to his own research, which led to writing documents, changes in his pedagogy, and participation in various meetings.

The role of coordinators was affected by the relationships between them and other teachers which had already been established before the project began. In all cases, the coordinator held a middle or senior position of responsibility in school and had some managerial responsibilities. In all cases where teams worked effectively, the coordinator fostered democratic participation in discussion and decision, rather than charismatic leadership. The project had brought teachers together voluntarily to work on tasks that were defined by themselves. When the school team did not get on well with each other, it was often because of the ineffectiveness of the coordinator (or change agent); instead of using his or her position to create and sustain democratic participation, it was used to sustain power relationships that were already entrenched in the school. The coordinator could not always be blamed for failing to overcome the conservatism, since some heads later admitted they had selected people for this position who they believed would "not rock the boat."

Some teachers evaluated their success by comparing their depth of involvement with other schools, as indicated by the production of documents and expressed at meetings and conferences. That is, there was a certain amount of friendly competition between schools, especially in the middle part of the project, to produce documents that reported their research. When the coordinator was ineffective, the team did not contribute to the project. In one case, the coordinator left before the project was finished and the team lost its drive and focus, although they had already done a lot of ambitious work. In another case, a new coordinator was appointed in the person of the teacher who had become most involved in the project.

School meetings. These kept the individual members in touch, exchanging experiences and information. They could discuss problems of constraints on research within the school and consider questions to ask members of the central team when they visited. The main purpose, as it transpired, was to keep morale high and sustain a collective identity within the school. This meant that in some cases teachers working on the project were identified by the rest of the school as being in some way different, but in no case was there any stigma attached. In some cases, other members of the school joined teams or gave complimentary reports about classes they had taken over from members of the team. Lewin's insistence on development through group discussion was substantiated in the school meetings, and those few teachers who were the only representatives of the project in their school joined with adjacent schools.

Regional meetings. These dealt with issues across schools, age, sex, and subject, and also across the secondary and primary boundary. They were events in which the school teams' experiences had to be made explicit and communicated to other teachers. They were often situations where some sort of chairperson was needed to facilitate communication. Regional meetings were held less frequently than school meetings, but provided situations in which more forward-looking decisions were made, to be communicated to the project as a whole through documents and at project conferences. Propositions and strategies could be compared and each team's progress monitored by other teams. In retrospect, it seems it was at these meetings rather than at the conferences that the primary and secondary insulation broke down, apparently because teachers from each type of school began to appreciate that they had many common problems.

Support for teachers' research and the constraints of time. The central team became involved in the school team's research problems far more than Document D had anticipated. Coordinators did ask for central team members to visit and help with problems that were arising. In only one case was the entire first-term schedule adhered to. Other teams worked through the case study principles, and all teams tried to compare their individual experiences with others. In many cases, timetabling prevented school team meetings from being held, except at lunchtime. In two cases, teams were given time to meet: one for half an hour and the other for one hour per week. The team that was allowed one hour found that meetings out of the immediate school environment—in the Teachers' Center—were more conducive to concentration and honest exchanges. In most cases, the sharing of experiences and findings took place at regional meetings. Here the school teams who had managed to co-ordinate were likely to attend regularly and contribute much more than those with weak coordination.

In the design of the project, the teams were comprised of three to four members but by the end of the project there were several pairs, four individuals, and one group of six. Although the individuals were at a disadvantage in that they could not compare their experiences with other teachers, the regional meetings and conferences seemed to have been frequent and informative enough to sustain—along with the visits of central team members—the isolated teacher. According to these individual teachers, their inner conflicts would not be talked over with colleagues, which added to the stress of their particiption.

When the case studies were to be written, lack of time and the rather slower development of the start of the project than the central team had expected meant the teachers were still unsure of their capabilities to write the case studies, even by the end of the third term. Subsequently, other action research projects reported the difficulties that teachers encountered in projects where they were asked to write accounts of their own practice, usually under the heading of "case studies." They found writing at length about a reflexive problem difficult. Initial drafts were fragmented and often in the form of notes. A lot of sensitive supportive guidance rather than criticism was required from facilitators. Harsh judgments from participating teachers were very disruptive to the group's cohesion as an action research unit. My experience is that only by the third draft, which usually becomes available after four to six months, does the writing begin to flow. There are a few exceptions, and these are not those who specialize in English or who have a particular talent for conventional writing; it is those teachers who are already highly reflexive about their practice.

Ten case studies were eventually received after the end of the fourth term. Two of them were written by whole school teams, rather than by individuals.

We think the lack of time is also reflected in children and teachers ceasing to keep diaries as a method of monitoring. Generally, recordings were used for this purpose, although many other methods, as set out in the project's booklet, "Ways of doing research in one's own classroom" (a final version of the original "Research Methods" document),were tried. The diary, although attempted in several classes, could not be sustained; however, in two cases, a questionnaire about the lesson was used as a substitute.

Conferences. Three residential conferences of three days' duration, at the beginning, middle, and end of the project, were occasions for consolidation. What had happened up until then was reported, discussed, and decisions made as to how much of the schedule, as laid out in Document D, could be fulfilled in the future. There was a progressive ease of discussion about classroom problems associated with inquiry and discovery teaching, starting with the first conference, which was rather tormented—people came away saying they did not really know what they were doing on the project or what the project stood for—to the second conference, where strong commitment based on understanding was expressed, and the final conference, where consolidation, reflection, and a feeling of achievement were evident. The final conference resulted in the establishment of working parties to organize the production of in-service materials that would help other teachers monitor their teaching. This outcome marked the strong orientation toward the problems of methodology for action research and teachers' research of their own practice. The initial substantive problem of inquiry and discovery teaching had been rewritten as more than the pedagogic problem. At the last conference, the talk was about self-monitoring schools and autonomous curriculum development, and there was a high level of confidence among the teachers in their writing and reflexive achievements and, thus, in their theorizing abilities. The teachers felt they had demonstrated their abilities to theorize about their own practices and had found that these abilities were necessary to conduct inquiry pedagogy.

Recent U.K. Developments in Action Research

The Ford T Project had sought democratic participation but found that most of the forty teachers were slow to actively participate; they waited to see what developed with those teachers who were more ready to take the risk of dissonance between their claims and practices and the expression of these in a public form. Although 'issues' from teachers were expected to arise from their reflection of their 'troubles,' the issues were often difficult to express. At those junctures, the participating teachers were vulnerable to interventions either by their colleagues, particularly those in a formal position of a higher status, especially the head teacher. The central team could not be sure that the issue was personal to the teacher and could not ensure, in spite of numerous documents giving guidance and meetings for discussion and decision, democratic, rather than autocratic, procedures. Elliott and I could not monitor every meeting nor the process of arrival at the issues and their analysis. The teachers' case studies were intended to provide such detail and their own research the systematic record.

We realized that Ford T had been successful in demonstrating that teachers are able to research and theorize about their own practices. The long reviews of Cook (1975a, b) attracted even more attention to the Ford T project. However, Elliot and I knew that a more pervasive and lasting influence would come through explicit support of HMI. After their invited visit to Norwich, the response was, "It is not the policy of HMI to provide funds for projects which they themselves have not initiated." It should be noted that at about that time funds for dissemination were made available to at least three DES/HMI projects in the areas of In-service Education of Teachers (INSET) and school management.

However, there was considerable interest in the project, particularly from those in INSET and in Local Authority School Advisory Services. Some Chief Education Officers sent their representatives to conferences, but HMI did not ask Elliot to attend any of their national or regional conferences. Further dissemination of the project was mainly in the voluminous writings of its participants. Productively, Elliot wrote overviews of these and earlier Ford documents (see, for instance, Elliot 1976), and these writings attracted particular attention in North America (where three Ford teachers, Elliot, and myself gave seminars in New York, Chicago, Ohio, and Toronto in 1976). The late Schools Council funded a compilation of action research endeavors in England and Wales. Stephen Kemmis, a colleague at CARE, took action research to Australia some four years after Rae Monroe (1974) had begun work in New Zealand.

This was the beginning of the Classroom Action Research Network (CARN), which now has an international membership (Adams 1980). Other regional initiatives in the United Kingdom include the Teacher Research Network of Northern Ireland, based at the University of Ulster, and the Avon Curriculum Review and Evaluation Programme. Like most programs, these are small-scale and brief with transitory funding. In an attempt to further establish action research, Jack Whitehead at Bath University, Pamela Lomax at Kingston Polytechnic, and Richard Winter at the Anglia Institute of Higher Education supervise master's courses that can include dissertations based upon teachers' research into their own practice. However, these studies are within the constraints of academic time and do not allow for the risk associated with group participatory research. However, since the 1970s, Colin Fletcher at Cranfield Institute of Technology has developed alternative ways of approaching supervision of participatory research.

I do not dismiss these efforts to promote reflexivity in professional practice à la Schon, but I question whether, in the medium and long term, they make any changes in the conduct of schooling. Sustained participatory research continues under the heading of Mutual Support and Observation (MSO) at Stantonbury Schools in Milton Keynes (Fielding 1989; Gates 1989). In MSO, three or more teachers observe an issue in their mutual teaching and feed back this information to each other. The observation, reporting, and changes made are discussed within the whole school among those who take part in MSO. These comprise about 15 percent of the teachers in any one year. MSO has continued since 1985.

In the United Kingdom, a few places in England have sustained action research by incorporating it into higher degree courses, as mentioned above, and I have criticized this framing of the risky in the structure and 'progression' of academic courses (Adelman 1989). CARN continues under the guidance of Bridget Somekh at CARE. An annual international conference and a bulletin are regular features. There are no individual Ford T teachers remaining in a membership of approximately 400. CARN keeps the most complete list of the small projects and dissertations in the United Kingdom.

The tendency to individual reflexivity using the selective work of Schon as the exemplar[4] rather than group research will not promote democratic participation, nor will the explicit yet convoluted distrust in teachers' accounts as ideologically distorted misrepresentations of reality. As Elliot (1991) argues in a volume published after this article was in its third draft, if claims are made to a distinction between 'practical' and 'emancipatory' action research, as do Carr and Kemmis (1986), they should not deny the possibility of critical reflexive practices arising out of the struggle by practitioners with their action research self-understandings. The problem of participation is, in the main, who is to define the issue for their investigation, theorizing, and relationships, and in whose name is the research publicized, if at all?

The lack of articulation with regional or national educational policy formation has been commented on elsewhere (Carr 1989). The means to sharing vocabulary and meanings as the antidote to alienation may be through participatory research, but the conditions for participation in that research are hard-won and harder to sustain. We in the United Kingdom may learn from John Goodlad (Sirotnik and Goodlad 1988), Herb Kohl (1990), and Colin Fletcher (1988) and the PALM project in these respects.

I do believe action research, or rather participatory research, could be a means to reconstruction (Simey 1985) and productive work (Wirth 1983). One of the urgent tasks is to bring together those who have concentrated on individual reflective practice, such as Schon, those who try to carry on Lewin's group discussion and decision making, and those who have worked with large communities following the examples of Horton and Freire. Participatory research may empower by raising the consciousness of teachers about the social context in which they work, but participatory research in its own right is still weak, lacking the kind of support that the Educational Priority

Area and Community Development Projects briefly attracted. Currently, planning and decisions about educational policy and practice are increasingly being taken away from the local authorities by central government. Teachers are seen as operatives in a system of line management, their work assessed and appraised, yet all of this without the local democratic politics of the North American school boards.

In this paper, I have argued that two deficient rhetorics have arisen since Lewin: action research for greater effectiveness with, but more often without, the link to democratic processes; and clarification of the principles of democratic practice without sufficient or adequate action research to demonstrate these claims. What has also been lost sight of in the more recent emphasis on individual reflection has been the essential inclusion of group and institutional relationships. Much of this individual emphasis is attributed to the person-to-person consultant work of Schon while his former co-author, Argyris, continues to investigate organization and group development in the Lewin tradition. The fruits of reflexive thought, if they are claimed to have potential for improving practice against stated criteria, have to be tested in joint and reciprocal social action in the context of constraints and conflicts.

It remains to be seen whether participatory research can influence social and educational policy in technocratic bureaucracies. There is every indication that in the United Kingdom the national curriculum and assessment have in no way been informed by participatory research.

Afterword

John Elliott wrote the following statement as part of the preface to his M.Phil. thesis (1980) for the University of London. This is included to corroborate some of the details about the Ford Project and the problem of democratic participation.

Statement About Conjoint Work

Although every word of this study was written by me, the project it is based upon represented a collaborative effort between two researchers—Clem Adelman and myself—and forty teachers. I hope I have made the contribution of the teachers clear. If the ideas expressed in this study are of any value, much of it is due to these teachers, listed in Appendix 1.

I owe an enormous debt to my research colleague Clem Adelman. It is difficult to assess our relative contributions to the theoretical and methodological aspects of the project, there being no rigid division of labor. Clem's contribution reflected his sociological interests, while mine reflected a philosophical stance. The interaction was wholly productive.

My interest in the philosophical literature about the nature of teaching and education, apparent in this study, tempted me to share it with teachers at an early stage in the project. Clem opposed me, insisting that we work from the ideas and beliefs already implicit in teachers' practices. Eliciting the schema, reported by me in the first half of chapter 4, was entirely his idea. He also devised the techniques employed in this particular aspect of the research, formulating the schema that resulted. The interpretation of the schema provided in the second half of chapter 4 and its translation into the typology of teaching, described in chapter 6, was largely, but not exclusively, my contribution.

Clem Adelman's second major contribution to the project lay in the development of the triangulation techniques reported in chapter 7. I had employed them rather crudely in the Schools Council Humanities Project, while Clem was familiar with their potential use in cognitive sociology. In working with teachers, we both employed them but Clem in particular, mainly in primary and middle school classrooms, was responsible for refining and developing them in ways appropriate to such contexts. He devised the tape and slide system of recording, which was particularly appropriate as an observation tool in decentralized classroom situations. Operating largely in secondary school classrooms that were more centralized, I tended to rely on tape-recording and note-taking techniques. Clem also devised ways of enabling teachers to take a more active role in the triangulation process, allowing the researcher to pass much of the initiative for collecting and processing information to the teacher. As will be seen from the example in chapter 7, I, as the outside researcher, tended to exercise far more initiative than I allowed the teacher.

Finally, Clem Adelman played a significant role with myself and other project teachers in generating hypotheses about the development of self-monitoring ability. These are reported in chapter 10, where I alone am responsible for the form in which they are presented.

In addition to the contributions cited above, I was largely responsible for the design of the project and its underlying rationale (reported earlier), helping teachers reflect about the aims and values of inquiry and discovery teaching (see chapter 5) and the systematic generation of hypothesis from the comparative study of cases (see chapter 8). Sections III and IV stem mainly from my own personal attempt to explore the implications of the project for educational research and teaching.

Notes

My thanks to Colin Fletcher, Derek Purdy, and Harold Silver for their constructive criticism of the penultimate draft of this paper. The author remains culpable.

1. Alfred J. Marrow, his biographer, was the secretary to the American committee.

2. Whose individualistic rather than group approach to development comprises just one of the differences between his work and participatory research. This may be a reason why Carr and Kemmis (1986) do not mention his work, albeit this absence is reciprocal.

3. The first triangulation, which I devised in 1972, appeared as 'The tins' in the Ford T booklets of 1975, and the methodology was discussed in Adelman and Walker (1975).

4. The process of reflexivity about professional issues through the study of individuals is just part of the work of Schon. The book *Organizational learning* (Argyris and Schon 1978) situates individual facts as part of reciprocating organization within the context of accountability. This aspect of Schon's work has been developed by Stanton (1988).

References

Adams, E. 1980. Ford teaching project. In *Curriculum research and development in action*, ed. L. Stenhouse. Heinemann Educational Books.

Adelman, C., and R. Walker. 1975. Developing pictures for other frames: Action research and case study. In *Frontiers of Classroom Research.*, G. Chanan and S. Delamont. Slough, UK: NFER.

Adelman, C., et al. 1983. *A fair hearing for all: Relationships between teaching and racial equality*. University of Reading, Bulmershe Research Publication No. 2.

Adelman, C., and C. Fletcher. 1982. Collaboration as a research process. *Quarterly journal of community education* 1(1) February:15–24.

Adelman, C. 1989. The practical ethic takes priority over methodology. In *Quality in teaching: Arguments for a reflective profession*. W. Carr. Sussex: Falmer Press.

Argyris, C., and D. A. Schon. 1978. *Organizational learning*. Reading, Mass: Addison-Wesley.

Argyris, C., R. Putnam, and D. McLain Smith. 1985. *Action science*. San Francisco: Jossey-Bass.

Baratz, S. S., and J. C. Baratz. 1970. Early childhood intervention: the social science base of institutional racism. *Harvard educational review* 40(1):29–50.

Bernstein, B. 1970. Education cannot compensate for society. In *Language in education*. London: Routledge & Kegan Paul in assoc. with the Open University Press.

Blake R. R., and J.S. Mouton. 1968. *Corporate excellence through grid organization development : A systems approach*. Texas: Gulf Publishing Co.

Carr, W., and S. Kemmis. 1986. *Becoming critical: Education, knowledge, and action research*. Geelong, Vic.: Deakin University Press.

Carr W. 1989. Understanding quality in teaching. In *Quality in teaching: Arguments for a reflective profession*, W. Carr. Sussex: Falmer Press.

Cartwright, D., and A. Zander. 1953. *Group dynamics*. London: Tavistock Press.

Cicourel, A.V. 1973. *Cognitive sociology*. Harmondsworth, UK: Penguin Educational Books.

Coates, K., and R. Silburn. 1970. *Poverty: The forgotten Englishman*. Harmondsworth, UK: Penguin.

Cook, M. 1975a. Where the action research is: A look at the innovatory work arising out of the Ford Teaching Project. London, *Times education supplement*.

———. 1975b. Bridging the gap between theory and practice: A review of Ford Teaching Project publications. London, *Times educational supplement*.

Corey, S. M. 1953. *Action research to improve school practices*. New York: Bureau of Publications, Teachers College, Columbia University Press.

Elliott, J., and C. Adelman. 1975. Teacher education for curriculum reform: An interim report on the work of the Ford Teaching Project. In *British journal of teacher education* 1(1) January:105–14.

Elliott, J. 1976. Developing hypotheses about classrooms from teachers practical constructs. *Interchange*. Ontario Institute for Studies in Education, 7(2):2–22.

———. 1991. *Action research for educational change*. Milton Keynes: Open University Press.

Fielding, M. 1989. The fraternal foundations of democracy: Towards emancipatory practice in school-based INSET. In *The democratic school*, C. Harber and R. Meighan. Ticknall, Derbyshire: Education Now Publishing Cooperative Ltd.

Fletcher, C. 1988. Issues for participatory research in Europe. *Community Development Journal* 23: 44–46.

Gates, P. 1989. Developing consciousness and pedagogical knowledge through mutual observation. In *Working for teacher development*, P. Woods. Durham, Norfolk: Peter Francis Publishers.

Halsey, A. 1972. *Educational priority*, 1. London: HMSO.

Kohl, H., and S. Kohl. 1990. *The long haul: An autobiography of Myles Horton*. New York: Doubleday.

Landsberger, H. A. 1958. *Hawthorne revisited: Management and the worker, its critics and developments in human relations in industry*. Ithaca, New York: Cornell University.

Lewin, K. 1920. Die sozialisierung des taylorsystems. Praktischer Sozialismus, No. 4.

Lewin, K., R. Lippett, and R. K. White. 1939. Patterns of aggressive behavior in experimentally created social climates. *Journal of social psychology* 10:271–301.

MacDonald, B., and R. Walker. 1976. *Changing the curriculum*. Milton Keynes, UK: Open Books.

Madaus, G. F., and D. Stufflebeam. 1989. *Educational evaluation: Classic works of Ralph W. Tyler*. Boston: Kluwer Academic Publishers.

Marrow, A. J. 1969. *The practical theorist: The life and work of Kurt Lewin*. NY: Basic Books.

Midwinter, E. C. 1972. *Priority education*. Harmondsworth, UK: Penguin Education Special.

———. 1975. *Education and community*. George Allen & Unwin.

Rowan, J. (1974). Research as an intervention. In *Reconstructing social psychology*, ed. N. Armistead. London: Penguin Books.

Sanford, N. 1970. Whatever happened to action research? *Journal of social issues* 26(3).

Schon, D. A. 1983. *The reflective practitioner.* New York: Basic Books.

Silver, H., and P. Silver. 1991. *An educational war on poverty: American and British policy-making 1960–1980*. Cambridge: Cambridge University Press.

Simey M. 1985. *Government by consent: The principle and practice of accountability in local government*. London: Bedford Square Press.

Sirotnik, K. A., and J. I. Goodlad. 1988. *School-university partnerships in action*. New York: Teachers College Press.

Smith, G. 1987. Whatever happened to educational priority areas? *Oxford review of education* 13:23–39.

Stanton, A. 1988. *Invitation to self management*. London: Dab Hand Press.

Stenhouse, L. (ed.). 1975. *An introduction to curriculum research and development*. London: Heinemann Educational Books.

———— (ed.). 1980. *Curriculum research and development in action*. London: Heinemann Educational Books.

Wirth, A. G. 1983. *Productive work in industry and schools*. New York: Universities Press of America.

Wright Mills, C. 1959. *The sociological imagination*. New York: Oxford University Press.

CHAPTER 5

Participatory Action Research in Colombia:
Some Personal Feelings

Orlando Fals Borda

When I resigned from my university post in 1970 and plunged into the initial quest of what today is generally referred to as Participatory Action Research (PAR), I never expected that such a decision would eventually take me into political action. The decision to leave the National University of Colombia— a painful one, as I had been professor and dean there for many years—had to do with a number of problems or dilemmas within the intellectual domain, which did not necessarily imply dealing with mass parties or movements. Nevertheless, this opened the way to unexpected events that broadened the points of view taken for my subsequent decisions.

Such problems started with the mortifying discovery that my university, in its actual condition, could not understand adequately the ever-present theory and practice dialectics. Like many other such institutions, it remained in an ivory tower, learning by rote without relating to surrounding social and cultural realities. Moreover, it fell victim to the fatal belief in science as a fetish with a life of its own, a notion that I was already connecting with Oppenheimer's denouncement of the atomic bomb. If I still wanted to be a good academician, I had to work with a different concept of science, more ethical and pertinent to the daily vicissitudes of the common people, which would place me on the side of peace and progress, not death and destruction.

Could theory and practice be combined indeed for such lofty purposes? I remembered the teachings of my professors on the history of social thought, the ways in which they extolled the achievements of founders like Saint Simon, Comte, and Marx. Certainly these intellectual giants showed some positive methods and philosophies for sociopolitical change that later scholars disregarded for the sake of Cartesian objectivity. Moreover, in the contemporary context, path analysis was the closest I had come to understanding feedback mechanisms; socialist central planning was another example of such possibilities. Later on, I also understood theory and practice dialectics in action in the medium of the Second World War, when John D. Bernal's group discovered the operationality concept and applied it to raise the dreadful efficacy of the armed forces.

Therefore, if the opposition between thought and action was only apparent, it was possible to conceive of practice as a source of theory-in-action, relegating to oblivion the separation between the two elements that was of daily acceptance in academia and which I rejected as artificial. This old Spinozistic discovery helped me in deciding to search for praxis and phronesis as an alternative to instrumental science, without ethical qualms. Besides, it was good to remember Sir Francis Bacon's dictum that science, like the life of the just man, can be judged mainly for its deeds.

Another personal problem, an existential one, dealt with the classic subject and object dichotomy. Natural scientists—at least until the work of quantum physicists—had no trouble in dealing with it as it fulfilled all Aristotelian conditions. But I as a social scientist found increasing difficulty in Spencer's organic analogy or in applying Durkheim's principles for interpreting social processes and actions as 'facts' or 'things.' This polemics today is obsolete, but in the 1970s it was heretical to preach horizontal relationships in the research adventure, even in professional life. It became clear to me however that sociological investigation should not be autistic but a rite of communion between thinking and acting human beings, the researcher and the researched. The usual formality and prophylaxis of academic institutions had to be discarded and given space to some sort of down-to-earth collectivization in the search for knowledge. This attitude I called *vivencia*, or life-experience (*Erlebnis*). For me, it became like litmus paper in determining authentic participatory practices in research and action.

The evidence that it is possible to produce serious, responsible knowledge apt to accumulate through group vivencias and symmetrical information exchange became so exhilarating for me and the colleagues who accompanied me that we started to compare the breakup of the subject and object relation in sociology with the fission of the atom in physics. Hence our increasing interest in a *Verstehen*-type idea of participation, which subsequently led us to reject liberal definitions of it. We finally came to see participation as a breakup of the relationship of submission, exploitation, or oppression between subjects and objects in most expressions of daily life. Finally, as our social commitment increased, the resulting participatory research concept opened the gate to the more ambitious idea of participatory democracy. This was premonitory for further work with political implications: in fact, participatory democracy became a central premise for Colombia's first Constituent Assembly in 100 years, the Assembly for which I was nominated and elected in December 1990.

A third intellectual problem experienced at the time dealt with the relation between Reason and Knowledge or, if you wish, between rationality and science. I had been told to be aware of my values and biases so a true scientific attitude would always be respected. No doubt this well-meant advice took cognizance mainly of the Newtonian tradition of science and technology based, as is known, on operational rationality. But, as we had questioned this rationality from the ethical and heuristic standpoints, as stated earlier, we discovered another line of reasoning, duly acknowledged by Galileo, Descartes, and Kant themselves, among others, that belonged to another level of science: that of the common people's knowledge (popular or folk science) based on practical reason and communicative sociability.

Therefore, the instrumental wish to shake up nature to dominate it gave way to questioning the value components of human action over nature and society. This led us to look for and respect the wisdom of peoples who had been forgotten, neglected, or despised by academia and elite groups in general, such as peasants and Aboriginal communities. Thus, we tried to establish direct contact with them and our social commitment then functioned as ideological cement for our field work.

Once outside the university, I was met in real life with a conflictive context ready to accommodate my subversive expectations. It was an ugly reality fraught with violence: Colombian peasants and Indians were in deep crisis, struggling for lands which had been monopolized by the wealthy and powerful. But disregarding implicit dangers, once personally involved with the people in my native region, sharing life in their miserable huts, I satisfied the need or concreteness in commitment and found an unknown universe titillating with discoveries, a challenge to build with the peasants some sort of alternative discipline designed to benefit them and a different style for communicating the findings.

Assisted by the late readings of Marxist literature, at first I thought we were discovering a 'science of the proletariat.' This soon disappeared like a phantom. What was left was a series of methodological and technical guidelines for local leaders which, apart from independent invention, surprisingly assimilated certain procedures from academia. Were we subsuming the two known types of knowledge (instrumental and practical) so a more complete, satisfying, and valid type of science, committed to people's progress, was in the making? This was confirmed by later work in many countries. Are we then on the brink of proposing, with PAR, a new paradigm in the social sciences? Some European colleagues did advance this idea, based on the work of many of us in Third World countries, but no satisfactory answer can yet be given.

While the knowledge front was not perfected for lack of enough analytical field work and comparative schemes, there arose the practical side of recognizing politics in the Colombian localities where the poor and the landless were still invading latifundia. Because the information systematically gathered with them regarding their recovered history of struggles and the sharp impact of popular culture on their organization and regional movements abetted such land invitations, this could be considered politics, too.

The peasants soon discovered they were gaining political clout with such theory-in-action. I too felt this whirl and unexpectedly started to gain regional visibility; such work took me to jail with the peasants more than once. Put against the wall, finally I had to decide whether to become a full-fledged politician, so be it with new orientations, or remain an out-of-the-way scholar attuned to the popular struggle. I chose the latter and invited local leaders to take up the political mantle themselves.

In any case, an important lesson in political science was derived from that practical experience: that the classical Lukacsian-Leninist conception of the vanguard party as supreme intermediary between the State and the masses had to suffer serious modifications. I had seen leftist organizations at work in the regions with such arrogance and sectarianism that I felt confused, often misunderstood, and once threatened. They talked the garbled language of the manuals and transferred foreign models in the hope of successful repetition. Such could not be a satisfactory way to revolution, nor even to the participatory democracy urgently needed. We were all heading toward frustration, thus I spoke out.

Then we discovered Rajni Kothari's seminal proposal for 'non-party political processes.' With this timely input, we could extricate ourselves from the dead-end street in which we found ourselves. It was possible for us to stimulate alternative social movements as demonstrations of people's power, as more constructive ways of doing politics, this time inspired by tolerance, altruism, and respect for life and diversity as most people want it.

The movements with which we became connected in Colombia (civic, regional, ecological, feminist, cultural, aboriginal, peasant, human rights, etc.) passed from short-lived acts of protest to visionary proposals, in great part inspired or guided by PAR procedures. They grew quickly. The movements eventually became persistent and formed networks, maturing in time and ideas to become feasible political alternatives for gaining State power and helping to change the world as Walter Benjamin wanted it: free from blood and horror.

Continuous field experience naturally conditioned my subsequent intellectual production and marked my style and personality to the present day. Even when the time arrived, after twenty years, of returning to the National University, I carried with me the early image and load of an iconoclast, a subversive scientist. Yet apparently the level in institutional tolerance for iconoclasm had likewise risen in the country. The critical situation of Colombia could not be solved with old ways and ideologies. The university had also changed in the meantime, advancing toward interdisciplinary conceptions akin to our original ideas.

Past symbioses also kept functioning. The peasants, for example, had never forgotten: they voted for me, along with intellectuals, social movements, and regional organizations for my present post in Colombia's Constituent Assembly. Now political parties formed by the new sociopolitical movements, aided by PAR ideals and techniques through 'self-reliance promoting organizations' (alternative NGOs), have become protagonists in Colombia today.

I feel this twenty-year adventure in praxiological vivencias turned out this way as a combination of conjuncture and will, with roots in the structural cleavages of Colombian society. Politics had not been my goal in life. Yet collective problematic circumstances led me to assume a commitment that combined a sociological discipline with a political role, with new meanings and increased responsibilities.

PAR assisted in this transition with constant bearings on science-making and ideological-ethical orientation. As a result, we have perhaps clearer insights into and richer knowledge about the predicament of humankind in many parts of the world and in previously neglected societies and cultures. PAR at this moment is probably helping many others in Colombia and elsewhere who are yet motivated by knowing and acting and full of illusions for a better world, especially for the underprivileged, just as I was in the previous stage of intellectual dilemmas and institutional shortcomings.

This is good. The work continues, not in vain, because PAR still remains a philosophy of life as much as a method, a sentiment as much as a conviction.

References

Fals-Borda, O. 1979. Investigating reality in order to transform it. *Dialectical anthropology* 4:33–55.

———— . 1987. The application of participatory action-research in Latin America. *International sociology* 2(4):329–47.

———— . 1988. *Knowledge and people's power*. New Delhi: Indian Social Institute.

———— . 1990. Social movements and political power: Evolution in Latin America. *International sociology* 5(2):115–28.

Fals-Borda, O., and Md. Anisur Rahman (eds.). 1991. *Action and knowledge: Recent views of participatory action-research*. New York: The Apex/New Horizons Press.

Goulet, D. 1974. A subversive agent from Colombia. *Worldview* (New York) 17(6):29–34.

Kemmis, S., and Fals Borda, O. 1990. *Investigating reality in order to transform it: A conversation with Orlando Fals-Borda and Stephen Kemmis* (Videotape 30 min.). Calgary: University of Calgary, Communications Division.

Kothari, R. 1984. The non-party political process. *Economic and political weekly* 19(5).

CHAPTER 6

Toward an Epistemology of Participatory Research

Anil Chaudhary

It was sometime during 1968, in my first year of college, that I read Dosto-evsky's *Crime and punishment*, which provided a passionate critique of money, economy, and a vivid description of the inhuman impact of money lending and interest. Once, in an economics class, while the teacher was explaining theories of interest, I could not resist raising certain questions about the attempt to rationalize an inhuman practice that was rampantly prevalent in our society. The point of debate in the classroom was about the Liquidity Preference Theory of Interest, which, as a natural consequence, led to the question of distribution. For about half an hour, the teacher tried to argue in a scholarly manner, but suddenly he became very serious. He confessed that although some of my arguments were making a lot of sense, he was being paid a salary to teach something different and that the students could receive grades only on writing the same theories during the exams. Thus the teacher suggested that I not waste others' time during class in such futile debates. As a democratic gesture toward me, he suggested that I not attend the class, yet promised me full attendance to fulfil the bureaucratic requirements of the university.

At this juncture, I stopped attending my classes for a couple of weeks and tried to reflect on my entire experience about the educational system. The scenario looked quite frightening. I realized that the values related to profit, accumulation, interest, and individualism are drilled into us from childhood. All four basic operations of mathematics, that is addition, subtraction, multi-plication, and division are taught to us through questions framed around these values during our primary and elementary education.

During my time, profit loss, simple interest, and compound interest used to be the core of arithmetic throughout school. As a result, most of my peers became insensitive to these issues and started considering these things sacrosanct.

In the absence of a clear ideological reference point, the world looked like hell in those days, thus one took recourse in reading history books to study the phenomenon in-depth.

Time has proven that I chose the right direction by seeking recourse in history and returning to the classics, as advised by the elders.

Today, since most of us from Asia, Africa, and Latin America are struggling with the same values, and the clutches of international monetary and market systems are instrumental in perpetuating 'status-quoism' and anti-people power correlations in most of our countries, we are obliged to place the philosophy of Participatory Research (PR) in this historical context. Even the journey of PR networks through the last fifteen years is full of experiences that provide ample evidence that PR is neither a mean critique of conventional research methodology nor a set of tools and techniques, as attempts in the past have been made to prove. It is necessary to develop an epistemological framework of PR with a historical perspective and vision of totality.

Lessons From History

Knowledge and the control over its production and use has been an effective instrument in the hands of rulers, ever since societies became divided into rulers and those who were ruled. If the armed organizations of the state have been instrumental in protecting the physical boundaries and control of power, the control over knowledge and information has been instrumental in providing the rational and moral basis for that power to perpetuate itself. The function of sustaining the psyche conducive for acceptance of a specific power-relation had been solely performed through control over knowledge and information throughout history.

The attempts by the custodians of knowledge (Brahmins, in the case of India) during the ancient period to prove that the 'King is a Reflection of God' or the attempts of officially sanctioned specialists in contemporary times to rectify and rationalize every act of 'power,' irrespective of its implication on societies, are the same phenomenon.

The industrial revolution in modern times led to the commercialization of all human values. Even knowledge was conveniently converted to a mere commodity. The conditions of knowledge production also acquired the characteristics of an industry, that is the production and distribution of knowledge was guided by the demands of the market on the basis of equations of input and output.

The directions of the formal knowledge systems were decided by the requirements of those controlling the power. All of the advances made in the field of information technology during the twentieth century tended to centralize control over knowledge production and its use in favor of those dominating the power correlation.

Historically, in most of the developing societies, the mode of control over formal systems of knowledge production and distribution is of a similar nature. Such controls may be categorized into three types: structural, linguistic, and thematic.

Structural Control

During every stage of social development throughout history there have been certain controls that debarred the entry of the common mass into the fold of formal systems of knowledge production and distribution. In ancient India, it was the prerogative of only 'twice-borns' (specific social strata) to indulge in knowledge production and its use. The people who were performing menial functions in the society were banned from even listening to the scriptures. The historical incidents provide ample evidence that whenever someone from the ranks of the lower strata of society tried to acquire knowledge, the person was severely punished. These types of structural control were certainly crude and got washed away in the post-industrial revolution wave of 'equality, fraternity, and liberty.' Certainly, when the dominant mode of production in society was not in a position to discriminate between human beings on the basis of their birth, how could the formal system of knowledge production do so? Even more so, the rise of industry demanded more and more skilled working hands, and the doors of formal systems of knowledge production were opened for everyone, to the extent of preparing them to operate machines, and so on. High levels of knowledge production and use still remained the prerogative of those who could afford the high costs.

A number of developing societies such as India claimed to hold on to the values of 'liberty, equality, and fraternity,' thus, in principle, opened the doors of the formal system of knowledge production and use for everyone. But the conditions of rampant poverty prohibited the masses from taking advantage of the gesture of goodwill made by the dominant sections.

In India, attempts have been made over the last forty years to create two tiers of non-formal systems of knowledge exchange. There is one set of facilities for the elite, which prepare technocrats, bureaucrats, and managers, and another set for workers, clerks, and consumers.

Thus, even today in our societies the strategy to perpetuate conditions of poverty through monetary and market manipulations marginalizes the majority of the populace from the formal systems of knowledge production and its utilization.

Linguistic Control

This relates to the medium of instruction used in formal systems. In India, the formal systems of knowledge production and use, throughout history, had a medium of instruction that was never the language of the masses. During the ancient period, we had Sanskrit, a language that only the uppermost strata in society was allowed to use. Even women were prohibited from using that language. In some parts of India today we see the introduction of Persian, which again was not the language of the masses. The colonial era, then, introduced English as the medium of instruction, which we are still faithfully following. At all points in history, this has helped to keep the field of knowledge production and usage inaccessible to the masses, which has been an effective instrument of monopolistic control over knowledge and information by those dominating the power-relations in our societies. It is this monopolistic control that leads to the ideological and cultural hegemony of dominant sections.

Another dimension of such linguistic control is related to the cultures linked with these languages and their impact. Even if some people work hard and transcend the linguistic barriers, they fall flat because of not being able to internalize the culture attached to that language. It is only the second- and third- generation users of these languages who attain entry into the cliques of the elite who monopolize knowledge and information.

The most apparent implication of such a process in today's modern societies is that the people who somehow obtain entry into the formal systems of knowledge production and usage begin to look down upon their own community, language, and culture, thus become alienated from their own people.

Thematic Control

The content or issues that the formal system of knowledge production and usage address also are the means to control, by those dominating the power correlation in our societies. Along with the structural and linguistic controls, the content of a formal system of knowledge exchange had always been of the status quo. During the ancient and medieval periods in Indian history, such controls were explicitly pronounced as policies of the formal system of knowledge production, but in modern times, due to the compulsion of democratic rhetorics, such controls are camouflaged and indirectly exercised through financial regulations and aids.

The example of mathematics education, which is projected as value-neutral yet revolves around profit, loss, accumulation, interest, and compound interest, clearly demonstrates the implications of thematic control in amply perpetuating the status-quo. The field of engineering and management education in most of the developing countries is another glaring example of such a control. In India, engineering and science education was heavily funded by the U. S. P. L. 480 grants and had influenced the whole curriculum in such a way that the engineers produced by such institutions were only useful for working in the West or with the technologies developed in the Western world. The local conditions and requirements have had no influence over our own engineers. They are trained to design only big buildings, large dams, super power stations and macro irrigation systems, all of which lead to a centralized control, serving the multinational business interests. The appropriate technologies, which would have helped meet the basic requirements of the masses, have no place in the curriculum of our professional and technical institutions. The curriculum of medical doctors does not include occupational health and safety issues that endanger the lives of millions of workers. By influencing the content of engineering education in our country, the interests of the developed world and that of big local business have been able to direct the course of social development as a whole to suit their needs.

Areas of social science and history are always made to serve the purpose of those holding the reins of power.

History also reveals that the formal systems of knowledge production and its use were never the only channels of knowledge created at any given point. Outside the purview of the controls of formal systems, there always existed systems and mechanisms where people themselves created knowledge relevant to them. Although there has never been much research or written work done on these systems and mechanisms for obvious reasons, the developments in historical writings during the last two decades do make tangible references to this phenomenon. For example, until recently, communities and villages in our society had some mechanism for gathering information every day which served the purpose of transfering knowledge from the elders to the younger generation and exchanging experiences, all of which led to the enhancement of existing knowledge. Most societies and communities in developing societies have a strong tradition of verbal knowledge transfer and the creation of a knowledge bank, which is the contribution of such a mechanism only.

Indian history, as it is available today, is full of instances where issues consequential to the lives of the masses were raised and resolved through these mechanisms. People sought recourse in these mechanisms for their problems, related to their livelihood and social relationships. All of the movements challenging the different aspects of 'status-quoism' in history grew and drew strength from such mechanisms.

Thus, history points out the parallel existence of two types of systems of knowledge production and its use: the first being the formal system, with all of its burden of serving sectional interests and mechanisms of control, and the second operating within the communities as part of larger social practices. While a lot is written about the former, the latter still needs to be explored in-depth. Both of these systems of knowledge production have distinctive means and relationships of production.

If we further analyze the means and relationships of knowledge production and its use, within the framework of such a historical perspective, we may be able to identify some broader characteristics of such modes of knowledge production. For better articulation purposes, I suggest we refer to the formal system as a 'dominant mode' of knowledge production and its use and refer to the latter as the 'popular mode.'

Characteristics of the Dominant Mode of Knowledge Production

A closer look at the formal systems of knowledge production and usage throughout Indian history highlights some of the following characteristics.

Isolation

The formal system of knowledge production in India has always been isolated from the day-to-day life in our society. In India, the tradition of *Gurukula*, where disciples came to stay for years with their teachers, was employed. They stayed in remote forests, totally cut off from the rest of society, as a rule. Suspending links with families and all other human relationships was a prerequisite for joining the ranks of those involved in the profession of knowledge production.

The basic element of 'isolation' in this tradition seemed to have percolated down from history to modern times. Today's formal systems of higher learning are organized in much the same way. Such organization of the system of knowledge production and its use makes isolation from real life imperative to those willing to join the elite club. This process makes them appear 'special' when they return to their communities; as a consequence, they become isolated from their own people.

Individualistic Pursuit

Throughout history, the act of acquisition and utilization of knowledge in our society has been considered an individualistic pursuit. The end of the pursuit of knowledge is always seen as an individual gain or a matter of personal satisfaction.

In modern times, due to the commercialization of values of life and the existence of a perpetual rat race to find a niche in the system, this element of our age-old tradition has compounded in many ways.

The issues of social relevance of knowledge created through these formal systems and of the social obligations of those in possession of such knowledge are thrown into the background, thus isolating the noble process of knowledge production even further and identifying it as a specialized profession.

Accumulative Nature

The first two characteristics contribute to creating a possessiveness about knowledge (and information) and encourage its use for carving out a position for the individual in power mechanisms. Thus, the people involved in knowledge production tend to accumulate more and more knowledge. Sharing this wealth of knowledge with others, for whom it may be more useful, is not part of the value system of the dominant mode of knowledge production.

Abstract Issues and Sectional Interests

The substance of knowledge produced and used in the dominant mode generally deals with abstract issues and serves sectional interests, those which dominate the power correlation.

In the ancient period of Indian history, the substance of knowledge production was devoted to metaphysical issues related to life and death, concentrating upon the learning scriptures and the use of arms. In modern times, the major thrust of the system is on projection of GNP and so forth, and on the development of 'Star Wars' programs, which are totally inclined toward perpetuating the control of a powerful few over the powerless many.

Centralized Control

An individualistic pursuit (of an accumulative nature) of abstract issues in sectional interests, creates conditions conducive to centralized control. The whole process of knowledge production and use in this mode leads to the creation of a class of specialists, with high stakes for survival that turn them into instruments of control. Financial support has been the most effective means of control throughout the history of humankind. The state and sections of society with a larger stake in state functioning are the ones financing the formal systems of knowledge production of this type. Such shared stake-holdings of those dominating the power correlation and those specializing in knowledge production have facilitated centralized control throughout history.

Perpetuation of 'Status-Quoism'

Perpetuation of 'status-quoism' has been the most basic characteristic of the dominant mode of knowledge throughout history, as elaborated previously. With the advancement and investment in information technology along the lines of the above-mentioned characteristics, the implications of this function of the dominant mode are becoming increasingly consequential, both nationally and globally.

Characteristics of the Popular Mode of Knowledge Production

Interaction

The process of knowledge creation and its use in the popular mode had always been likened to a social event. People acquire knowledge, contribute to the development of knowledge, and make use of that knowledge while carrying out their daily chores. For them, this process is a part of their daily routine.

Interaction in terms of the exchange of experiences, ideas, stories, songs, anecdotes, and so on is the core of this process of knowledge-creation. It is this characteristic that makes the popular mode an interactive mode of knowledge production and use.

Collective Pursuit

In the popular mode, the function of knowledge acquisition and use becomes a collective pursuit as opposed to being an individual pursuit in the dominant mode. The interactive nature of the popular mode makes it imperative upon the process of knowledge production and its use to be a collective process. It is through mutual sharing and collective action that people generate or increase new knowledge.

Disseminative Nature

The popular mode, by its basic nature of being interactive and collective, ensures the dissemination of knowledge and information as opposed to the accumulative character of the dominant mode. Dissemination, in a way, is built into the process of knowledge-creation. Along with the interactive and collective nature of the popular mode, its disseminative character works as a source of its strength.

Concrete and Common Issues

Historically, and by virtue of its nature, the popular mode tends to address itself to concrete and common issues. The interactiveness and collectiveness of the process ensures the concreteness and commonness of the issues it tackles. These issues generally relate to the livelihood and survival of the common people and the common interest of the masses.

Decentralization

Due to the basic characteristics explained before, the popular mode tends to create a decentralized system which may be developed as a system of

knowledge production and usage. Because of its inherent situation and cul-
ture-specificity, the popular mode operates in conditions that are not at all
conducive to any kind of centralization or control. The popular mode, due to
its tenets, defies the creation of any kind of monopoly over knowledge, its
production and use. It is a decentralized mode in letter and in spirit.

Questioning 'Status-Quoism' (Seeking Transformation)

Although one does not have enough evidence from history to proclaim
that the popular mode of knowledge production and its use is the sole factor
responsible for any kind of transformation in our societies, the evidence from
history does suggest that in every effort of social transformation the basic
tenets and processes of the popular mode of knowledge production and use
have substantially contributed to strengthening the efforts.

From Indian history, several instances, ranging from challenges to the
ancient Brahmanical control to struggling against colonial rule, can be cited
where elements of the popular mode were extensively used.

The writings on PR available to date suggest that, in a way, PR is an
attempt to reinforce, refine, and enhance the popular mode in the contemporary context. The practice of PR during the last fifteen years has explicitly
highlighted the need to further explore the existence and role of the popular
mode in different societies, and draws strength from this heritage. Although
the term *participatory research* in present times may have been coined only
fifteen years ago, the roots of its epistemology lie in the age-old traditions of
the popular mode of knowledge production and its utilization.

The characteristics of the popular mode of knowledge production provides PR with the epistemological basis from which to draw strength.

What Is To Be Done?

Centuries of systematic undermining of the popular mode of knowledge
production had successfully paralyzed people's faith about their own systems.
The power of printed works and the supremacy of institutional expertise had
invaded the mass psyche, following the flag of industrialization and market
economy in the most remotely possible communities.

Despite our faith in people, their willingness and capacity to learn and
change, and our wish to reinforce the people's systems of knowledge production and use, it is almost impossible to reverse the direction of history. But the
frustrations and disillusionment among some of those professionally trained
as experts in their respective disciplines led to a critique of the dominant mode
and ventured to transcend the boundaries to initiate a process of interaction,

through which strategies for reinforcement of the popular mode evolved. Linking knowledge production to the field of people's action was definitely a starting point in this direction. The concepts of praxis, organic intelligentsia, and action research are important landmarks in such chain reactions.

The experiences surrounding all of these concepts have produced some fundamental questions, such as, Who sets the agenda for social inquiry? Who is involved in the process of inquiry? and, In whose interests is the outcome of inquiry used?

The underlying thrust of such questions has remained an issue of control by people over the systems of knowledge production and its use. Previous attempts in this direction point to a gradual movement from the "use of research in favor of people's interest and actions" to "involving people in the process of research," then preparing people to set up the agenda for social inquiry.

Substantial contributions have been made in the acceleration of such movement by the processes of appropriation, adaptation, and incorporation of knowledge produced through the dominant mode in strengthening the base of people's knowledge for the creation of their own knowledge.

To enhance and strengthen the processes facilitating people's control over knowledge production and its use, the precondition is to break the 'culture of silence' by enhancement of people's self-concept, self-esteem, and self-confidence.

This is precisely the reason why PR should situate itself in the processes of people's empowerment and organization.

What Are We Doing?

In the beginning of the 1980s, we began an organized effort to promote the practice and enhance the understanding of participatory research in the Asian region. The first step in this direction was to develop the roots of our own practice in India, before playing a wider role. The analysis of the situation at that time made it clear that thousands of small grassroots initiatives were already in existence, devoted to facilitating the process of empowerment and organization among the urban and rural poor. This has helped evolve a strategy of enhancing the capacities of such grassroots initiatives through educational interventions based on participatory research philosophy.

We began by becoming involved in the issues that the grassroots initiatives were adopting, that is, people's access and control over natural resources, women and development issues of the urban poor, workers' education, occupational health and safety, and many other related areas.

The basic thrust of our work focused on capacity building within grassroots initiatives for strengthening the knowledge base of their own actions, thus reducing their dependence on expertise from the dominant mode. Within a couple of years, our interventions had acquired three distinct dimensions: first, sensitizing the initiatives to different aspects of the issues; second, assisting the initiatives in building the capacity to understand and analyze their reality with a view to evolve appropriate action; and third, to support a strengthening knowledge base of their actions and struggles. Involvement of this kind has helped tremendously in building credibility, by taking stands on the issues on the one hand and by being responsive in times of need on the other.

While facilitating such educational intervention, we have enhanced our own understanding of participatory research, training, and evaluation. We became clearer that, along with the enhancement of the knowledge base of people's action, it is important to strengthen the grassroots initiatives of organizations in order for them to play the role of vehicles of peoples' aspirations for directing the process of change to their advantage. This realization made us interpret the theories of organizational dynamics and development within the framework of grassroots initiatives and participatory research framework, and intervene to build capacities in grassroots initiatives to guide the processes and directions of their organizational development by themselves.

The application of a pedagogy based on experiential learning that helps create respect for their own experience and knowledge and facilitates the process of building understanding on that base has helped to initiate a process of empowerment among those involved in empowering the marginalized and powerless. This also has helped in creating a sense of ownership of, and responsibility for their own learning.

Challenges For the Future

Specificity of Context

Participatory research needs to be interpreted and defined in the specific context of each situation and culture. It needs to establish a coherence and linkage with the heritage of the popular mode of knowledge production in each community.

Evolution of Techniques and Tools

Participatory research needs to reduce its dependence on the techniques and tools of social inquiry borrowed from the dominant mode of knowledge production. The techniques and tools should not be taken as value-free phenomena, because that tends to dilute and distort the basic tenets of our epistemology.

Reference of Validation

At this stage, PR should stop seeking validation from the frame of reference of dominant modes of knowledge production. Instead, it needs to seek validation from the tenets of its own epistemology. Since individuals representing the dominant mode are constantly criticizing and browbeating the reinforcement and refinement of popular modes of knowledge production, this task becomes more urgent, in spite of its complexities. Falling back on the frame of reference of the dominant mode for validation creates conditions for co-option of participatory research into the dominant mode of knowledge production and use. Participatory research may become just another set of techniques, for example, in some forms of participant observation and action research.

CHAPTER 7

Participatory Educational Research in Australia: The First Wave—1976 to 1986

Shirley Grundy

This chapter attempts to provide an account of the beginnings of a tradition of participatory educational action research in Australia. It was written at a time of intense action research activity across the school education sector. This present upsurge of interest and activity is reminiscent of the interest and activity evident in the mid-1970s. There are, however, a number of crucial differences between the educational action research movements of the mid-1970s and mid-1990s. The continuities and discontinuities within these periods of activity make it possible to speak of 'two waves' of action research in Australian school education. This chapter describes the period of the 'first wave,' from approximately 1976 to 1986.

It is beyond the scope of this chapter to trace the development of the second wave of activity, although some of its features will be sketched in conclusion. My contention here, however, is that it is only possible to speak meaningfully of an 'action research tradition' if the development of that tradition is understood. Moreover, it is important to see the way in which that tradition has developed as a response to particular historical moments and opportunities. Thus, the present wave of participatory educational research cannot be seen as either uninterruptedly continuing a tradition or as an imitation of an earlier period, for it is neither. The present interest in action research has its own integrity, sources, and manifestations. However, it has not developed *ex nihilo*. While the current wave might not have grown directly out of the earlier work, it can stand firmly upon the foundation laid then. It is the purpose of this chapter to trace and document that earlier history.

The account presented here makes no claim to being the definitive story of participatory educational action research during this period. Rather, it is an interpretive account that attempts to discern the extent to which it is possible to talk in any meaningful way about a developing tradition of participatory action research. In relation to this project, Gadamer's (1979, 236) account of the hermeneutic task of understanding is pertinent:

> A person who is trying to understand a text is always performing an act of projecting. He (sic) projects before himself a meaning for the text as a whole as soon as some initial meaning emerges in the text. Again, the latter emerges only because he is reading the text with particular expectations in regard to a certain meaning. The working out of this fore-project, which is constantly revised in terms of what emerges as he penetrates into the meaning, is understanding what is there.

In the case of the act of interpretation that is being undertaken here, the 'text' to be understood is the practice of participatory action research in Australia. Because of my own knowledge of and involvement in the action research movement in Australia, I will be interpreting this text with certain expectations of meaning. As such, this account is a celebration of participatory research in the recent history of education in Australia and a chart of the beginnings of a strong tradition.

A wholly celebratory account will not, however, represent an authentic interpretive reconstruction. As Gadamer (1979, 238) again reminds us:

> The hermeneutical task becomes automatically a questioning of things and is always in part determined by this. . . . (A) person trying to understand a text is prepared for it to tell him (sic) something.

Thus, while the writing of this chapter has been an attempt to engage in the process of uncovering the source and course of the educational action research tradition in Australia, a number of questions need to be addressed. These questions relate to whether participatory action research in Australia is a sustainable tradition and whether it has the potential to be regarded as legitimate research.

All attempts to retell history are, of course, partial. The antecedents of any historical phenomenon always lead further back than we would have imagined. So it is with the story of participatory educational research in Australia. The 'beginnings' merely reveal themselves as emerging patterns, drawing our gaze back to other people and places. But this telling must begin somewhere, so it will begin in the mid-1970s with the Commonwealth Schools' Commission and the Curriculum Development Centre.

Before proceeding with this account, however, it is important to establish a shared understanding of 'participation.' For the purposes of this history, McTaggart's principles for participatory action research (1989) will be utilized.

McTaggart (1989, 3) cites the determinants of authentic participation in research identified by Tandon:

- people's role in setting the agenda of the inquiry
- people's participation in the data collection and analysis
- people's control over the use of outcomes and the whole process

McTaggart applies these principles to participatory action research:

We use the term *participatory action research* to differentiate it from kinds of research which typically involve researchers from the academy doing research on people. . . Participatory action research engages people from the academy and the work-place in an entirely different relationship. . . . (they) are joined by a thematic concern—a commitment to inform and improve a particular practice. (1989, 3)

Elaborating on this project, he notes:

The common project of participatory action research has several aspects. Each participant . . . must undertake:

- to improve his or her own work
- to collaborate with others engaged in the project . . . to help them improve their work
- to collaborate with others in their own separate institutional and cultural contexts to create the possibility of more broadly informing the common project, as well as to create the material and political conditions necessary to sustain the common project and its work.

. . . Participatory action research is concerned simultaneously with changing individuals, on the one hand, and, on the other, the culture of the groups, institutions and societies to which they belong. (1989, 4)

These, then, are the principles that have been used to determine what should count as participatory educational action research for the purpose of this account.

The First Wave: The Commonwealth Fosters Participation

The early 1970s were a time of great optimism in Australia. The election of the Whitlam Labor government signaled a quickening of the Australian spirit. It was a democratic time, a time when "the men and women of Australia," as Whitlam so stirringly addressed them in his election speeches, caught a new glimpse of themselves as mature participants in government and society rather than simply being 'the governed.' It was, however, a time, like any time, of great contradiction. Of relevance to the story of participatory action research are the contradictions that emerged in relation to the facilitation of participatory ways of working in educational settings. Interestingly, it was the entry of the Commonwealth government into education through the Commonwealth Schools' Commission that was crucial to the fostering of participatory decision making, teacher-initiated curriculum development, and, ultimately, participatory action research at the school level.

The Commonwealth would not have been successful in intruding into an area of States' rights, however, if its *modus operandi* was not in harmony with a wider social orientation. There was a prevailing ethos of teacher and grassroots control that manifested itself in a revitalization of teacher unionism and the flourishing of alternative and community schools.

In this story, I will consider three Commonwealth-initiated participatory educational initiatives that were significant in shaping participatory action research,[1] including the Innovations Grants, the Language and Learning Project, and School-based Curriculum Development and Evaluation.

The Innovations Grants

The Innovations Grants Program, which was one of the early initiatives of the Commonwealth Schools' Commission, was designed to encourage innovation in education by providing funds directly to teachers who had ideas about educational change that they could initiate. It was not, as such, an action research-based project. It was not self-consciously research-based at all, but it was participatory to the extent that it relied upon initiatives from practitioners who were not usually consulted about educational change. I vividly recall being a teacher in a Queensland primary school in 1975 and listening with interest to the principal telling us about the call for applications for Innovations Grants. My colleagues and I were amazed that as classroom teachers we could come up with proposals for funding 'good ideas.' Being so used to implementing ideas provided from somewhere else rather than generating them ourselves, we found it difficult to accomplish, but we all thought it was an excellent scheme.

The Innovations Grants program fulfilled Tandon's first determinant of authentic participation, referred to earlier. It also provided many teachers with their first experience of reflectively evaluating an initiative they had taken and making that evaluation public. In this respect, Tandon's second and third determinants were satisfied to some extent.

Language and Learning

Perhaps the most significant impetus to participatory action research in Australia during this phase of the Schools' Commission's sponsorship of teacher initiatives in education was the Language and Learning Project. This project, which began in 1974, involved teams working within education systems in four states (South Australia, Victoria, Western Australia, and Tasmania) and two territories (the Northern Territory and the Australian Capital Territory). These respective Education Departments cooperated with the Schools' Commission to sponsor initiatives in individual schools and among groups of schools.

The Language and Learning Project encouraged teachers to look closely at their own pedagogical practices and at the learning practices of children, documenting and reflecting on classroom problems in learning. In 1978, the Curriculum Development Centre established the National Working Party on the Role of Language and Learning, which had the task of "gathering together and sharing the best of state enquiries and of collaborating in on-going work." (Boomer 1982, ix)

The projects fostered by these initiatives in language and learning introduced a large number of teachers to the idea of investigating their own practice; in short, becoming educational researchers. Teachers were encouraged to relate and reflect on their classroom experiences through diaries and journals and to examine the language of their classrooms through transcriptions of taped classroom interactions. Typical of some of the investigations fostered by this project are those published as *32 Voices* (Cook 1979).

From the reports of these early language and learning investigations, a number of features are discernible. The inquiries were classroom-based and participatory, that is, they focused on children's language and learning as it occurred in classrooms, with the teachers being the investigating agents. This was the first time many of these teachers questioned the received knowledge of the profession and engaged in the production of their own knowledge.

The inquiries were collaborative, to the extent that the participants shared their investigations and reflections with a group of similarly interested teachers. In the main, however, the project did not involve strategic action to systematically change practice through a cycle of action and reflection. Reflection on data for improved understanding was the usual focus of the studies.

School-based Curriculum Development and Evaluation

The movement toward SBCD[2] was fostered strongly in the 1970s by the Commonwealth through the Schools' Commission and the Curriculum Development Centre (CDC). The SBCD movement provided yet another impulse toward teachers taking initiatives in relation to their own practice.

Not all school-based curriculum development during this period employed an action research approach. There were, however, many examples of groups of teachers who engaged in curriculum development as a research enterprise. One such example is that reported by Newson (1981), a teacher at Mount Barker High School in South Australia:

> The appointment of a new principal gave the staff . . . the opportunity to become involved for the first time in major moves towards staff participation in decision making. . . . During an examination of the philosophy and objectives of the school, the idea of sub-schools arose. . . . Staff investigated organizational alternatives . . . [from which] the staff selected the four types now in existence.
>
> By the . . . following year it had become evident that there were several aspects of the functioning of the sub-school system which required examination. . . . A formative evaluation exercise was undertaken by the staff. [The report indicates that two further evaluations were conducted, resulting in strategic changes to the school curriculum and organization.]

Examples such as this provide instances of participatory curriculum development that conform to the principles cited above—simultaneously changing the practice of individuals and the culture of the institution in which the practice was located.

One line of development in the SBCD movement found its expression under the label of "negotiating the curriculum." This approach to curriculum development was fostered by the National Working Party on the Role of Language in Learning and became particularly associated with the work of Garth Boomer through his edited collection of teacher accounts of their experiences of negotiation (Boomer 1982). Negotiation of the curriculum extended the idea of participation to include students as joint decision makers and researchers of changes in practice (see, for instance, Cosgrove 1982).

The Commonwealth also took initiatives to foster participatory approaches to curriculum evaluation. Of particular significance here was the "Teachers As Evaluators" project, sponsored by the National Curriculum Development Centre and the Education Research and Development Committee (ERDC), the national body charged specifically with funding educational research. This project was grounded in two important principles:

- that judgments in relation to education need to be made about teachers' work as well as about student outcomes
- that teachers themselves should be the ones making such judgments about their work

School-level evaluation was not, however, conceived as merely backward-looking. In 1981, the Schools' Commission provided "Guidelines for School Level Evaluation Projects." School-level evaluation is described as an action research process, although the term is not used.

> School level evaluation embraces all the means by which schools examine what they are doing, set targets for improvement, plan action to achieve those targets and review and adjust action in the light of experience. (Commonwealth Schools' Commission 1981, 1)

It should not be assumed that all school-level evaluation incorporated this prospective as well as the retrospective focus. In many cases, evaluation became a legitimating exercise, focused on past practice rather than a learning experience incorporating research into changing practice. Nevertheless, the principle of participatory evaluation was established. Interestingly, but not surprisingly, these developments were paralleled by a questioning of the role of the traditional 'inspectors' in schools. That is, the idea that an outside 'expert' can pronounce judgment upon the work of the practitioner came under severe criticism. The concept of the outsider as 'adviser,' 'consultant,' and 'facilitator' was reinforced during this period.

State Systems Facilitate Participatory Approaches

I have concentrated above on the way in which the Commonwealth fostered participatory approaches to educational change. In Australia, however, the Commonwealth has no power to intervene directly in school education. School education is a state responsibility. Thus, all of the initiatives discussed above were, in various ways, collaborative ventures between the Commonwealth and the states. Various state departments of education were, however, also fostering participatory action research among teachers, particularly through changes in approaches to in-service education. Action research began to be recognized as an in-service approach, which made more sense than the traditional one-off in-service days in which curriculum experts imparted policies and ideas to grateful, but passive, practitioners.

Participatory approaches to in-service education were grounded in the idea of the teacher as learner about her or his own practice. Not, however, as a learner in the sense of passive recipient of information about practice, but as a producer of professional knowledge through processes of action and reflection; in short, 'participatory action research.'

The following is a list of in-service projects, all in operation around the turn of the decade (around 1979–1980), which demonstrate a wide-range commitment to participatory research-based approaches to in-service education across a variety of states:

- the ACCESS Teaching Skills project (Victoria)
- the Victorian Education Department's Curriculum Services Unit project, 'Investigating Learning in Classrooms'
- projects facilitated by the Curriculum and Learning Unit of the Wattle Park Teachers' Centre, South Australia
- the 'Principals and Change' project, sponsored by the Queensland Education Department and the Queensland In-Service Education Committee
- the Western Australian school-based curriculum development workshops
- the Kewdale Project, a teacher-initiated, school-based, in-service project in Western Australia

While all of these projects had a finite life, they, and others like them, forever changed the conception of 'good' in-service education for teachers. While there have remained 'outsider' initiated programs, 'best practice' in-service programs include opportunities for action and reflection by teachers in the process (Maxwell et al. 1988). From this time, the meaning, if not the universal practice of in-service, was more commonly acknowledged as being participatory to the extent of expecting some practitioner engagement in and control of the outcomes of the experience. This has become an important aspect of the second-wave of educational action research.

Tertiary Institutions Foster Action Research

During this 'first wave' action research movement, Deakin University acquired the reputation of being the Australian 'home of action research.' I will elaborate in more detail later about the importance of that work. Meanwhile, it is important to recognize that the idea that practitioners were crucial players in the educational research game was being fostered within a number of Australian tertiary institutions around the beginning of the 1980s. This idea was being legitimated in the courses being offered at both the undergraduate and postgraduate level.

Such courses fulfilled a dual purpose within tertiary institutions. On the one hand, they introduced action research concepts and methodology to teachers, but at the same time they contributed to the legitimation of action research within the research community. This legitimating work was most important. In the mid-1980s, when I began to supervise postgraduate research, a number of students complained to me that they wanted to conduct their thesis research within their own schools and classrooms, investigating aspects of their own practice, but had been told that these were not legitimate topics for educational research. Such students greeted the news of action research with relief and enthusiasm.

Of course, there are limitations on the authenticity of action research undertaken for accreditation purposes; the issue addressed may be contrived for the purposes of the exercise, and course deadlines and assessment procedures may impose an artificiality on the learning process. Despite such problems, however, courses offered by tertiary institutions continued to provide an important introduction to the theory and practice of participatory action research.

Some Significant People Foster the First Wave of Action Research

The account of the fostering of educational participatory action research in Australia during the late 1970s and early 1980s has traced some of the institutional support which was offered. It is important to recognize, however, that it is people, not institutions, who promote ideas and construct practices. The imprimatur of an institution may be important in legitimizing changes in practice, but it is people who drive initiatives. It is, therefore, important to understand the role played by persons in the early movement toward participatory action research.

Once again, the selection of people for identification as significant contributors to the development of a participatory action research tradition in Australia is partial and, in some cases, arbitrary. It is possible to identify some obvious 'players,' but there is no suggestion here that those mentioned are the only ones to have influenced the development of participatory action research. If an action research 'honor roll' was to be written, it would be much longer and would represent a far richer story than the one given here.

An aspect that must be noted regarding this account of the influence of persons on the early history of educational action research in Australia is the gender imbalance. This is principally an issue of 'voice.' Those who were best placed to be the advocates of and to articulate a legitimating discourse for action research were those from the university sector or those in leadership positions within the educational system. In the period of the mid- to late-1970s, these were predominantly male. This does not mean that action research was entirely a male domain. Indeed, as noted later, within the practitioner-based action research field there were some significant women, such as Marie Brennan (in Victoria; see Brennan 1982), Heather Felton (in Tasmania), Susan Kling, Susan Cosgrove, Lorraine Riordan, and Beverley Beasley (in

South Australia; see Riordan 1982; Beasley 1981a, b), and Jo-Anne Reid (in Western Australia) who were developing and sustaining action research and contributing to the development of the action research discourse through participation in conferences and research projects. Their writing about action research was circulated mainly through the informal networks of the practitioner communities. Moreover, their work was largely facilitative of the action research and writing of others, so their voices remain muted within the record of history.[3]

Early in this chapter I characterized the 1970s as a time of democratic regeneration in Australia. This democratic commitment was expressed in the work of a number of Australian educators who helped provide an environment in which participatory approaches to curriculum change could occur, thus also paving the way for participatory action research in education.

One such person was Malcolm Skilbeck, who returned to Australia from a professorial post overseas in 1975 to head the newly formed Commonwealth Curriculum Development Centre (CDC). Skilbeck had a strong commitment to participatory decision making in curriculum development. In a paper addressing the subject of school-based curriculum development in the United Kingdom, Skilbeck (1975, 80–1) wrote:

> The curriculum is, for the learner and the teacher, made up of experiences; these should be experiences of value, developed by the teacher and learner together from a close and sympathetic appraisal of the learner's needs and his (sic) characteristics as a learner. . . . Freedom for teacher and for pupils is a necessary condition for the full educational potential of these experiences to be realised. . . . In the simplest terms, school-based curriculum development claims that of all our educational institutions and agencies, the school and the school-teacher should have the primary responsibility for determining [the] curriculum.

This strong advocacy of the rights and responsibilities of teachers and students to make educational decisions signals a commitment to participatory decision making that became characteristic of the early years of the CDC.

Another person who was in a position to foster similar democratic approaches to education was Syd Dunn, chairman of the ERDC, the organization referred to earlier as being responsible for funding educational research. Reflecting on the role of Dunn in supporting action research in the early 1980s, Stephen Kemmis commented:

> Syd Dunn was a great democrat, he was a great Australian federalist, and he believed that multilateral negotiations between people would advance education. He was a practical man. . . . Far from him being a representative of

the positivistic establishment (although he could do that stuff as well as any-body else), he was interested in the improvement of education and in the democratic improvement of Australia. (Interview, 1990)

So it was that in at least two significant Commonwealth organizations, people with commitments to democratic ways of working occupied influential positions with the potential to influence educational change in Australia.

At the state level, there was also a number of people with similar commitments to democratic decision making for teachers and students. Of particular significance was the work of Garth Boomer.[4] In the late 1970s, Boomer was director of the Wattle Park Teachers' Centre in South Australia. He later became director of the CDC, then was appointed chair of the Commonwealth Schools' Commission and the Schools' Council before returning to South Australia as Associate Director-General of Education in that state.

It is through Boomer that some of the links between the Australian action research movement and the British 'teacher as researcher' movement can be traced. In the early 1970s, Boomer worked with Britton at the London Institute of Education, undertaking a study entitled "Teachers Learning" (1973), which employed documentation and commentary by teachers reflecting on their own practice.

Boomer's work in fostering the Australian Language and Learning Project was noted earlier. This project was built on the work he had undertaken in Britain, adapting the principles of teacher research to an Australian context. There were other significant links with the British 'teacher as researcher' movement in Britain. Stephen Kemmis was deeply influenced by the work of Stenhouse and others at the Centre for Research in Education (CARE) at the University of East Anglia. He brought inspiration from that source back with him to Australia and was able to build on that experience within Deakin University. David Tripp arrived at Murdoch University in 1978, having had an association with the Ford Teaching Project, directed by Elliott and Adelman. He incorporated action research into courses at Murdoch University.[5]

Thus, the Australian participatory action research tradition developed with a direct link to its British counterpart; but, as I will indicate later, it developed its own practices and epistemology.

It is, however, wrong to see the development of participatory action research as a missionary venture in which the gurus, who had come to see the light in a far country, now brought the good news to a waiting population. It is clear from what was said earlier that there was, both socially and educationally, a milieu already oriented toward teacher participation in the production of educational knowledge. Although the likes of Boomer, Kemmis, and

Tripp were able to give voice and rationale to the work already being fostered, their success in the promotion of action research clearly depended on the foundation that had already been laid.

Deakin University Fosters Action Research

Mention was made earlier about the link between Australian and British action research, forged by Kemmis through his work at Deakin University. I wish to describe in further detail the part that was played in the development of action research by the Deakin School of Education, for it has provided an important focus and legitimation for participatory action research in Australia.

The way in which Kemmis was able to promote action research at Deakin University following his appointment in 1978 is an interesting example of the confluence of historical circumstances. Coming from a strong psychological background, Kemmis had undertaken postgraduate study in the United States in the area of evaluation. During that period, he became increasingly disillusioned with the capacity of quantitative evaluation to provide legitimate insight into practice. The growth of evaluation as a representational art rather than a measurement science began to take hold of Kemmis' thinking. Kemmis describes this early period:

> I came out of Sydney [University]—[an] educational psychologist, went off to Illinois. By the time I left Sydney I was worried about questions of explanation and understanding in educational research. [At] Illinois [I] began to understand more about . . . interpretive research . . . I realised that a lot of the problems of doing research were political problems . . . I saw Stake's [1975] responsive evaluation, Parlett and Hamilton's [1976] illuminative evaluation, MacDonald's [1975] democratic evaluation and I knew we were getting close to the politics. I had the opportunity of going over to East Anglia and while I was there John Elliott and Clem Adelman [1973] were working on the Ford Teaching Project and Rob [Walker] and others had been influenced by Lawrence talking about teachers as researchers. Soon after Lawrence Stenhouse's [1975] *Introduction to curriculum research and development* came out arguing the case for teachers as researchers and I agreed with Lawrence that the Ford Teaching Project action research thing was the way to go.

> At the time of writing up my Ph.D., which was the end of '75 and the beginning of '76, I was reading Habermas and I began to see a conjunction between the politics of evaluation as described by McDonald in terms of bureaucratic, autocratic, democratic, and Habermas' technical, practical, and emancipatory interests. . . . But the problem about democratic evaluation was that . . . we democratic evaluators were still doing the work for the participants. We were the people who held the pen. . . . What Ford T was point-

ing in the direction of was . . . that instead of us having a representative democracy where we were the representatives of participants, of course, who never asked to be represented, the question was could you have a participatory democracy and Habermas was showing me a way. . . .

When I came back to Australia, I was interested in developing more participatory forms of evaluation at CDC in relation to the evaluation of curriculum projects. Then I was asked to come down for an interview for the job at Deakin. I was told by a friend of mine that there were a whole lot of people down here who were very good on knowing about schools . . . but they didn't know very much about research and what was needed was someone to develop curriculum research at Deakin. . . . I realised that here was an opportunity to use the expertise of the people [here]; draw on their expertise and develop more participatory projects, so I made a big play on action research, based upon what I knew about Ford T at the time.

To be sure action research could be done, I knew that, I knew how it could be done in broad terms, but what did it really mean to do it? I didn't know anything about action research, other than working from the instance of Ford T and the general principles from Habermas. So we applied to ERDC for money [to undertake the Research on Action Research project]. I was appointed in October 1978 and we made the application in 1980.

ERDC gave us the money . . . [and] we started getting into the literature and started connecting the sort of things that I had previously done; the epistemology of education and democratic evaluation and research methodology much more to what had been going on in action research and it didn't take us long to get back to Lewin . . . So we began to get into the history of action research at that time and you came to Deakin just at the time when we were getting our story together. (Interview, 1990)

The ERDC project, "Research on Action Research," with which I was associated as a research assistant, was highly significant in developing an epistemology of action research, in legitimating action research as a research methodology, and in developing an Australian 'critical' action research. The project was significant in that it provided a data bank of reports of participatory research, curriculum development, and evaluation that had been undertaken by teachers in Australia. These data, together with the theoretical work being done in the area of critical theory and the history of action research, enabled the development of an Australian form of action research, one grounded in the practice of teachers and supported by critical theorems developed from the work of the Frankfurt School, in particular, Habermas.

There were a number of significant features and outcomes of the project. In May 1981, near the beginning of the project, a National Invitational Seminar about action research was held at Deakin. This seminar was at one level a recognition and celebration of the action research that had been occurring all over Australia; at another level, it provided a forum for debate through which a common understanding of the epistemology and methodology of participatory research could be developed. The shared understanding of action research, which was developed through the deliberations of the seminar, is expressed well in the definition of action research contained in the Notes that were subsequently published:

> Action research is a term used to describe a 'family' of activities in curriculum development, professional development, school improvement programs, and systems planning and policy development. It is an approach to the improvement of practice which may be employed by anyone . . . who is engaged in an educational practice. . . . Action research in any of these activities has as its central feature the use of changes in practice as a way of inducing improvement in the practice itself, the situation in which it occurs, and the rationale for the work, and in the understanding of all of these. Action research uses strategic action as a probe for improvement and understanding. (Brown, Henry, Henry and McTaggart 1982, 338)

Two issues stand out from the Notes on the National Seminar (Brown et al. 1982) as overriding concerns at that time. The first of these is 'collaboration.' The participatory and collaborative nature of action research was accepted as part of the definition just described and was elaborated upon later in the paper:

> Action research is distinguished by its adherence to a collaborative ethic. It is a collaborative endeavour in which groups of practitioners work together to understand better their own practice and to increase their awareness of the effects of their practice and of their control over the situation within which they work. (Brown et al. 1982, 340)

Another issue that was of intense concern to the participants in the seminar was the role of the outside 'facilitator.' A number of roles was identified for facilitators of action research. These roles were to provide:

- an outsider's perspective
- a focus for a group of researchers
- a teacher of action research
- a critic in the process
- a group recorder
- a representative of the group
- a source of personal support
- a source of practical assistance
- a resource person (Brown et al. 1982, 341–3)

It is interesting that, while the role of the nonparticipant facilitator was critically scrutinized and legitimated, 'participation' itself was left unproblematized and undertheorized at this point.

The other major issue to emerge from the seminar was that of action research as 'research.' The importance of this issue reflects the need for the legitimating of action research within the research community. However, while the seminar contributed somewhat to this agenda, the focus was more on action research as an educational practice rather than as research, perhaps reflecting the balance of interests of the participants (thirteen of the twenty-two participants were from educational systems, nine from tertiary institutions).

The project continued to provide an important focus for action research in Australia following the seminar. Three papers, which have been important in providing a basis for legitimating and understanding action research, resulted from the project. The first of these, "Action Research and Group Dynamics" by Grundy and Kemmis (1981a), traced the roots of the participatory and collaborative nature of action research back to the group dynamics movement in the United States in the late 1940s. Grundy's (1982) paper, "Three Modes of Action Research," used Habermas' theory of knowledge constitutive interests to analyse the action research reports of Australian teachers. The paper argued that, although action research is ideally an emancipatory educational practice, it can be applied in both technical and practical modes, so while an emancipatory form of educational practice would be expressed in a participatory, self-reflective way of working that is characteristic of action research, not all practices that call themselves action research are necessarily emancipatory.

The paper arising from the project that was most influential in providing a legitimating discourse for action research is the Grundy and Kemmis (1981b) paper, "Educational Action Research in Australia: The State of the Art (An Overview)." This paper, presented at the Annual Conference of the Australian Association for Research in Education in 1981, provided a summary of the epistemological foundations of action research and an overview of the practice of action research at that time.

As was noted in an earlier section of this chapter, a number of institutions were fostering participatory approaches to educational research through a variety of courses. This happened also at Deakin University but with more visibility than at other institutions. This increased visibility was the result of the collaborative nature of the course development and delivery systems at Deakin University, the fact that there were a number of young and enthusiastic academics wanting to establish themselves within a teacher-centred research tradition, and because the distance education mode of course delivery meant that course content and materials were publicly available, independent of the course itself. This latter feature is exemplified in the wide circulation and use of the *Action research planner* and the *Action research reader*. Both of these works (which each have appeared in three substantially revised editions) were produced as course materials but both have had wide circulation outside of the courses themselves.

Thus it was that Deakin University became established as the Australian intellectual home of action research, and Stephen Kemmis became known as the Australian 'father of action research.' However, as I hope this account has already shown, the ascendancy of Deakin as the champion of action research was made possible by the work that was already going on across a number of sites in Australia.

The Development of an Action Research Tradition

The account provided thus far here is the establishment of action research as a legitimate form of participatory educational research. The Research on Action Research project was very important in that quest for legitimacy. That legitimacy was (and is) still contested, but increasingly teachers and other academics undertaking higher degree work began to use action research methodologies to investigate aspects of educational practice in which they were participants. So the legitimacy of action research *qua* research was being established.

It was, however, just as well that the historical moment to establish action research as a legitimate form of educational inquiry and practice had been seized, for the climate that had nurtured this development was changing. This change is documented in the "Notes on the National Seminar" (Brown et al. 1982, 337):

> The seminar achieved some historical significance even before it began. The ERDC, the funding authority for the seminar, had its last meeting only two days earlier. The Federal [Liberal, Fraser] Government's decision to disband the ERDC and to reduce funding levels to the Schools' Commission and the Curriculum Development Centre clearly indicated a substantial realignment of its educational priorities.

Thus, while there was a clearly established practice of action research in Australia by the early 1980s, our understanding of that practice was in many ways still in its infancy. The action research story of the 1980s is in essence itself the story of an action research project, for it is the story of a network of practitioners engaged in the process of improving both their understanding and their practice of action research and engaged in the political struggle to improve the situation in which that practice occurs.

It is ironic that, while much of our understanding of action research was achieved through learning from practitioners who were engaged in systematic reflection upon and change of their practice, those understandings became translated into a 'methodology' of action research. The cycle of 'plan,' 'act,' 'observe,' and 'reflect' took on a mantra-like quality, as practitioners were facilitated in their application of the methodology. There was a distinct danger at this time of action research being technologized. This tendency is well-illustrated by the first Deakin University *Action research planner* in 1982, which was a step-by-step guide to successful action research (Kemmis and McTaggart 1988a). The same could be said for my own "Three modes of action research" paper (Grundy 1982), which incorporated ever more complicated and precise diagrammatic representations of the relationship of theory and practice.

The potential of action research is evident, however, in the ability of the Australian action researchers to resist the methodological trap. Since understanding rather than efficiency underlies the theory and practice of action research, constant critical reflection kept the practice problematical. The self-reflective cycle of the development of participatory research at this time found a tangible expression in another seminar sponsored by the Deakin School of Education in 1986. The title of the seminar, "A Fourth Generation of Action Research," embodied the retrospective and prospective aspects of action research. The earlier 'generations' of action research were understood to be the early post-war 'positivist' manifestation in the United States, the 'practical' British action research exemplified in the Ford T Project, and the 'critical' orientation of the developing Australian tradition. The Fourth Generation Seminar posed the question of "where to from here?"

A comparison of the Notes from the 1981 and 1986 seminars (Brown et al. 1982 and McTaggart and Garbutcheon-Singh 1986) reveals a significant change in the discourse of action research. The earlier seminar was concerned with carving out the action research territory, developing shared understandings of ways of working, hence the concern with definition and the laying down of guidelines for facilitation. In 1986, there was a concern to make problematic what had become established practice. This time the distinctions were finer; nor was there merely a concern for defining ways of working, but of identifying ways of talking. So it was that much of the discussion centered on developing a discourse of action research through which taken-for-granted ideas such as 'practice,' 'collaboration,' and 'critique' could be better understood.

The final paragraphs of the 1986 Notes (McTaggart and Garbutcheon-Singh 1986) provide an interesting summary of the 'state of the art' (to borrow a phrase from the previous generation) of action research:

What will action research look like *now* as a form of life? . . . Action research will focus on a more broadly understood conception of practice. It will be conducted more by *groups* interested in social *and* educational amelioration. It will be better informed and tested theoretically . . . The authenticity of its probes and gains will be critically examined in language communities ranging from the local action group to those trying to make gains in the articulation of social theory.

Action research will become *part* of a form of life for groups broadly committed to social action and educational reform. It will often be associated with specific projects committed to equality of access to education and legitimate participation. It will be *emancipatory* or it will not be called action research at all. (1986, 426, 427 emphasis in the original)

A number of concerns are evident here; the emphasis on the problematizing of practice and collaboration, the identification of action research as a form of emancipatory social action as much as a form of educational practice, and the concern with "equality of access to education and legitimate participation."

However, despite the prediction of the seminar that action research "will be emancipatory or it well not be called action research at all," from the mid-1980s until the second wave of action research in the early 1990s, the label "action research" appears to have become less and less useful for describing emancipatory and participatory educational projects and practices.

The Mediation of Theory and Practice in the
First Wave of Australian Educational Action Research

It has been impossible here to provide an adequate overview of the development of this first wave of the Australian educational action research tradition. The early part of this account, while providing some insights into the practice of participatory research, did not provide an adequate account of the theory which informed that practice. Similarly, the latter part of the account has focused more on the developing action research discourse, rather than the practice. This suggests some temporal division of practical and theoretical concerns; that in the 1970s, people just got up and did it, while in the 1980s, they all sat around and talked about it. Such an interpretation does not do justice to either the theory which informed the work of the practitioners or to the practice in which those engaged in the theoretical discourse also were engaged.

What the division of emphasis does, however, is it allows for an exploration of the mediation of theory and practice in participatory research in Aus-

tralia. It is my contention that this first wave of participatory research provides an interesting example of Habermas' (1974) theory and practice mediation functions, but also illustrates the nonlinearity of that mediation process.
Habermas argues:

> The mediation of theory and praxis can only be clarified if to begin with we
> distinguish three functions . . . the formation and extension of critical theo-
> rems, which can stand up to scientific discourse; the organization of
> processes of enlightenment, in which such theorems are applied and can be
> tested . . . by the initiation of processes of reflection . . . within certain
> groups . . . and the selection of appropriate strategies, the solution of tactical
> questions and the conduct of the political struggle. (1974, 32)

It is possible to distinguish traces of these three functions in the account
of the first wave of participatory action research in Australia provided here.
There was a strong discourse relating to participatory research. Through this
discourse, a critical theory of action research was developed, debated, and
defended. The volume by Carr and Kemmis (1986) is one example of this critical discourse, and my own work (Grundy 1984, 1987), as well as the 1981
and 1986 Action Research Seminars, provide other examples of the development of this discourse.

It also is possible to discern aspects in the aforementioned account that
could be called the 'organization of enlightenment.' Of interest here is the
work done by tertiary institutions in mounting courses that encouraged the
theoretical exploration of and practical experimentation with action research.
'Enlightenment' was, however, not the preserve of the universities alone. It is
interesting to note in the documentation of practitioner research from this
period that teachers were also engaged in theorizing as well as recording their
work. The educational consultants often were active in promoting such reflection.

Habermas' account of the mediation of theory and practice tends to suggest that the mediation functions referred to are linear; that is, critical theory
comes before enlightenment, which in turn precedes action. What this analysis of the development of theory and practice of action research in Australia
has shown, however, is that the relationship is not linear. It is quite clear that
the practice of action research in Australia preceded the development of a
coherent legitimating theory. That does not mean, however, that the early
practice was completely atheoretical. Indeed, the contribution of a number of
practitioners to the development of a theory of action research as well as its
practice has been noted.

Furthermore, it should not be expected that with the development of a
coherent critical theory of action research, action research practice would nec-

essarily be transformed into an emancipatory practice. McTaggart and Gar-butcheon-Singh's (1986) pronouncement that "Action research . . . will be emancipatory or it will not be called action research at all" misconstrues the theory/practice mediation process. Habermas (1974, 33) warns that "decisions for the political struggle cannot at the outset be justified theoretically and then be carried out organizationally." The practical world is a political world in which there are all sorts of encumbrances to acting 'rightly.' All that can be expected is that we act 'prudently' (Habermas 1974, 32).

The identification of the decade from the mid-1970s to the mid-1980s as a 'wave' makes sense because the period of the late 1980s is discernible as a 'trough.' It is not that there was a lack of action research activity altogether, but rather that it is difficult to find evidence during this period of widespread organic educational action research. By 'organic' action research, I mean research which has an intellectual link with the participatory research move-ment, but has not been specifically generated by people from tertiary institu-tions. There was, for instance, a strong school improvement movement being developed during this period, which located responsibility for improvement with school principals and teachers. School improvement was not generally conceptualized and/or practiced as participatory action research.

A New Wave of Action Research

During the decade of the 1990s, there has been a regeneration of organic action research in schools. It is this renewal of interest in action research that has formed the 'second wave.' In concluding this account of the development of an action research tradition in Australia, therefore, some of the features of this new wave will be explored.

Readers of this account who are not familiar with Australian geography may not have noted the absence of reference to New South Wales (the most populous Australian state) in the previously mentioned account. The absence of a vigorous action research tradition in New South Wales is notable. Just as notable, however, was the influence of some key educators from New South Wales in generating and supporting the second wave of action research. Inter-estingly, however, we also once again see the influence of the Commonwealth in the facilitation of a climate to foster action research, while another key player in the second wave has been the teachers' unions. It is not possible here to provide more than the briefest of sketches about some of the features of this new wave.

Between 1991 and 1996 the Commonwealth Department of Education sponsored two large-scale projects, each of which provided a vehicle for participatory action research. These included the National Project for the Quality of Teaching and Learning (with its subproject the National Schools Project and its successor the National Schools Network) and the National Professional Development Project (with its subproject the Innovative Links Project). Interestingly, these initiatives have been promoted and supported by the Australian Education Union and the Independent Education Union through an 'accord' between the teaching profession and the labor government.

The teaching accord was adamant in its support of collaborative partnerships to foster and promote educational improvement. A strong player in the development of such an environment in which participative action research could flourish was the national president of the AEU, Sharon Burrow, a former secondary school teacher and union representative from New South Wales.

Another key player in the facilitation of the second wave action research was Viv White, a former NSW primary school teacher and the national coordinator of the National Schools Project and National Schools Network. White also was the instigator of the development of an academic reference group that gave rise to the Innovative Links Project, an action research project designed to facilitate the support by university academics for teacher-based action research.[6]

This second wave action research movement has some important continuities with the action research tradition described in this chapter. Specifically, the emphasis on collaboration and joint action for participatory research by practitioners in schools continues the traditions of action research. Moreover, the development of the academic support networks has provided a continuity of theoretical understanding of the action research tradition.

This next wave, however, also has extended some of the practices of action research. In the first wave, while the theory of action research emphasized the importance of focusing on the organization of work and the situation in which practice occurs when considering change, the earlier experience of action research more often addressed practice itself. In the second wave of action research, however, the emphasis has been firmly on work organization as an important arena for research and action.

What is not yet clear about this second wave of action research is the extent to which the critical edge of participatory research has been maintained. As action research becomes widely accepted and adopted, the possibilities of maintaining it as a vehicle for the opposition to oppression and the critique of unjust institutionalized practices become problematic.

From this analysis of the development of action research in the last two decades, it is clear that while it is possible to identify a strong tradition of participatory research in Australia, the nature of that tradition is complex and somewhat perplexing. Far from being a cause for concern, however, such perplexity merely serves to identify participatory action research as a vibrant part of Australian educational work. Kemmis and McTaggart (1988b, 21) highlight this dynamic in their introduction to the most recent edition of the *Action research reader*:

> What [action research] is, what and who it is for, and how it should be done are all matters which are *contested* . . . This is characteristic of most fields of new and exciting intellectual endeavour. Despite a forty-year history, action research has managed to retain its sense of intellectual excitement. It has passed through several phases and exists in a diversity of forms in a variety of contexts, but it still has a lively 'breaking edge' of intellectual work as its various protagonists attempt to define and refine the field and its work.

Notes

1. The reports upon which this early history of educational action research in Australia are based were accumulated as part of the Research on Action Research Project, directed by Stephen Kemmis in 1981–82. Many of these reports are analyzed in greater detail in Grundy (1984).

2. The following abbreviations have been used in this text:

> SBCD—School Based Curriculum Development
> CDC—Curriculum Development Centre
> ERDC—Educational Research and Development Council
> PEP—Participation and Equity Program
> ACT—Australian Capital Territory

3. There were also a number of males working within departments of education, fostering action research among practitioners; for instance, Lynton Brown in Victoria, John Annals in Tasmania, Jon Cook, Bill Green, and Bill Louden in Western Australia. (Reports of the work of many of these consultants and practitioners are contained in the references for this chapter.)

4. Garth Boomer died prematurely in 1993.

5. It is to Tripp that I owe my own introduction to action research.

6. A description and evaluation of the Innovative Links Project can be found in Yeatman and Sachs 1995. Information about the Innovative Links Project is accessible through the World Wide Web at http://cleo.murdoch.edu.au/echalk/innovlinks/ u&s.htm, and to the National Schools Network through http://www.schnet.edu.au/nsn/ Welcome.html.

References

Beasley, B. 1981a. *A case study of a school-based curriculum development in a primary school.* Adelaide: Wattle Park Teachers Center.

————. 1981b. *A case study of a school based curriculum development in a secondary school.* Adelaide: Wattle Park Teachers Center.

Boomer, G. (ed.). 1982. *Negotiating the curriculum.* Sydney: Ashton Scholastics.

Brennan, M. 1982. *Investigation as in-service.* Melbourne: Curriculum Services Unit, Education Department of Victoria.

Brown, L., C. Henry, J. Henry, and R. McTaggart. 1982. Action research: Notes on the national seminar. *Classroom action research network bulletin* 5:1–16. Reprinted in S. Kemmis and R. McTaggart. 1988. *The action research reader.* 3rd ed., 337–52. Geelong, Vic.: Deakin University Press.

Carr, W., and Kemmis, S. 1986. *Becoming critical: Education, knowledge, and action research.* Geelong, Vic.: Deakin University Press.

Commonwealth Schools' Commission 1981. Guidelines for school-level evaluation projects, 1981. Canberra: Circular 9/80, November.

Cook, J. (ed.). 1979. *32 Voices.* Perth: Education Department of Western Australia.

Cosgrove, S. 1982. Negotiating mathematics, in *Negotiating the curriculum.* ed. G. Boomer. Sydney: Ashton Scholastics.

Elliott, J., and C. Adelman. 1973. Reflecting where the action is: The design of the Ford Teaching Project. *Education for teaching.* 92.

Gadamer, H. G. 1979. *Truth and method.* London: Sheed & Ward.

Green, B. (ed.). 1982. *The Kewdale Project: Theory into practice.* Perth: Education Department of Western Australia.

Grundy, S. 1982. Three modes of action research. *Curriculum perspectives* 2(3):23–34.

————. 1984. *Beyond professionalism: Action research as critical pedagogy.* Ph.D. thesis, Murdoch University.

————. 1987. *Curriculum: Product or praxis?* Barcombe: Falmer Press.

————. (in press). Beyond guaranteed outcomes: Changing the discourse for educational praxis. *Australian journal of education.*

Grundy, S., and S. Kemmis. 1981a. Action research and group dynamics. Paper presented at the Annual Conference of the South Pacific Association of Teacher Educators, July. Adelaide.

————. 1981b. Educational action research in Australia: The state of the art (an overview). Paper presented at the Annual Conference of the Australian Association for Research in Education, November. Adelaide. Reprinted in *The action research reader*. 1988. eds. S. Kemmis and R. McTaggart. 3rd ed., 321–337. Geelong, Vic.: Deakin University Press.

Habermas, J. 1974. *Theory and practice*. London: Heinemann.

Kemmis, S., and R. McTaggart (eds.). 1988a. *The action research planner*. 3rd ed. Geelong, Vic.: Deakin University Press.

————. 1988b. *The action research reader*. 3rd ed. Geelong, Vic.: Deakin University Press.

MacDonald, B., and R. Walker 1975. Case study and the social philosophy of educational research. *Cambridge journal of education* 5:2–11.

Maxwell, T. W. et al. 1988. Early literacy in-service course (ELIC) and literacy teaching practices. *The South Pacific journal of teacher education* 16(1):13–35.

McTaggart, R. 1989. Principles for participatory action research. Paper presented at the 3rd Encuentro Mundial Investigacion Partipativa (The Third World Encounter on Participatory Research), Managua, Nicaragua, September.

————. 1991. Action research: Issues for the next decade. *Curriculum perspectives* 11(4):44–6.

McTaggart, R., and M. Garbutcheon-Singh. 1986. A fourth generation of action research: Notes on the Deakin seminar. Mimeograph, School of Education, Deakin University. Reprinted in *The action research reader*. eds. S. Kemmis and R. McTaggart. 1988. 3rd ed. 409–28. Geelong, Vic.: Deakin University Press.

Newson, T. 1981. Teachers as researchers at the school level. Paper presented at the Annual Conference of the Australian Association for Research in Education, Adelaide.

Parlett, M., and D. Hamilton. 1976. Evaluation as illumination: A new approach to the evaluation of innovative programs, in *Curriculum evaluation today: Trends and implications*. ed. Tawney. London: Macmillan.

Riordan, L. 1982. *Towards cooperative curriculum development in a teacher network: Reflection on the Language Development Project in South Australia*. Adelaide: Education Department of South Australia, Directorate of Research and Planning.

Skilbeck, M. 1975. School-based curriculum development. Mimeograph. Reprinted in Department of Social, Cultural, and Curriculum Studies (1990) *Curriculum development and schooling*, 80–90. NSW: University of New England.

Stake, R. E. (ed.). 1975. *Evaluating the arts in education: A responsive approach.* Columbus, Ohio: Charles E. Merrill.

Stenhouse, L. 1975. *An introduction to curriculum research and development.* London: Heinemann.

Yeatman, A., and J. Sachs. 1995. Making the links: A formative evaluation of the first year of the Innovative Links Project. Murdoch University: Innovative Links Project.

CHAPTER 8

Participatory Research in Venezuela: 1973 to 1991

John Dinan and Yuraima Garcia

Introduction

Given the fact that little has been published on the development of participatory research in Venezuela, the authors seek to outline the principal socioeducational, economic, and political processes surrounding and influencing this development. The original document was published in Spanish in July 1990 and circulated to a number of Venezuelans and foreigners associated with the subject matter, as well as to some of the respondents mentioned in the text.[1] Their detailed commentaries and observations have been incorporated into this English-language text, without deviating from the original document. The majority of these contributions have identified valuable complementary research areas, derived from the contents of the study.[2]

In Venezuela's present critical condition, participatory research is one of the methods most named in recent socioeducational literature as an important research and organizational contribution.

For social projects and movements in the present 'strengthening of democracy' to become significant, alternative, and operational choices, they must identify and confront specific problems in today's social, economic, and political structure. Two fundamental requisites must be satisfied: using a clear, effective method, and having the organizational capacity for long-term action in present dramatically changing circumstances. However, there is little documented material on the specific tasks, strengths, and weaknesses in the national context from a historical perspective.

The principal objective of this study is, therefore, to present a critical historical analysis of the introduction and expansion of varied points of view and activities, generically termed 'participatory research,' since 1973. Thus, we do not seek to define 'participatory research' either in methodological or epistemological terms, nor to classify the quantity or results of educational programs using this technique. The authors have not set out to report a study of the impact of participatory research, but rather to initiate a record of certain indicators to determine its potential, defined as the recognition of the present state of participatory research in light of the country's actual sociopolitical interplay. This interplay can only be determined within a framework of those social strategies, which render them a creative process for valid knowledge and as an organizational procedure.

In light of these considerations, the study is both descriptive and interpretative. Beginning with the development of participatory research in the last twenty years, there are three periods: 1973–1983, 1984–1989, and 1990–1991. For ease of comprehension, three fields have been isolated: adult education, socioeducational research, and participatory research activities. We have worked against a background frame of reference, including certain social, economic, and political factors, in order to highlight the interaction among the areas mentioned, as well as to facilitate interpretation of national development for those unfamiliar with these facets of Venezuela.

In the analysis of these periods and the development of participatory research, the shifts in the socioeconomic and historical processes are outstanding, especially those that involve this type of research in Venezuela. This begins as academics and researchers from all parts of Latin America introduce participatory research projects in Venezuela, of their own volition, extends for a period in which a certain organization or structure was attempted for the development of participatory research, and is finalized in a period of considerable economic and social crises, which, in turn, is the initiation of a more critical period for participatory research efforts.

Venezuela in the 1973–1983 decade had unimaginable income levels, a strong centralized state, a sociopolitical structure firmly based on the redistribution of oil wealth, and alternate power control between the leading political parties. Later, following the collapse of oil revenues, Venezuela was characterized by a drastic budget reduction, a large foreign debt (one of the largest in terms of per capita income in Latin America), an alarming drop in employment level and living standards, a discredited political system and public administration, almost universally perceived as corrupt, and the ordinary citizen's despair with the dwindling purchasing power of salaries, personal insecurity, and inefficient public services, among other factors. All of these elements provoked the manifestation of strong social tensions, culminating in the 1989 violence and leaving an uncertainty regarding the future of Venezuelan society in the 1990s.

Within this context, what role has participatory research played and how has it been influenced by these changes? Within the historical framework mentioned in this study, some answers can be found comparing participatory research's efforts and tendencies with the scenario of each period, with emphasis on socioeducation, precisely where participatory research was used as an instrument of social intervention since it was introduced into Venezuela.

Beginning from the methodological principle, which maintains that whatever the problem of interest, it is to be analyzed in context in order to be able to understand it specifically. From this vantage point, we structured our study of participatory research in Venezuela. From this perspective, the above-mentioned principle was applied in the analysis of social, political, and institutional conditions, the rise and development of participatory research in Venezuela, and its repercussions on actual sociopolitical and economic reality, more than from a Latin American viewpoint. It also has been useful in the research process per se, permitting precision and disposition of the type of information required for understanding the present state of participatory and action research in Venezuela.

There have been no previous studies of this kind in Venezuela because, up to the present, theoretical and methodological predispositions have seriously limited collective critical analysis, as well as the scope and effectiveness of participatory research. Thus, the methodological purpose of this study is to promote participatory research as a shared experience, starting from a descriptive and interpretative overview, involving interviews with researchers and members of grassroots projects. This first report will be discussed by interviewees and other interested parties.

The compilation of significant relevant documentation, as a parallel task, has become increasingly difficult and important. Biographical material and the results of interviews present a diversity of interpretations within participatory research, such as: militant; action; participatory action; biographical; collective; group self-research; thematic; and emancipatory action research. Nineteen people who were related to participatory research in Venezuela were interviewed over a three-month period. Criteria used in selection included: the authors' firsthand knowledge of their work, involvement since 1970, and more recent participation, as well as presentation of papers in national and international seminars. Further interview candidates were recommended by the initial respondents.

Information analysis involved designing a series of charts, each pertinent to a specific study aspect: researcher's role; project beneficiaries; methodology; conceptual framework; participation ideas and practices; project definitions; application areas and goals; and views on the effectiveness of the organizations and associations engaged in disseminating participatory research in Venezuela.

This initial report contains three sections:

1. *Economic bonanza.* This deals with Venezuela's economic bonanza period, starting in 1973 and continuing to 1983, characterized by a crucial lack of means to effectively relate participatory research to social processes.

2. *Economic crisis.* The period from 1984 to 1989, analyzed in the light of implications for participatory research in the context of the intense social and economic changes that took place.
3. *Socioeconomic uncertainty.* This last section discusses participatory research potential in a situation of acute social, economic, and political uncertainty from 1990.

Economic Bonanza: 1973–1983

The Weak Link Between Participatory Research and Socioeducational Processes

Rise and fall of oil income and its repercussions. This is a summary covering boom years and the consequent imbalance arising in the late 1970s in society, the political system, and the state (Lopez 1986, 166–83). From 1930, oil and other public revenues allowed the state to promote and regulate development. Oil price rises reemphasised the already centralized system. By the end of 1973, state income more than doubled (from Bs 24,000 million to Bs 55,600 million—at Bs 4.3 = $U.S.1.00). International revenues went from $U.S. 2,412 million (1973) to $U.S. 9,243 million (1975). From 1973 to 1987, GDP rose from 6 to 7 percent to 8.4 percent in 1976; in 1978, 6.3 percent annual growth in domestic economy, with a 12.2 percent maximum inflation rate, and an annual unemployment rate of under 7 percent (Silva Michelena 1987, 46–9).

The state launched development programs to accelerate industrialization while contracting a massive foreign debt. Subsequent changes were quantitative, though essentially qualitative. Sociologist Héctor Silva Michelena wrote:

> In effect, the role of the State considerably increased in weight throughout economic and social life. The explosion in fiscal income and the nationalization of the iron and oil industries relieved the State of its complementary function in the supply of basic goods, placing it as the decisive axis and dynamic centre of the cumulative process in general with its export-oriented basic industries. The State . . . without abandoning its role as shareholder, protector, and benefactor, becomes an important producer of goods and services, establishing itself through multiple State agencies as the main financier and generator of capital. (Silva Michelena 1987, 158–9)

Surplus oil income, combined with the left wing's political defeat at the end of the 1960s, are the principal factors in the rise of the 'populist-paternalistic-clientist nature' of Venezuela's democratic system. (Uribe and Lander 1988, 223). Acción Democrática (Social Democrats) and COPEI (Christian

Democrats) were virtually the only political forces signing an 'institutional pact' allowing them, at the beginning of each constitutional period, the election of public servants to high posts (Lopez 1986, 178). This led to party politics in all spheres of life.

Giving rise to a strategy for handling social conflict that defused direct confrontation between social sectors, Venezuela appeared to be one of the few Latin American countries with a functioning democracy, despite the unequal distribution of wealth. Government spending neutralized autonomous action by various social groups through the homogenization of social expectations. In this sense, the official program of 'democratization of education' was most influential.

Adult education. Bolivar and Marrero (1989) reviewed the official adult education program, as it did not implement the policies in the 1969 Decree No. 208 (Ministry of Education 1980). It presented, for the first time, integrated adult education, including literacy, secondary schooling, special education, and cultural extension programs. These authors pointed out that the need for careful teacher training was ignored; that there was a marked incidence of absenteeism among instructors; that there was a high dropout rate and a lack of requirements and resources of the physical plant. Thus, experiences were trial-and-error and left a bad image of official performance in this area. In 1980, the Organic Education Law renewed the principles of Decree No. 208. In 1985, an evaluation of the *Parasistema* (Navarro 1982; Marrero 1977) alternative showed grave planning failures.

Centro de Recursos y Asistencia Técnica (CRAT) was an alternative introduced in 1973–1974 for industrial works in the Guayana region. It was a good proposal, however, it succumbed to party political interference and poor planning. In 1975, the Ministry of Education closed the center and initiated Educación Básica Acelerada para Adultos, which covered sixteen states.

In a structural and historical analysis, Gonzalo Tapia et al.'s (1981) study of adult education in Venezuela during this period affirms that there has been a wide range of experiences in adult education. Approaches range from broad cultural experiences within literacy programs and labor focus in job training to grassroots self-improvement programs with a critical awareness focus. Their goal analysis was the redefinition of the liberating and transforming role of adult education as a means of changing society. Based on an analysis of fifty programs, they made recommendations relevant to this study. They concluded that adult education, through historical development and official sponsorship, was a marginal activity, relegated to an inferior position relative to state financing, as in content and methodology.

Certification in adult education did not help adults obtain jobs, enter further training courses, or compete with secondary school graduates in the

job market, and it was not an aid to social mobility. Financially, adult education received 3 percent of the 15 percent allocation of the national education
budget. Thus, life expectancy of new programs was uncertain at best. In content and method, perceived as deficient, no changes were made, but rather the
social status quo was promoted through job training, general education, and
community development projects. In most programs, the adults concerned did
not participate in program planning, execution, or evaluation.

However, there were exceptions: plans carried out by the Centro al Servicio de la Acción Popular (CESAP) and the Fundación para el Desarrollo de
la Comunidad y Fomento Municipal (FUNDACOM) were initiatives
approaching social problems from a participatory and global stance. According to Tapia et al., such valid endeavors should be a base, integrating all agencies into an independent 'coherent, participatory, democratic and pluralist,
system,' (1981, 172) to respond to changing needs in social, economic, and
political fields. The content of the FUNDACOMUN-CESAP programs gives
clear popular education-action orientation to adult education. To carry out
these programs, a total legal and political restructuring of the educational system would be necessary. Among other things, connections with the Consejo
Internacional para la Educacion Adulta (ICAE) should be sought as it promotes change in adult education.

The authors of this paper add to these recommendations the necessity
for an installed organizational and research capacity at the grassroots and nonformal educational levels. In 1975, the Oficina Sectorial de Planificacion Pre-
supuesto (OSPP planning and budget office) of the Ministry of Education
commissioned a wide study (Droogleever and Oud 1977) on the functions of
the formal and nonformal educational systems. This study, conducted by
Droogleever and Oud of Amsterdam's Sociografisch Institut, together with
the Venezuelan Centro de Futurologiá (CEFU), covered the period 1974–1976
and confirmed the success of national policy in the quantitative area of the
democratization of education. It also noted the exaggerated confidence in education in tackling national development problems, while revealing the fragmented structure of the system itself.

They also stressed the contradiction between decentralizing education
and a *cacique* (chieftain) tendency in Venezuelan culture, whereby all bosses
impede the delegation of responsibility. Sufficient examples of effective interaction between school directors and teachers were found to be of special interest to this study. This base-level interaction could become strategy with long-
range program design and administrative implications. However, in an
analysis of popular education in Latin America, Parra et al. stated that local
institutional cooperation is insufficient (Parra et al. n.d., 68). Change will
occur they said when educators associate with political currents of social
transformation and a global social project incorporates their educational

ideals. Not even micro support systems existed at this level, and even less so between nonformal and community self-help programs.

Haydée Garcia's study of job training (Garcia 1987, 163–202) asserted that industry needs were covered during the period 1973–1977. There were 'efficiency problems' which did not become fully evident until the recession period, despite government subsidies and foreign technical aid. Garcia emphasizes the role of the Instituto Nacional de Co-operacion Educacional (INCE) as the leading nonformal training agency. Ascribed to the Ministry of Education, INCE was to provide job training and interrelate the different educational subsystems. In the transition from boom to recession, agriculture, manufacturing, and construction lost ground to commerce, finance, and services as employment areas, and INCE had major difficulties adapting its financing, planning, and instructional format to the changing employment market. INCE's constituent members only weakened its role. The private sector questioned its capacity to satisfy their needs; unions criticized courses without full credit and, along with the state, did not uphold job training as a priority. With this sectorial crisis, Garcia referred to alternatives within Francisco Vio-Grossi's definition of popular education. The author named Fé y Alegria (Faith and Happiness) and the Asociacion para la Educacion Popular (APEP) as local examples. Relevant to the present study is Garcia's affirmation that popular education in Latin America is very restricted and, especially in Venezuela, it does not go beyond an isolated experience. She maintained that popular education places the worker in the center of the educational process, stimulating creativity and capacity to make him or her less vulnerable to job market fluctuations. In practice, there are limitations, among them, financing and industrial relations. Garcia stated that the political aims of popular education conflict with private enterprise, that state subsidies would be reduced, and that popular sectors lacked the means to support these programs. It is then that the church can play an increasingly important role. Community orientation could frustrate specific employer needs, and popular education should further penetrate the job market, allowing the worker diversified opportunity.

Without debating whether Fé y Alegria, APEP, and Vio-Grossi share the same interpretation of popular education,[3] the main point is the implications of Garcia's analysis in the field of professional development on the recommendations that Tapia et al. mentioned in their work, "Socioeconomic conditions in the adult education programs in Venezuela" (1981). Garcia implied that in the 1970s and early 1980s popular education did not rely upon adequate financing, depending more heavily on the church and/or those auto-financing alternatives they might find (1981, 192).

Furthermore, Garcia added that popular education is extremely locality-community oriented. Both considerations, combined with a lack of coordination between base-level organizations and disassociated research activity concerning socioeducational processes at the time, reveal the real limited capacity existing for the introduction of the profound changes visualized in Tapia et al.'s document in 1981.

Socioeducational research in the 1970s and early 1980s. Carmen Garcia-Guadilla (1986, 85–104) stated that 1973 was a crucial year for the economic and political scene in Venezuela, with direct consequences for the development of educational research, such as, a drastic reduction of foreign financing for educational research, the arrival here of exiled Marxist intellectuals from Argentina, Chile, and Uruguay, and the introduction of new international paradigms in the interpretation of social and educational phenomena (1986, 99).

However, of interest to the present report is that, although esteemed in academic circles, the theories they brought did not materialize in work trials or experiences. Furthermore, virtually all of these southern professionals returned to their own or other countries. Both of these factors contributed to a fundamental deficiency in continuity, necessary for the organizational and evaluative ends they contributed.

It is necessary to make this point to understand the complex process of apparent lack of continuity of some efforts in Venezuela. In many senses, Venezuela is perceived as a place of transit, even for nationals. Cultural identity crises contribute to this 'passing through' effect (Vilda 1984; Montero 1984); what has been learned has relevance elsewhere, either in academic or applied terms. However, for many Latin American social or educational theorists and activists, Venezuela reflected little in common with other Latin American countries at this time. That professionals like Yolanda Sanguinetti-Vargas (Chile, Mexico), Tomás Vasconi (Argentina, Chile, Cuba), Eugenio Ormeno, Gonzalo Tapia, and Francisco Vio-Grossi (Chile), Paloma Lopez de Ceballo (Spain), and Mario Kaplun (Uruguay), came, worked, and left is to be grasped within the subcontinent reality and Venezuela's place therein.

Other local organizations and individuals introduced participatory methods in different educational areas with more continuity and more measurable results.

1. Intellectuals of the Movimiento de Izquierda Revolucionario (MIR), a left wing political party, committed to militant investigation. Even the Laboratorio Educativo (Educational Laboratory), a cooperative educational publishing venture based on the works of Freinet, identified with this interpretative tendency in social action from the viewpoint of class differences and the position of the researcher as an academic in this role (Segovia and Santiago 1980, 5–40).

2. Founded in 1967, the Centro de Investigacion Aplicada para el Desarrollo y Entrenamiento de la Comunidad (CIADEC—Applied Research and Training Centre for Community Development) was the result of an agreement between the Venezuelan government and the United Nations (Project Ven 13). This Centre resulted from the National Program for Community Development, offering training services to promoters and professionals in diverse careers at a local and Latin American level through a multidisciplinary group of professionals. The Centre closed in 1974 due to financial problems.[4]

3. The Simón Rodriguez National Experimental University, which, from 1973 to 1975 embodied in a Venezuelan context current Latin American radical ideas and attempts to change higher education.

4. The Centro Experimentaal para el Aprendizaje Permanente) (CEPAP—Centre for Experimentation in Life-Long Learning) was Simón Rodriguez University's nucleus set up in a former *barrio* school. CEPAP played a decisive role in the dissemination of participatory research. From 1974 to 1976, CEPAP was a center of research and action discourse for currents of educational thinking from Latin America, Europe, Canada, and the United States. An intense debate was held in CEPAP, as occurred in other institutions (Garcia-Guadilla 1986, 95–8). The effects were provocative but poorly understood by CEPAP members and outside agents, although basic to alternative educational thinking, which later was extended nationally. Lucio Segovia (1989) points out that from 1976 the integration of theory and practice took place in this field in Venezuela. The author identifies this integration as a result of the interchange among the Zavala group, René Garcia's workshops, and a more profound study done by Orlando Fals-Borda, all in Colombia.[6]

5. The Centro al Servicio de la Acción Popular (CESAP—Educational Centre at the Service of Popular Action), in its founding document in 1973, called for the need to redefine work with popular sectors, with real, effective participation aimed at developing the individual and consolidating grassroots organizations. Based on the psychosocial methods of Paulo Freire and the group dynamics of Carl Rodgers, they initiated women's group programs, centers for popular education, youth groups, cooperatives, and small manufacturing units (Tapia 1981).

Cartagena, Colombia, hosted the World Symposium on Active Research and Scientific Analysis in 1977, with the aim, says Lucio Segovia (1989), of giving an ethical and a political, as well as a scientific and professional dimension to the social sciences in Latin America. This meeting had little effect on daily community development activities in Venezuela.

In 1978, Chilean lawyer and adult educator Francisco Vio-Grossi joined the postgraduate staff of the Universidad Nacional Experimental Simón Rodriguez (UNESR), strengthening participatory research in Venezuela. In 1979, members of CEPAP collaborated with him on the organization of the first Latin American Participatory Research Seminar, held in Caracas, sponsored by Simón Rodriguez University and the International Council for Adult Education (ICAE). As a result of the seminar, the Consejo para la Educacion Adulta en la America Latina (CEAAL) was established in Caracas, where they promoted a Venezuelan network of participatory researchers and the Venezuelan Council for Adult Education (COVEP). From this point on, staff and members of CEPAP and CESAP benefited from the whole Latin American movement of participatory research.

From 1974 on, CEPAP and CESAP worked together to provide relevant ideological, conceptual, and methodological contributions to adult education and participatory research in many parts of the country. Throughout this period, CEPAP was the only higher education institute working with an open curriculum and a project learning format with action research components (Dinan et al. 1978; Leon et al. 1981). This attracted people who required flexible, in-service studies. Besides CESAP, other groups included: Federacion de Asociaciones de la Comunidad Urbana (FACUR); Federacion de Organizaciones y Juntas Ambientalistas (FORJA—Federation of Environmental Groups and Organizations); Fé y Alegria, a church-sponsored popular education movement; Churuata, a popular cultural promotion program group; CECONANVE, representing Venezuelan cooperatives; Centros Communitarios de Aprendizaje (CECODAP—Community learning centers) for *barrio* children; the Confederacion General de Trabajadores (CGT), a progressive workers' union, and directors and teachers of more innovative private schools in Venezuela, such as Apune, Rondalera, and Colibri Dos.

While CEPAP was developing as a training and accreditation center for social action, CESAP was involved with popular action networks, styled after the International Council for Adult Education (ICAE). These centers, the mainstays of COVEP, were the principal promoters of the participatory research discourse, from 1980. Between 1980 and 1985, they organized eight meetings of researchers and action groups, national as well as international,[7] in an attempt to establish a Venezuelan participatory research network.

In a report on six of these meetings, up to 1983 (Martinez and Dinan 1983), one can find a wide range of popular action experiences in Venezuela during this period. Although in other Latin American countries, grassroots organizations and networks were well-developed by the 1980s, this was not the case in Venezuela, which implied serious limitations in setting up any kind of participatory network.

Ernesto Schiefelbein (1981, 371) stated that the 1970s saw the foundation of socioeducational research capacity in each country of the region and in the 1980s, it "should be preserved from destruction and that diffusion and use of it must be developed" (1981, 371). In the case of Venezuela, efforts made in the early 1980s promoted participatory research, assuming there existed an academic and organizational capacity, favoring the introduction of other participatory research experiences from Latin American countries.

Did Venezuela really have these given conditions for consolidation? The answer was no. It was still a period in which participatory research was promoted in an adverse academic climate. Efforts were directed to exploring channels for the distribution of explanatory materials. The CEAAL network was in a formative stage and COVEP was undefined, relative to popular education in Venezuela. COVEP, according to Lucio Segovia of CEPAP, grouped five or six small organizations, keeping their own identities while associated with CEPAP.

The principal founders of COVEP were staff of CESAP and CEPAP. These were seen as reinforced by their connection to the international network (CEAAL), having direct access to data on participatory research and exercising certain control over its handling, and thus, over members of COVEP. This produced tension and criticism of the way in which the central role was administered in a complex grassroots situation. Schiefelbein referred to this process (1982) whereby national entities supported by international networks provided conditioned assistance to newer organizations, both stimulating and restricting them.

Schiefelbein defined a network "as formed by institutions or individuals who are linked together through information transfer or collaborative action" (1982, 30, note 24), and another, "educational projects and plans and the critiques prepared by non-government centres are dealing with education in a more comprehensive and complex way" (1982, 24).

The logic of interrelating the CEAAL-COVEP national participatory research network produced, in Venezuela, a hegemony of the leading parties involved in COVEP. Thus, in the mid-1980s, when the principal COVEP members discontinued participation in the network, this ceased functioning. Therefore, Venezuela lost its only network which related academic and grassroots protagonists in action and research in socioeducational areas, while the Asociacion Venezolana de Investigadores Educacionales (AVIED—Venezuelan Association of Educational Researchers) continued to interrelate professionals in academics. Leonor Pulgar[8] stated that out of all the national information networks in this period, none covered the socioeducational field. Today, only those covering medical and socioeconomic matters continue. Externally, Venezuela lagged behind other Latin American countries in the grassroots and supportive research areas. Among other explanations, Lucio Segovia (1989) of CEPAP said in COVEP, "We are not interested in participating in these experiences because at this moment we do not see any sense to it, and we prefer to achieve a higher degree of theoretical, conceptual, and methodological development ourselves."[9]

In concluding this section, it is necessary to point out that the time factor was restrictive, but there was a central idea that moved all debate on participatory research: the problem of relating practice to theory, in such a way that neither the action nor the development of the participants is impeded. Another influential element was the differing work styles. Network tactics basically contributed to better awareness of alliances that were formed by interested groups as, because the time, the majority worked from their own positions and their understanding of the positions of other groups—an attitude that Pablo Latapi classified as "whose side are they on?" (Latapi 1981, 311).

As a result of this situation, differences were accentuated, which was detrimental to the strengthening of total commitment to network philosophy. This was rated by Latapi as 'a social process' in Latin America, as opposed to the orthodox sense of 'invisible colleges of professionals' (1981, 29). We infer from Latapi's comments that the tendency in Latin America to form networks was based on the commitment between researchers and activists, more than between subscribers and readers of printed matter.

The network format, as involving COVEP, was to be wide-ranging and heterogeneous. Later, CEPAP held a series of meetings among its own students, graduates, and associates, relating participatory research to the university context. Formalism appeared, much involved in learning projects and curriculum discourse, albeit flexible and innovative. Participatory research had limited rural applications[10] (Carmona 1977). Note that rural adult education was the area in which it had made its presence felt in Latin America.

This formalist tone was reflected in a short-lived structure to gather research professionals in the Venezuelan Association for Research and Action (AVIA). Though short-lived (1980 to 1986), this association introduced to Venezuela Professor Henri Desroche, the founder and promoter of the International Cooperative University (UCI), who established a research-action style and permanent formation based on reasoned, centered autobiography in the 'life and action' project. The Desroche/UCI inheritance remained in the Creation and Management of Participatory Projects in the Higher School of Practice in Social Research (EPSIS-CISOR). However, AVIA never established a coordinated corps of researchers in this area. Militant investigators opted for a separate line of action, holding meetings among professionals regarding their commitments to and functions in social action,[11] while they could have contributed greatly to the participatory network.

Economic Crisis:Implications for Participatory Research 1984–1989

Recession and Standard of Living Crisis

The 1970s saw alternative research in a context of economic expansion and weak political organization in popular sectors, and the 1980s were marked by profound social and economic crisis. The early 1980s showed important organizational developments in civil society, and the later years were politically and organizationally disjointed.

Despite considerable new resources generated by higher oil prices from 1979 to 80, the economic crisis soon became evident. Héctor Silva Michelena (1987) reported that from 1979 to 1982

> the Gross Domestic Product showed no growth; the employment rate, which was 4.3 percent at the end of 1978, rose to 6.3 percent in the first semester of 1981 and was nearly 10 percent at the end of 1983 . . . oil income slipped steadily, internal activities remained static or grew very little . . . only agriculture and manufacturing showed positive growth despite the recessive climate. (Silva Michelena 1987, 152)

In 1982, the fiscal and budgetary deficit was accentuated by falling oil prices and a public foreign debt of $U.S. 25 000 million, and a rapid spiral that reached $U.S. 33 000 million by the end of the decade.

In 1983, the GDP fell by 5.7 percent to the lowest point ever registered in the economy. Due to a resultant lack of confidence, private sector investment dropped from almost 60 percent in 1979 to less than 30 percent in 1984. That year, the national currency was devalued by 70 percent, slowing the GDP decline to –1.7 percent. Inflation climbed to 12.7 percent and basic food prices rose by 33 percent. These combined factors led to increased unemployment and a stagnation of nominal salaries (Silva Michelena 1987, 155).

In 1986, oil prices and therefore national revenue plunged violently and economic decline accelerated, a pattern also seen from 1987 to 88, becoming acute from February 1989 onward. As part of the economic measures adopted by the Venezuelan government to meet its foreign debt obligations, public transportation fares were increased, thus igniting public wrath, and, in the sacking that followed, a still undetermined number of people died.

In 1989, the economy deteriorated further and, as a consequence, so did the standard of living, especially among lower- and middle-income people. The following indicators serve as an illustration:

1. *Poverty level increase.* From 1984 to 1985, the critically poor population totaled 5 percent. In 1987, 15.1 percent were in extreme poverty and 30.1 percent were critically poor; a total of 45.2 percent were extremely/critically poor. However, more recent indicators show the increase in poverty. In 1989, 31.3 percent of total families were critically poor and 30.5 percent were in extreme poverty—61.8 percent of Venezuelan households (Cartaya 1989).[12]
2. *Decline in real income.* The progressive deterioration of income is a structural problem in Venezuelan society. In 1978, 66.3 percent of fami-

lies earned incomes below the level of the Basic Food Basket;[13] by 1984, that rose to 73 percent (Garcia Guadilla 1986, 176) and by 1989 it was nearly 80 percent. The resultant drop in consumption is approximately 50 percent.[14] It is evident that serious malnutrition was produced by less quantity and quality of food, especially in those homes classified as in extreme/critical poverty.

3. *Rising unemployment.* Officially 9.2 percent; unofficially estimated at 20 percent for the end of 1989 (Rodriguez 1989, see note 14).

4. *Economic activities.* A 13 percent decrease in economic activities (Rodriguez 1989, see note 14).

5. *Growth of the informal sector.* In 1985, more than five million people (34.4 percent) worked in the so-called 'informal sector.' By 1989, there were a million more people at work, 43 percent (OCEI 1989, 706). Such data refer to the informal sector as defined as 'self-employed' or as domestic help, without counting those underage or holding informal jobs. Indicators for the informal sector are difficult to determine, however, identification and dissemination of this socioeconomic data is important to ensure realistic management with rising levels of critical poverty in the nation and Latin America.[15]

Social Response

Although social unrest could result from this social and economic deterioration, many were surprised how Venezuela, 'asleep' in the 1970s and 1980s, finished the decade. As well as the looting of shopping centers in major cities, small *barrio* groceries run by foreigners were sacked. No specific political orientation seemed involved, but unrest served as a catalyst in the political system (Graham 1990, 7). Venezuela showed signs of a radical difference entering the 1990s. Emigration was greater than immigration. After thirty years of democracy, the Confederacion de trabajadores de Venezuela (CTV), the government's labor arm, called a national strike.

The apparently dominant Acción Democrática party lost nearly all of the state and municipal elections in 1989 for the first time. In sharp contrast to the 1970s, it was possible to see the growing protests from teachers, parents, students, and the production, agricultural, and transport sectors. The right to social and political participation was the common factor.

Government failure to join social policy to its economic plans was highly criticized. Immediate official social planning appeared as a spontaneous initiative of an emergency nature.[16] However, as recession and inflation hit the already poor strata of society, public administration lacked the experience and means for the coordination and implementation of plans based 'on greater discrimination of social needs.' Government, independent institutions, and grassroots organizations have had to define their across-the-board functions in light of the present complex social environment. Counting on a trend to armed repression, the government has swung between conceptually defined authority and lack of any strong leadership. In contrast, agents of alternative education and social proposals have increasingly shown their strength. Some women's and neighborhood movements have participated with public and private representatives in national forums, part of a coordinated effort to face present difficulties. They were present in the debate sponsored by the Latin American Institute for Social Research (ILDIS) to discuss repercussions in employment, wage policies, and social security.[17]

There has been a substantial increase in technical and financial agreements signed between independent, private, and official entities. For example, the Ministry of the Family has signed credit, training, and technical assistance accords with five institutions and organizations which work with cooperatives and small merchants in the lower social sectors.[18] CESAP, for example, has organized frequent seminars and workshops on cooperatives involving FONDACOMUN, the Fundación para el Desarrollo Centro-Oriental (FUDECO—Foundation for Central-Western Regional Development) and others.

In the late 1980s, the term *nongovernment organization* (NGO) was incorporated into the social action milieu, given that Venezuela was losing its privileged economic position vis-à-vis other Latin American countries. The term NGO has been diversely understood by increasing numbers of independent groups, but has at no time been referred to as an organized capacity for social response. The financial and technical support implications of an NGO created new alliance groups and links between them and official and international bodies. There was also a growing awareness of GONGO agencies (government/ nongovernment organizations), where the lines between official and alternative social planning become confused.

A CESAP coordinator pointed this out, referring to the necessity for cooperating with official plans, while not losing sight of the tension of differences.[19] However, the real significance is at an operative level, where the emphasis on efficient project management can sometimes mirror the official sector's philosophy of global social management. For NGOs today, the question is not "what side is the other on?" but "who is doing what?" Specifically, members of the Comisión del Sur suggested that NGOs collaborate in systemizing data on social needs and realistic solutions derived from grassroots experiences to consolidate these agencies' autonomy and to influence social planning. The real lack of statistical data requires that measurement in the socioeconomic area be a series of indicators that can be used for the definition of parameters in this field. It is necessary to use a combination of factors for true indicators.

It is evident that in Venezuela there is a social planning vacuum, both theoretical and technical, which contributes to broadening the distance between those who delineate these policies and the ever-changing social reality. Very little has been done in this field and, from this perspective, what can be hoped from adult education and socioeducational research to support this task?

Adult Education and Socioeducational Research

The fluctuating socioeconomic scene has not shown any redefinition of the formal educational system. Even today, despite reform pressure from intellectuals and educators,[20] there is no National Education Plan. Researchers affirm that the state is losing ground with the increase of elitist private sector influence in education (Albornoz 1987; Casanova and Brofenmayer 1987). However, compared to the first period studied, abundant evidence gathered for the 8th National Plan, shows the near collapse of the educational system. Thirty-eight percent of students finish basic education, while 66 percent of the budget goes to higher education, administration, and supervision, yet represents only 9 percent of enrollment (Cordiplan 1990). In 1989, the National Education Congress set in motion regional and metropolitan seminars to examine the decentralization of education, in the context of local government authorities. Also, in 1989, SUMMA (the leading teachers union) carried out a series of parallel meetings throughout the country to update and resubmit its proposals for educational change.

Foreign creditor pressures like the World Bank advocate accelerating decentralization of state administrative functions and involving independent agencies and NGOs in national educational work. For example, the Asociacion Venezolana de Educacion Católica (AVEC) is involved in the managerial and administrative functions of the Ministry of Education in farm schooling and city *barrios*. Venezuela's educational system appears as international support programs of the World Bank and UNICEF, no longer as pilot project partial funding. Private sector attitude shows change, as evidenced in the Mendoza and Bigott Foundations' support for programs, with a popular education focus in barrios and rural communities.[21]

Some authors argue that the state is the only valid means of implanting a national popular education plan, using the school as a fundamental base for the democratic process per se (Brofenmayer and Casanova 1987). In the area of adult education, papers presented at the National Education Congress continue to make recommendations for strategy and methodology. Their ultimate value depends on a political decision to establish an independent adult educational system that supports and builds on existing examples of independent adult education activity, mentioned by Adams and Marrero (1989, 126) who cite rural and women's programs as evidence of substantial self-financing, achieved by involving participants in productive activities. Adult education continues to be a marginal activity, as it is not included in the 8th National Plan.

In socioeducational research, Schiefelbein affirms that NGOs deal with education problems in a more complex and comprehensive way than do research institutes, which is extremely relevant to this report. The majority of new social groups involve adult education, varied personnel, and action fields. Of interest is how many NGOs can handle the complexities of formal and nonformal education; what are their action research focuses and needs, and what relationship exists with other grassroots organizations?[22]

Research methodology varies in these groups, either by the members themselves, or in contact with universities. Very few, such as CESAP or the Centro de Investigacion para el Niño y la Familia (CENDIF), have an infrastructure to stimulate productive research. Venezuelan formal socioeducational research tends to parallel educational processes. The majority of studies are dedicated to system shortcomings, but alternatives are seldom provided (Piñango 1987). Research theory categories, cited by Carmen Garcia Guadilla (1986, 9–10) are relevant: the 1960s as the 'age of innocence' (education as a means of overcoming social differences); the 1970s, the 'age of skepticism' (education creates social differences), and the 1980s, the 'age of activism' (acting on the possible within what is socially just). Present educational research tends to lag behind in the chronological framework.

A possible explanation is that the actual procedure of NGOs and private institutions is very much of the 1980s, but without permanent research support. Research pilot experiences tend to be joined to the schools or the students involved. Also to be considered is that funding agencies emphasize impact studies. This implies that research and action in the socioeducational field are separate activities, a dichotomy that participatory research attempted to correct in the 1970s. In the 1980s, participatory researchers, in an attempt to 'justify upwards' were tied to producing conceptually explanatory works. Today, a certain priority is placed on participatory research as being fundamental for alternative education forms (Brunner 1985, 84–5; Garcia Guadilla 1986; Piñango 1987; Gianotten and Dewit 1982),[23] particularly in the present crucial social circumstances. However, no significant paper on the subject was presented at the Latin American and Caribbean Sociology of Education Conference in Caracas in 1987, and since COVEP closed in mid-1986, there is no promoting body. Thus, is there a sufficient body of knowledge and practice of participatory procedures acquired by a sufficient number of people to affirm what Schiefelbein says about NGOs handling socioeducational problems in a comprehensive way? Answering this involves reference points on the 1990 social, economic, and political circumstances, as background for a description of the state of participatory research in Venezuela.

Socioeconomic Uncertainty: The Potential for Participatory Research in the 1990s

Social Uncertainty, Socioeducational Research and Adult Education

The effects of the economic changes in Venezuela since 1989 are of an irreversible nature, especially in the social and educational fields. According to the Venezuelan Society of Puericulture and Pediatrics,[24] the country "is on the border of a social disaster with unpredictable implications." The Ministry of Education[25] revealed that 19 percent of children between the ages of six and twelve (628,000) have no formal education, and, furthermore, 50 percent of students abandoned their education at the secondary and/or technical level.

All basic services are in near collapse. Previous subcultures of under-development are modus vivendi for the majority of Venezuelans. In this sense, social and educational researchers refer to this decade as one of uncertainty to offer alternatives that at least contend with, if not solve, problems of macro social dimensions.

In an article published by Heinz Sonntag (1986), he refers to future uncertainty in terms compatible with 1990. Sonntag states that from the social, economic, and political points of view, the country is living a profound crisis. Writing before the riots in February 1989, Sonntag noted the absence of social conflict comparable with other countries. He credited this calm to civilian society's weakness as a political entity and concluded that the challenge which faced Venezuela was in overcoming citizen apathy, especially in young people. The role of the Venezuelan social movements he criticized as weak, both in their aims and penetration.

By contrast, in a 1988 publication, Sonntag expressed belief in the positive role of social movements in Latin America, to reinstate themselves in world affairs to contest existing hegemonies (Sonntag 1988, 162). He identifies these movements as transformations affecting all classes, groups, sectors, and social categories (1988, 146). The difference is not only local, but regional, also involving utopian thinking into social analysis in the second text, in which Sonntag affirms that the social sciences will resume their traditional commitment (1988, 163).

It is worth noting that this is what participatory research has been attempting to do in Venezuela over the last approximately twenty years, which confirms its utopian content as a knowledge-creating and social organization process and underlies the poor impact it has had on social science thinking at a national level.

The identification of social movements as an expression of emerging new social subjects, in less utopian terms in the present Venezuela, tends to place a generic term over and above a reality that seems to have little correlation. The term *social movement* in Venezuela is used to group diverse social actors, not the sharing of social or educational propositions (Sonntag 1986). Each group, with its own history, does not, as Uribe and Lander (1988) stated, function in a value vacuum, nor are groups impervious to the cultural milieu in which they operate. It would be particularly interesting to know how much participatory research, in its double role, has contributed, first, in producing information about the drastic modifications in the social classes (Sonntag 1988, 147) and second in elaborating the conceptual structures derived from national reality, to identify the 'emerging social actors' with greater precision.

Focusing on education and educational research in Venezuela in the 1980s and for the 1990s, Ramón Casanova and Carmen Garcia Guadilla (1990) defined this decade of singular importance in national history as the combined effects of the recession and radicalization of the democratic system. Change and conflict will invade education and research, and it will have to get used to austerity and uncertainty. They analyze the anticipated impact in problem areas such as access, management, organization, and politics, highlighting the term *new sensitivity surrounding educational action* (1990, 13). From their detailed study, it is worth recording some observations. Casanova and Garcia Guadilla refer to an incipient nonuniversity 'project market,' stimulated by the opening of demand for educational research among diverse sources (1990, 19). This list included groups interested in setting up popular education networks, multidisciplinary centers for personnel, and training schemes related to development and administration, and official units to cover social and educational planning needs, as well as offering consultancies to large economic and cultural institutions within an 'educational engineering' context. Far from constituting an integrated network, the internal operative logic is to inter- and intra-institutional atomization.

Casanova and Garcia Guadilla state that educational research will have to relate to new patterns of conduct due to growing competition in educational financing, opportunities, control of establishments, improvement in learning, and the promotion of cultural and regional differences (1990, 14). Competition becomes increasingly acute with more belligerent action from teachers' unions, deterioration of curricula content, teaching practice, equipment, overall school working conditions, and broad structural changes, such as state reforms and industrial reconversion.

Given that, on the one hand, there are no up-to-date studies about adult education in Venezuela comparable to those carried out by Droogleever and Oud (1977) and Tapia (1981) and, on the other hand, there is a recognition of the growing level of critical poverty, it is possible to extrapolate observations from articles by Pablo Latapi (1985) in which he analyzes adult education in Latin America as a response to the dramatic conditions of poverty and exploitation. For those who conceive and practice participatory research as an expression of adult education in Venezuela, Latapi's opinions, although they did not include Venezuela, are pertinent as they reflect one of the principal areas directed to achieving a minimum consensus on the actual definitions and applications of this methodology (Segovia 1989, 14 (26); Lima 1988; Fonseca,1982).[26] The authors mention that the necessary reconstruction of educational research paradigms, method options, and problem selection must take into account conflict and social action as a dimension of change, as well as of theory itself. They anticipate a certain refocusing of the innovational and mobilizing capacity of education research, making particular reference to the possible value of participatory and action research methodologies in this area.

The relevant questions are: How do participatory researchers in Venezuela interpret their activities within this perspective? What forum exists where researchers may analyze social strategies that incorporate conflict?

Schiefelbein provides a condensed version of alternative social strategy that promotes the complete review and development of socioeducational research, adult education, and participatory research, which at the same time is a guide to future action and hypotheses (Casanova and Garcia Guadilla 1990, 22). A final point of interest made by Casanova and Garcia Guadilla is the notable separation between educational research institutions and those whose activities initiate and develop educational responses and/or solutions. In this sense, they see the need for serious efforts to establish organizational patterns for transferring results from educational research centers to the field of action.

Current State of Participatory Research

By classifying and reflecting on the opinions of people with ties to action and research, we could then count on a first approximation to participatory research in Venezuela. The following are excerpts from interviews conducted with people within the participatory research field and their ties with action and research, which constitute a base for the realization of the objectives of this study. The classification and analysis of these opinions are only an initial approximation to the present state of participatory research in Venezuela. There is sufficient material to provide more specific analyses of many facets of this research method. Given the space limitations of this report, experience descriptions have been summarized. Also, it is necessary to point out that each entity represented by the respondents has a quantity of varied and important material which they applied (or not) for the organization of their own programs.

One can find important coincidences between conceptual and methodological sources used by social promoters and academics linked to the development of participatory research in Venezuela. For example, references to

Fals-Borda, Paulo Freire and, more recently, to CEAAL[27] and the methodology developed by CESAP for courses for popular facilitators.[28]

In Venezuela, participatory research is undertaken in three areas: universities, private entities, and sociocultural groups supported from a social base. Its nature and goals are different in these areas.

Academia. Some institutions and researchers work on the theoretical-interpretative side of participatory research: Arnaldo Esté, professor of Philosophy at the UCV; Ramón Piñango of IESA; Alberto Gruson of CISOR; Boris Lima of the School of Social Work at UCV and consultant for Cordiplan; and, in the social area: Pastor Mendoza of the Liberator Pedagogical Experimental University and Mariano Herrera of the Educational Post-Graduate School of the Simón Rodriguez National Experimental University. In this group, some emphasize effective unity between academia and social-educational experiences, while others undertake systematic studies from a strictly scientific standpoint.

Academics and socioeducational promoters. Arnaldo Esté organized a group of students to carry out participatory research in three communities on the central coast. Esté said, "We did not agree on a research method . . . the three communities were unable to overcome their dependency on the investigators and the project lapsed." Mariano Herrera at present is involved with teachers in a satellite town near Caracas, to improve children's self-expression and relate that to reading and writing. The other community-proposed project is the involvement of the parent-teacher's association in the school. Another example illustrating efforts made to join the academics and the social actors is provided by teacher Pastor Mendoza. He participated in setting up a rural education project, ". . . a study program seeking solutions by the community itself and stimulating its participation, but not with the idea of forming (local) promoters of education. . . ."

Within this orientation we may identify CEPAP, but under sui generis conditions, as the center was created to reinforce experiences in socioeducational development by means of an apprentice system. Julio Valdez stated

> . . . a participant undertakes an apprentice project in . . . [his or her] place of residence, singling out a problem together with people who work or live in the community and seek . . . an alternative. The participant puts forward objectives and strategies . . . it also affects the apprentice who analyses, reflects on, and systematises the experience . . . CEPAP cannot directly control the effect which the project has in the community. . .

Academic researchers with a stricter scientific approach. Within this sphere, Alberto Gruson says, ". . . those who remain on the level of common sense or routine (without) achieving an epistemological and practical break in order to go from the routine to the requirements of a search for truth. . . ." For his part, Ramón Pinango explains that IESA "develops research for organizations which intend to use the results for their own ends . . . it is not made public . . . action research, then, is a process of inquiry, undertaken with certain rigour and intended for publication. . . ."

Private institutions and participatory research. Who is presently undertaking this research in Venezuela? The basic role is filled by foundations, the most important being the Eugenio Mendoza Foundation, the Polar Foundation, Centre for the Child and the Family (CENDIF), Asociacion Venezolana para la Educacion Sexual Alternativa (AVESA), and the Instituto de Asesoramiento Educativo (INDASE—Institute for Educational Consultancy). On the staffs of these institutions are people with experience in participatory research who are working on projects with certain techniques and training elements in organized social action, seeking short-term alternatives in these times of crisis. The fields covered in these projects are strikingly different.

Sociocultural and community development. Marcos Brito points out that the Polar Foundation has supported community development in San Joaquin, Carabobo state, for the past ten years. ". . . San Joaquin conserves its traditional architecture and economic structure . . . using the self-research method, certain goals have been obtained: a sociocultural centre and the incorporation into local high school studies of a historical sketch of San Joaquin written by a member of the community."

Professional services to popular sectors. Elisa Jimenez of the Venezuelan Association for Alternative Sex Education (AVESA) explains that the aim of their work is ". . . to give psychosocial, medical, and educational help in the areas of sex education, . . . reproductive health, and sexual violence . . . thus forming an alternate answer for the community. . . ." The interviewee also mentions that "AVESA attempts to continuously renovate . . . members of AVESA maintain an investigative attitude as to updating their theoretical framework."

Community training. José Ramón Llovera of the Mendoza Foundation says it is undertaking "projects . . . to seek actors who can generate social projects, becoming researchers themselves . . . It was not created as a research design but as a work program . . . there is a methodology, context, beneficiary, and concrete proposals made to the community, everything else is subject to change, and the level of action rises to very dynamic programs. . . ." Llovera emphasizes "for example, to take training, and the response is one of impact, such as the granting of credits . . . people may or may not want the credit because they may have generated their own answers or made their enterprise more efficient."

The work of CENDIF (Metropolitan University—Van Leer Foundation) is also community training, operating from an institutional base. Researchers, together with Ministry of Education personnel, seek to establish informal preschool centers in urban *barrios*. For Carlos Leighton, director of CENDIF, emphasis is on action-research-action, with an ethnographic-illuminative approach, an integrated form of participation.

Industrial training. Henry León, contracted by INDASE in 1989, is working on a research-action program in industrial training in the steel industry, aimed at establishing "methodology for training personnel in the context of the mounting and start-up of a special steels plant . . . to supply methodology for optimising quality . . . so that each member sees himself as participant, facilitator, and researcher in the learning and work processes."

The projects and experiences described above, besides showing the role of participatory research in different fields, reflect the aim of consolidation, a self-taught capacity for proposing solutions in the face of social, economic, cultural, and value crises. Such diversity shows change in participatory researchers in Venezuela. We may cite Henry León and José R. Llovera, both informed by the CESAP-CEPAP experience and both education graduates through CEPAP. In the words of Llovera, between 1972 and 1980 ". . . the question was having people participate . . . [it] . . . was mistaken for activism. . . ." Henry León said that industrial training experience: ". . . can begin to open the field for demonstration . . . ideology is necessary in forming movements with social commitment . . . in order to react to the crisis we are living, we need to go beyond ideological currents . . . we are trying to make a real transfer, at least in two micro-enterprises." Lucio Segovia mentions that "I associated [participatory research] with political action. Today I consider it a very versatile concept."

Participatory Research As Developed By Sociocultural Centers, Teams and Grassroots Movements with a Social Base

Popular education. Edgar Martinez defined Fé y Alegria as "a movement of integrated popular education in which the option for the type of research-action-participation is clear and necessary . . . we are striving toward that, even unconsciously, because we work in popular sectors, both for the individual and the collective function of these population strata, positioning our centres in strategic places, forming . . . workforces from the residents . . . heads of families, representatives, teachers, students, directors, nuns . . . it has been a necessity to work with this focus, but it represents a historic moment in the development of the Fé y Alegria reality, if we remember that Fé y Alegria started at a point where 'assistance,' philanthropy, help for the poor, was fundamental . . . a series of characteristics which we now know were limited. At this time of integrated education, it is necessary to join the research-action-participation movement."

Community training and development. This consists of two areas. The first area includes people and institutions that initially proposed participatory research in Venezuela, such as CEPAP, presently reemphasizing from sociopolitical content to a search for practical alternatives to meet the current economic crisis. The interview with Ada Martinez reflects some of these changes.

We always worked on organizational efforts . . . beginning with women's, youth, and literacy programs . . . although we wanted to give organization equal strength, it was a more difficult job . . . we have emphasised courses which contribute to the popular movement and development of civil society . . . we can see how projects are working in the community. Right now, the situation we are living requires more training as to how to improve the quality of life. CESAP's connections with the International Participatory Research Network mean that in 1990 CESAP is able to take part in various forums and events, in addition to a popular support program. The craftsman and micro-businessman will benefit from CESAP's program of Support for Economic Units (AUGE) [Asistencia para Unidades Economicas], reinforcing their work 'by means of courses on costing and accounting . . . backed by small loans to artisans. . . .

The second area includes the Community Learning Centres (CECO-DAP). Fernando Pereira says it

. . . was born as a result of a research action program in El Cipres, a *barrio* in Caracas, within a CEPAP Accreditation Degree Program in Education. They are still linked in guidelines and methodology used . . . CECODAP develops community programs. The aim is to promote organizations in popular communities to train community agents in diagnostic and analytical promotion tasks, recording and interpreting data, execution and evaluation of actions.

Training in the rural environment. From its beginning, CESAP's work has been based on these programs. Coordinated by Roque Cardona, the Acción Campesina program was established to provide rural support and training. The objective of Acción Campesina is the formation of rural promoters and the training of peasants in different spheres, as their needs are identified. With projects scattered geographically, ". . . this implies a quantitative and qualitative growth of the base, signifying needs which now exceed our means . . . we must respond." "Today we are involved in a series of projects which are beyond our capacity . . . [we must] face up to them, because otherwise we would be outside concrete reality. . . ." As in the case of Ada Martinez, a change in emphasis by Acción Campesina is evident.

Sociocultural promotion. This area attracts many action groups, including Churuata, "a team offering professional service in methodology and networking in the country for the past ten years." Its aims are to train various entities in the "methodology of open recording." Hernán Peralta of Churuata states: ". . . Churuata's approach is to explain to people that they know their own reality and to offer methodology which helps uncover and systemise this knowledge. He does not believe in participatory research (they) do not attempt to translate or systemise experiences for the communities and various social sectors. . . ." Churuata was developing programs with children in 1982, promoting crafts as a popular expression involving artisans, sellers, and consumers, and offering a program on 'patrimony and the community.'

All of these are at a national level. Some outstanding points of this first report on the actual state of participatory research include:

1. The projects and experiences are significant in that in addition to showing that participatory research is being developed in various areas, they reflect the purpose of consolidating through different instruments and in varied contexts the capacity to promote solutions in the light of diverse manifestations in the social, economic, cultural, and value crises burdening the country at present.

2. Moreover, this diversity shows 'transition' processes that have been addressed by some of the respondents, Henry León and José R. Llovera, both formed in the CESAP-CEPAP axis and both titled from the Education Program, fully accredited from this last-named institution; they point out that the marked sociopolitical content of participatory research in the first years became a limitation, in the sense that between 1972 and 1980 ". . . the gist was that people participate . . . and nothing happened, participation was confused with activism. . . ."

Henry León stated that industrial training "can begin to open the field of demonstration . . . it's true that ideology is necessary for shaping movements with social ties, but the same ideology is weakening if it restricts honest transference of human resources in any application situation . . . to react to the crisis we live, it is necessary to go beyond ideological currents; this is said in words, but we are trying to make a real transference in at least two micro companies." Lucio Segovia of CEPAP says, "Today I maintain a more heterodox interpretation [of participatory research] compared with earlier years when I associated it strictly with political action." Ramón Pinango, director of the Educational Research Direction (DIE) of the Ministry of Education states, ". . . Research-action tries to influence action and thus to obtain data for better understanding of reality . . . the goal is to increase actor consciousness of the results and unforeseen consequences of action. The researcher and the actor are not always separate, and when they are not, participatory research takes place. . . ."

A last comment on this feeling of 'transition' could be understood with reference to Boris Lima, one of the more constant theorists and communicators of research-action since the 1970s in Venezuela and a speaker at many national and regional forums on participatory research. Today, he is a social projects consultant to Cordiplan (Venezuelan government planning agency) and expressed that ". . . I have not been linked to any practical experience in research-action [participatory] for a long time."

We have abbreviated opinions in this section due to space limitations, however, these are representative of the numerous professionals involved. However, more cooperation is necessary to be able to respond to the needs detected by the respondents through their experiences in this field. In keeping with this premise, interested groups should concentrate their efforts in general importance areas and in those prime areas identified in the course of this study. There are four general areas:

1. lack of communication between promoters and researchers;
2. poor theoretical production in participatory research;
3. social recession and its implications for participatory research; and
4. the necessity for participatory research to confront present problems.

There are three priority areas for attention:

1. Difficulties in systemizing and in making experiences of the public domain. This limitation was pointed out by the majority of the promoters in participatory research—with the exception of the academics and the Churuata group. For example, Inocencia Orellana from the Women's Program of CESAP states that "the problem is the difficulty in systemising the experience: basically time problems and the fact that practice, action, and daily occurrences prevent it. . . ."
2. Preparation for social training. Roque Carmona says that for project promoters to satisfy qualitative and quantitative demands from rural leaders, they should receive more rigorous training that will permit them to go further than the immediate or circumstantial.
3. Systematic experience interchange. Although this was not expressly pointed out by the interviewees, it is an element of common concern among them and has implications for the discussions already established on how to orga-

nize this interchange. All of the respondents have had experience in interchange attempts. Some show less tolerance for repeating the same procedure. It is necessary to reestablish the debate and carry out more consistent endeavors to demonstrate that it is the oral tradition among socioeducational researchers and not journals and documents that guarantees continuity and transcendency in this discourse (Schiefelbein 1981, 371).

It is interesting to note that essentially these areas of concern are the same as those detailed in reports of the participatory network, functioning up to the mid-1980s.

Considerations and Proposals

Central to this study is an approach questioning the potential of participatory research under present social, economic, and political conditions. Potential is the capacity of participatory research to contribute to positive change due to its incorporation into social strategies as a knowledge-generating, formative, and organizational procedure. A historical review with approximate dates shows the following sequence:

- *1973–1980:* Consolidation of interaction among grassroots organizations through networking and too much emphasis on participatory research as a slogan-type solution to problems of relating social science to social action.
- *1981–1985:* Grassroots and popular independent groups. These develop some focus and method elements from participatory research and apply them to the perspective of popular education.
- *1986–1989:* Transition of grassroots organizations to NGOs, a process that includes new alliances based on technical, financial, and intersectorial alliances. There is minimum consensus to reactivate participatory research and lack of a strategy to determine how to reach this goal.

The present effort to reconstruct a history of participatory research in Venezuela is evidence of interest in setting up a basis for further exchanges on these subjects. People who were related to participatory research in the 1970s and now express renewed interest bring to the present debate sufficient organizational and conceptual maturity to reach a functional or operational accord regarding identification of specific participatory research tasks (planning, training, organization, etc.) and how to satisfy these identified needs.

What follows is a series of additional considerations derived from this study, which should be considered:

- Division between those who emphasize practice versus theory can have an evident 'paralyzing' effect on any collective attempt to discuss this research.

- The need for collaborative action in Venezuela is urgent in 1990. Participatory research as a progressively accumulated body supports diverse work styles and attempts to interrelate participatory researchers themselves.
- A tendency lingers to engage in polemics over differences in techniques and methods. These problems were recurrent in the 1980s, when the terms *participatory research* and *action research* were so confused by those who questioned them. Paradoxically, among these are those who actively promote knowledge-creating and organizational processes, essentially participatory in nature.
- A rivalry for institutional territories and available social territories occurs within a spreading NGO modus vivendi.
- Diversity enriches as well as confuses approaches to participatory research. It is a question of extremely different operational bases from the human and financial aspects: universities, private enterprise, popular movements, and grassroots organizations.

Any serious attempt to answer all of the questions posed presupposes a clear delimitation of the reasons why interest should be reactivated in participatory research. What purpose would be served attempting to do what was not accomplished in previous periods?

Since the early 1970s to the present, it has not been possible to evaluate participatory research as it has not been incorporated into any specific, consolidated, and recognized social strategy. The result has been a disparate rehearsal of methods. There has been poor dissemination of the results and little or no discussion on content and evolution, particularly after disbanding the national participatory network. Participatory research can, and should, respond in the 1990s to certain challenges of an organizational and knowledge-creating type. Which social strategy(ies), existing or to be developed, can rectify the imbalances detected over the last two decades between the organizational and research dimensions of participatory research?

Compared to the 1970s, which we believe is a weak link in research and social processes, the 1990s present a different profile—a growing independent sector, with evident capacity to relate to international, official, and private entities, in both research and planning tasks. Venezuela today appears on international financing agency lists; the state withdraws from previous social commitments and, at the same time, private sector groups have appeared in social areas, including elements of popular education strategies. On the other hand, since the international encounter, 'The state and non-government strategies on the family,' which took place in Venezuela in 1988, sponsored by the Ministry of the Family and UNICEF, the independent NGOs, private institutions for development, and promotional organizations have shaped a new, diverse situation where it is possible to include coordinated action. A notable advance is seen at an organizational level. There is NGO coordination in areas such as the child and the family, led by CECODAP; popular education, promoted by Fé y Alegria and the Funación para el Aprendizaje Permanente (FEPAP); popular economy, led by CECODAP; human rights, whose central figure is Provea; and extensive experience in the field of women. In fact, Fé y Alegria, with the backing of IAF and the regional commission of the EEC, has initiated a promoter force in an NGO coordinating entity in the country. Added to this organizational dimension—evidently different from that of the 1970s and 1980s—is the access of these and other organizations to international sources of financial and technical aid. Fé y Alegria has been particularly active in this area, organizing encounters since 1989.

In the 1990s, participatory research seeks to play a dual role as a viable integrating factor for the eclectic contributions of research and as a mediator for socioeducational research in general, capable of producing guidelines for action generated by the experience of that same action, which can serve as 'hypotheses for the future.' To advance in this direction, there are some tasks which must be undertaken by institutes, organizations, and other interested centers. These initiatives should take into account the following necessities:

1. Establish regular channels of communication between independent entities to further ongoing analysis for shared plans and aims.
2. Set up organizational forms which progressively convert socioeducational action centers into research centers, promulgate their status as such, and relate them to other educational research centers.
3. Organize an adequate document support system to counteract the negative effects from the dispersed nature of the production and interpretation of biographical material and other problems relating to the classification of data.
4. Generate a minimal operational consensus on participatory research discourse, contents, modes, and promotional strategies.
5. Support independent initiatives in the design and implementation of alternatives in formal as well as informal educational spheres at local and regional levels.
6. Introduce participatory research into the official sectors plans for educational research for 1990 (National Council for Science and Technology (CONICIT) 1990).

Notes

1. We are grateful to the following people for their important contributions: Marcos Brito, Professor at the School of Education at Andrés Bello Catholic University (UCAB), Caracas; John Elliot, Assistant Director of the Centre for Applied Research in Education (CARE), University of East Anglia, England; Carmen Garcia-Guardilla, Researcher with the Regional Centre for Higher Education in Latin Amer-

ica and the Caribbean (CRESAL-UNESCO), Caracas; Ivan Giradin, Director of North-South Management, Montreal, Quebec; Alberto Gruson, Director of the Social Science Research Centre (CISOR), Caracas; Armando Jansen, Founder of the Centre for Popular Action Services (CESAP), Caracas; Stephen Kemmis, Professor, and Robin McTaggart, Associate Professor, School of Education, Deakin University, Victoria; Maritza Montero, Professor at the School of Psychology, Central University of Venezuela (UCV), Caracas; Jesus Orbegozo, Assistant Director General, Fé y Alegria, Caracas; Ramón Pinango, Academic Director of the Institute for Higher Studies in Administration (IESA), Caracas; Euclides Sanchez, Professor of the Psychology Institute of the Central University of Venezuela (UCV), Caracas; Yolanda Sanguinetti, Professor of the School of Social Work at the Catholic University of Chile, Santiago, Chile; Ernesto Schiefelbein, Regional Office for Latin America and the Caribbean (OREALC-UNESCO), Santiago, Chile; Lucio Segovia, Professor at the Permanent Centre for Learning Experimentation (CESAP), Simón Rodriguez National Experimental University, Caracas; Rafael Strauss, Professor at the School of History, Central University of Venezuela (UCV), Caracas; Antonio Valbuena, Member of the Board of Administration of the Educational Institute of the UNESCO, Hamburg, Germany.

2. The Spanish language report is available from the Instituto de Asesoramiento Educativo (INDASE), Apartado Postal 2477, Caracas 1010 A, Fax: (58-2) 326644; Tel: 261-3666.

3. The term *popular education* is used to denote the feeling of popular action, which is well-associated with the concept of popular power as a social alternative for social justice. (Vio-Grossi et al. 1987), and at the same time it is used to refer to basic education at all popular levels of the educational system (Brofenmayer and Casanova 1987). Although the first connotation is both formal and nonformal, the second only applies to formal education.

4. Interview with Marcos Brito, Polar Foundation (July 1989), and information provided by Maria Josefina Gonzalez, founder and ex-director of CIADEC.

5. This subject requires a special study. In very general terms, we may group these thoughts which have served to stimulate this area in the following manner: Freire-Freinet-Illich in Latin America; Acker-Knowles-Kidd in the United States; Zavala-Garcia-Bora in South America; Dearden-Hurst-Peters in the United Kingdom, and others. Also necessary is a follow-through of the discourse so the general panorama of the process will not be lost.

6. The Zavala method constitutes a methodological synthesis, a variant of participatory research, developed in Colombia by the mathematician German Zavala and his brother, Manuel Zavala, a social worker who lived in the city of Barquisimeto, Venezuela, where he was highly involved with the cooperative movement in Lara State. An active exponent of this method was the ex-priest from Bogota Rene Garcia Lizarralde, who directed a seminar-workshop on research-action in the CEPAP-UNESR between October and November 1977. For more information on the Zavala method, see Borls Lima: *Contribution to the methodology of social work*, UCV, 1977,

and Manuel Zavala, *Method without methodology*, ECRO, Buenos Aires, 1974, and tapes made of the seminar-workshop, in the Information and Documentary Unit (UNIDOC) of CEPAP-UNESR.

7. Anton de Schutter (Mexico); Francisco Vio-Grossi (Chile); Ton Dewit (Peru); and Orlando Fals-Borda (Colombia).

8. L. Pulgar, Director de Redinse, Conferencia Agosto 1989. The four subjects discussed were: medicine (Sinadeb); socioeconomic (Redinse); agriculture (Rediagro); and engineering and architecture (Redinara). Only the first two groups were still working in 1990.

9. Lucio Segovia Interview, June 1989.

10. Given that these promoters are also farmers, Carmona noted that it was difficult for them to reconcile activities in productive seasons with the academic requirements necessary to obtain a certificate from CESAP. (Interview in June 1989.)

11. As a reference, the Sixth Meeting of Militant Research in Valencia, Carabobo, Venezuela, in October 1989, used "The intellectual's commitment" as their central theme.

12. The author defines "poor families" in three categories: extreme poverty, in which total family income does not buy the basic necessities, such as daily food; critical poverty, in which total family income covers the daily diet, but does not satisfy other basic necessities; and poor families, whose total family income covers only the minimum necessities.

13. Cesta Basica. This concept covers both food and other basic necessities. This constitutes, along with other estimates related to basic services, an indicator used to quantify income and to classify a population within the aforementioned poverty categories.

14. Data supplied by Enrique Rodriguez in a course on design and social program evaluation, Venezuelan Planning Institute (IVEPLAN), Caracas, Venezuela, November 1989.

15. Suggested recommendations from the specialists of Third World countries who attended the reunion of the Southern Commission, Ateneo de Caracas, Caracas, Venezuela, November 1989. Taped on cassettes (INDASE).

16. Presidential Commission to Confront Poverty, February 1989. An interinstitutional organizational plan that requires various sectors to:

1. designate policies and programs destined to face the accelerated increase in poverty levels;
2. form and consolidate an effective 'social network'; and
3. stimulate and fortify participation of civil self-improvement programs, as the established Socio-Cultural Participation Programme, Ministry of p.8, February 1990, Caracas, Venezuela. There is no sufficient information or results to report about this plan at this point.

17. Workshop on 'Labor Elasticity,' Latin American Institute for Social Research, Friedrich Ebert Foundation, Caracas, Venezuela, January 1990.

18. *El Universal* newspaper, Section I, p. 30, May 19, 1990.

19. Santiago Martinez in the Inaugural Address of the Annual Reunion of the Latin American Association of Promotion Organizations (ALOP), Caracas, Venezuela, May 1990. Rajesh Tandon, coordinator of the National Participatory Research Network of India, used the term *GONGO* in a conversation held with John Dinan in 1982 in New Delhi, India.

20. An example of this is the Presidential Commission Report on the National Education Project (COPEN), presented to Dr Jaime Lusinchi, ex-president of the Republic. (Caracas, Venezuela, 1986.)

21. Mendoza Foundation, part of a corporation involved in diverse manufacturing businesses, in which at present a training program for small businesses located in the *barrios* of Caracas is in progress. Bigott Foundation, an affiliate of the British-American Tobacco Corporation, contracted INDASE in 1989 to design and apply a rural training program.

22. The Centre for Social Science Research (CISOR) prepared a publication to commemorate twenty-five years of foundation in 1991. This publication includes information on current projects in the participatory and action research fields, social management, facilitation processes, and teaching projects.

23. Gianotten and Dewit say, "the actual problem with participatory research, in our opinion, is in the 'upwards orientation'; that is to say, we are entering a discussion which endeavours to satisfy academic styles and obtain a theoretical recognition, while the strength of participatory research should be in social practice."

24. *El Nacional* newspaper, Section C, p. 1, 31 July 1990.

25. *El Universal* newspaper, Section I, p. 5, 17 July 1990. *El Nacional* newspaper, Section C, p. 2, 27 July 1990.

26. This interesting document emphasizes the original bases of participatory research, within the limits of the 'deviations' generated by these bases. In this sense, the piece of work falls within the boundaries of 'what is' and 'what is not' participatory action research.

27. Of the nineteen interviewees Julio Valdez arld Lucio Segovia cited as their conceptual sources CEAAL, Fals-Borda, Paulo Freire, Ivan Illich, the Zavala Group, Andres Blackwell, and Rene Garcia. Edgar Martinez, Mariano Herrera, and Fernando Pereira spoke of Fals-Borda, Pedro Demo, and Paulo Freire. Inocencia Orellana, Ada Martinez, José Ramon Lovera, and Roque Carmona attributed CEAAL as their source.

As well as the authors listed, Marcos Brito mentioned Alain Touraine, Lebret, and K. Lewin. Edgar Martinez cited Mario Kaplun (specialist and author in the popular communications field) and Mariano Herrera mentioned K. Lewin and the School of Action Research in Chicago, Illinois, U.S.A.

28. In Section 1.3 of this study, reference is made to the fact that the representatives of practically all local organizations and social movements in the country have been through CESAP. In the same way, it can be said that the methodology used by the majority of participatory research practitioners in Venezuela is related to the CESAP-CEPAP sphere of influence.

References

Adams, F., and S. Mannero. 1989. *Policies and prospects for adult education*. In *Congreso nacional de educacion*, 126. Caracas, Venezuela.

Albornoz, O. 1987. *The state and the disposition and effects of educational policies*. Inaugural speech at the Regional Reunion of the Social Research Association (AIS), Caracas, Venezuela. November.

Bolivar, R. C., and J. R. Marrero. 1989. *Fundamentacion de la educacion de adultos*. In *Congreso nacional de educacion* 14–48. Caracas, Venezuela.

Brofenmayer, G., and R. Casanova. 1987. Culture, popular education, and the future of Venezuelan society. In *Venezuela toward the year 2000: Challenges and options*, Editorial *Nueva Sociedad*, Caracas, Venezuela: ILDIS.

Brunner, J. 1985. *Some considerations on educational research in Latin America*. Report prepared for IDRC, Toronto, Ontario. Also in *Planiuc*, Year IV, 8:84–85, Carabobo, Venezuela: Carabobo University.

Carmona, R. 1977. *Anotacion sobre la difusion de investigacion educativa* (A note on the diffusion of educational research). Mimeo. Toronto, Ontario: Research Review & Advisor Group.

Cartaya, V. 1989. Poverty and the informal economy: Coincidence or causality. Paper presented at a symposium in 1989 by IESA. Caracas, Venezuela.

Casanova, R., and G. Brofenmayer. 1987. Education, state, and society: Apropos privatization. Paper presented at the Regional Reunion of the Social Research Association (AIS), November. Caracas, Venezuela.

Casanova, R., and C. Garcia Guadilla. 1990. Research and educational challenges in Venezuelan society in the 90s. March. Mimeo. Caracas, Venezuela: CENDES/ UCV/ CRESALC/ UNESCO.

Cordiplan 1990. *The great turn: Lineaments for the 8th plan for the nation*. Jan. 106–10, Caracas, Venezuela.

Dinan, J. et al. 1978. (Methodological Aspects of the Academic Process of the Accreditation Programme for Learning through Experience)—Aspectos metodológicos referentes al proceso académico del programa de acreditación del aprendizaje por experiencia. Mimeo. CEPAP-UNESR, Caracas, Venezuela.

Droogleever, F. E., and P. J. Oud. 1977. *Reflexiones sobre el funcionamiento del sistema educativo en Venezuela.* Publicacion no. 31 del Proyecto de Investigacion Estrategia de Desarrollo. Amsterdam: Los Recursos Humanos como Factor Catalizador, Instituto Sociologia Aplicada, Universidad de Amsterdam.

Fonseca, L. 1982. Emancipatory Action Research and Transforming Popular Conscience. Mimeo. March. Caracas, Venezuela: School of Social Studies of the UCV.

Garcia, H. 1987. Formacion profesional en Venezuela: Puntos de vista sobre su conceptualizacion y practica. In Editorial, *Nueva Sociedad*, 163–202. Caracas, Venezuela: ILDIS.

Garcia Guadilla, C. 1986. La investigacion socio-educativa en Venezuela. In La educacion, revista interamericana de desarrollo educativo, no. 99, 85–104. Caracas, Venezuela.

Gianotten, V., and T. Dewit. 1982. Participatory research orientation toward practice: The role of the organic intellectual. Mimeo.

Graham, R. 1990. Government on probation. *The financial times*, Section III, 7, February 21.

Latapi, P. 1981. The effectiveness of educational research. *Prospect* (UNESCO), *11*(3):311.

———. 1985. Expectations for adult education in the light of Latin American poverty. In *La educacion: Inter-American magazine for educational development*, 97.

León, H. et al. 1981. (Minimum Common Methodological Factors for Elaborating Learning Projects)—Mínimos comunes metodológicos en la elaboración de proyectos de aprendizaje. Mimeo. CEPAP-UNESR, Caracas, Venezuela.

Lima, B. 1988. The categories which give action research a profile. VI Seminar: New methodological alternatives in the social science and policies. May. Caracas, Venezuela: CEAP/ UCV-CLASCO,

López, Maya, M. 1986. Conformacion del estado y sistema politico (1958–1985). In *Poder dominacion: Perspectivas antropologicas*, ed. Villa Aguilera, 166–183. Caracas, Venezuela: URSHSLAC, El Colegio de Mexico.

Marrero, J. R. 1977. *Consideraciones acerca de los liceos nocturnos, el parasistema, y el CRAT de ciudad Guayana.* Caracas, Venezuela: Colegio de de Venezuela, no. l, Profesores.

Martinez, A., and J. Dinan. 1983. *Conocimiento y acción popular: Proyecto de investigacion participativa en la experiencia Venezolana, 1980–1983.* Mimeo. Caracas, Venezuela: COVE.P.

Ministry of Education 1980. *Fundamentacion legal del programa de educacion media para adultos*. Caracas, Venezuela: Enero.

Montero, M. 1984. *Proceso de la cultura en Venezuela, I, II, III*. Caracas, Venezuela: Curso de Formacion Socio-Política 31. Centro Gumilla.

National Council for Science and Technology (CONICIT). 1990. *Third national plan of science and technology*. Preliminary document, July. Caracas, Venezuela: CONICIT.

Navarro Torres, C. 1982. *Una vision de la educacion de adultos*. Caracas, Venezuela: Ministerio de Educacion, Direccion de Educacion de Adultos.

OCEI (Central Office of Statistics and Information) 1989. *Statistical summary of Venezuela, population calculations during the last 15 years, 1986–1989*. Caracas, Venezuela: OCEI.

Parra, R. et al. (n.d.) *La educacion popular en la America Latina*. Buenos Aires, Argentina: Kapelusz, UNESCO-Cepal-Pnud.

Piñango, R. 1987. Towards a sociology of transformation of the Venezuelan educational system. Paper presented at the Regional Reunion of the Social Research Association (AIS), November. Caracas, Venezuela.

Rodriguez, E. 1989. Design and evaluation of social programmes. Caracas: Venezuelan Planning Institute (IVEPLAN).

Schiefelbein, E. 1981. Research Trends in Latin Seminar 1980. *Prospect* (UNESCO), 11(3):371.

———. 1982. *Educational networks in Latin America: Their role in the production, diffusion, and use of educational knowledge*. Ottawa, Quebec: IDRC.

Segovia, L. 1989. *Investigacion participativa: Practica clientifica o quehacer politico?* Caracas, Venezuela: UCV, Fases.

Segovia, L., and M. Santiago. 1980. La investigacion en la educacion. *Cuadernos de educacion 74 y 75*, 5–40. Caracas, Venezuela: Laboratorio Educativo.

Silva Michelena, H. 1987. El estado, la crisis y muletas para la afliccion. In *Economia y ciencias sociales*, 26, Abril–Junio, 146–9.

Sonntag, H. R. 1986. Venezuela, An uncertain future. *Nueva sociedad*, August, 10–15. Caracas, Venezuela.

———. 1988. Doubt/ certainty/ crisis: The evolution of the social sciences in Latin America. Editorial *Nueva Sociedad*. Caracas, Venezuela.

Tapia G., et al. 1981. *Condicionantes socio-economicos de los programas de educacion de adultos en Venezuela*. Caracas, Venezuela: FUNDACOMUN & ICAE.

Uribe, G., and E. Lander. 1988. Acción social, efectividad simbolica y nuevos ambitos de lo politico en Venezuela. In Imagenes desconocidas: La modernidad en la encrucijada postmoderna, 223, CLACS0.

Vilda, C. 1984. *Proceso de la cultura en Venezuela, I, II, III.* Caracas, Venezuela: Curso de Formacion Socio-Política 31. Centro Gumilla.

Vio-Grossi, F. et al. 1987. *Participatory research and rural practice: New concepts in education and local development.* Santiago, Chile: CEAAL.

CHAPTER 9

A Background to Action Research in Spain

Maria Saez Brezmes

This article is centered on the work I have undertaken in educative research projects over the last ten years, during which time I was also a professor of biology at the School of Education at the University of Valladolid. I should say, as an autobiographical point, that my background in the field of biochemistry, during which time I took my first steps as a researcher while doing my doctoral thesis, trained me in the experimental scientific method in the 'best' positivist tradition. My work in teacher training encouraged me to look for a methodology that would allow me to face the problems inherent in teacher training in a scientific way, and later to face the problems that affect the educational system and, indeed, the whole field of education with a more global and political perspective. I tried to discard the experimental scientific approach derived from the field of psychology and applied as the educational approach, which, at that time, was and still is the dominant educational research method in our university. This led me, on the one hand, to consider the nature of education as a social science and, on the other hand, to question the type of research that our social system demanded in the precise political moment, given the character of public service that a nationally financed research program should have.

It was these considerations that without doubt made me opt for a type of methodology that for the time being can be called action research and that, later, will be defined with greater detail, to begin to clarify the panorama where this kind of work is being developed. However, what really made me decide to begin working on this project was its applied character and the possibility of having some kind of influence on educational reality, therefore on society at a time of large-scale political change. I am talking about the beginning of the 1980s, when the democratic preamble began to take place in my country, at the hands of a so-called socialist party. However, I believe that this article should deal with the 'participatory type of research' that is being undertaken in Spain. A short, historical summary of our political context is necessary to make the article accessible, basically because I understand that the word *participation* is by nature a political term, independent of the substantive entity that it qualifies, whether it be, for example, research, teaching, or organization.

Later, I will develop the idea of what can be considered participatory research, how it was born, and how it has been developed in my country, so that finally I can discuss the characteristics of current action research and the difficulties and consequences that the instigation of this kind of research is causing.

The Political Context

The end of the 1970s in Spain meant the end of a dictatorship and the beginning of a period of political change during which a new constitution was drawn up. This new constitution defines the Spanish state as a group of Autonomous Communities, some of which possess a clearly defined cultural and historical identity that had been repressed during the years of dictatorship, as is the case of the languages of communities such as Galicia, the Basque Country, and Catalonia. However, this political and administrative decentralization has been established as a gradual process and in this way the three above-mentioned communities and a few others have achieved a certain degree of autonomy through their rapid ability for decision making. Others, in spite of having local governments designated through an electoral system, have not reached the same level of autonomy as the above-mentioned communities. This is the shape of the national reality with some of the characteristics of a federal state, and it causes a series of tensions, which up to this day still have not been resolved between local governments and the central government, especially when the local governments and the central government are of a different political standpoint.

As a result of the democratization process, the political isolation to which our country had been subjected began to disappear and a new transitional phase began, one of integration into the international institutions and, more particularly, into the European community.

One can speak at great length about the characteristics of the social situation before the beginning of the democratization process, but there are three aspects that fundamentally interest me:

1. the absence of socially representative organizations of a professional type;
2. the absence of dialogue between the institutions and civil society; and
3. the lack of credibility in the institutions.

The consequences of this state of affairs can still be appreciated and manifests itself as individual intolerance in the face of alternative positions and opinions: a very small capacity for maneuvering to create a more participatory atmosphere on the part of the institutions beyond a simple vote in the elections, as well as a certain incapacity in many social groups to outline their opinions coherently and to argue and defend them. In a situation of such social disorganization, the religious organizations (Catholic in majority) supplied the social basis to a political regime by way of a leadership system that little-favored participation or autonomous and independent thinking. Other political organizations that acted clandestinely also were based on the leadership system with a certain connotation of being on a 'mission,' which was justified as necessary to attain a political impact with a reduced number of militants in an adverse situation. These organizations, with their hierarchical and not very participatory internal structures, also created an endless number of problems among the actors with a greater degree of autonomous thinking because of the lack of 'participation.' It is possible to conclude from this that participation, the way people belonged to different social groups, and their understanding personal autonomy, were not characteristics given by the different ideological focal points in the organizations and institutions for a long time. That was the political situation when the democratization and administrative decentralization period started.

Let us now look at its effect on the educational system. The decentralization process affects education insofar as the country is divided into two zones; those that belong to a territory where there is educational decision making and those that continue to depend on a central government, which we will call zones of 'territorio MEC.' This has required the definition of the affairs that are of a national ambit and those of a local responsibility that appear numbered in the OCDE Report on Education in Spain (OCDE 1986). The national affairs include the following:

- school certificates and professional qualifications
- basic rules safeguarding the fundamental rights in education
- general organization of the education system, including duration of compulsory schooling, regulation of levels, specialization, the length of the courses taken at each level, and the requirements for higher education, and the minimum content in the curriculum and the authorization of textbooks for the different levels
- minimum requirements regarding the teacher qualification, pupil-teacher ratios, resources, and facilities in the schools
- Upholding the right and obligation of all people to learn Castellano.

The issues in which the responsibility is shared with the Local Authority are:

- research in education
- improving the standard of teaching
- correspondence courses
- the interchange of information to make a general plan of availability of resources

The Central Government maintains a body of High Inspectors to ensure that the general rules are observed.

However, and in spite of the autonomy which some communities possess (those in which the control comes from the same political party as the government), the initiatives that are adopted are fairly similar. Having said this, in the communities in which the control comes from the opposition parties, the initiatives also are very similar, which leads to a blanket uniformity. In spite of the alternatives adopted by the Central Government, they can be considered as having the greatest impact in terms of innovation compared to those of the Autonomous Communities, which are governed by the opposition parties.

The democratization of the system was undertaken as a reform project that affects the entire educational system insofar as laws are passed with the intention of reorganizing not only university education but also primary and secondary education and vocational studies. These laws define education as obligatory and free until the age of sixteen and are centered around the new approach of the curriculum, teacher training, and the characteristics of research which the educational system requires as contributions toward the change. Assuming that an educational reform is a social change and, as with every change it has three stages of development, invention, diffusion, and consequences, ultimately it is the result of communication. How this communication system is established indicates the dimension of the innovation and the degree of participation of the different sectors involved in the educational system, particularly that of the teachers. Taking into consideration that the action research which has been developed is circumscribed to the field of education, let us analyze the nature of the reform that is being undertaken in that part of the system.

The Reform

The reform was undertaken through an 'experimental stage' in which the new ideas are developed concurrently with the beginning of the implementation. This experimental phase is being developed with the intention of evaluating the errors and difficulties arising from the implementation. The experimental phase could be used to highlight the errors that are made when the change is introduced, without providing a means of identifying and confronting the situational constraints and without attempting to understand the values, experiences, and ideas of those people who are essential when implementing any change. As Fullan (1982) stresses, the central practical question is how best to plan for and cope with change in settings that are not now successful. This takes us into the vicissitudes of the theory of change and contingency theory in which improvement, rather than resolution, is the name of the game.

If we look at the documents and blueprints edited by the MEC 'Vida Escolar' (229–30) regarding curriculum innovation, we can see that they begin with a brief diagnosis of the educational situation at that moment and focus on the main aspects to be changed. The 'schooling failure' is analyzed in depth and the areas where the situation must be corrected are explained at length.

In the first general elections, the manifesto presented by the socialists included the necessity for broad educational change. I suppose that political change of such dimensions always implies educational change. I would like to emphasize how they resolved the problems of the experimental phase implementation and dealt with the widespread feeling among teachers, who were organized into professional associations during the late franquismo period. The most influential association and the one with the highest level of membership is called the 'Renewal Movement Pedagogy.' It had the explicit goal of renewing the pedagogical approaches and strategies in the classroom. Their principal leaders became the policy makers in curriculum development in various ministerial departments when the socialists won the election.

At certain levels, the originators of the innovation were the teachers themselves. This meant the 'receivers' were the teachers, but the formulation of the problem was carried out by the developer, who also undertook the institutional process of change. However, in this case, the developer has the following peculiarity: the 'need for change' of the receivers, as they used to call it, was focused on and identified collaboratively with the more politically active teachers during the dictatorship. In this context, the initiative was taken by the developers who were university professors in their majority. In that sense, the process was given the receiver's perspective in terms of identifying the main areas of concern, although in the end a theory of change exists in formulating specific approaches to improve schooling, using the research findings and practice-based knowledge about what leads to success and failure. To be effective, the innovation theory must concentrate on those factors that define the situation and should be altered. The big difference that I see between research, development, and diffusion (RD&D) and Problem Solving (PS) of Havelock's model is that in the RD&D the receiver-population is dealt with as a nonactive population and only the developer (in a wide sense) is the one who is sensitive to the problematic situation and the need for change. This is certainly the case in Spain. But we need to take into consideration that some

of the receivers are actively involved in finding a way to solve their own problems and that that perspective is more coherent with the PS model.

At present, the receivers of the experimental phase are teachers and are
spread around the domain of the MEC and represent the different types of
schools. This experimental phase will last about three or four years and, in my
opinion, is another important peculiarity of the Spanish model, which could
contribute to the innovation theory because the receivers are still working on
the background process of drawing up the curriculum that will be diffused in
the near future.

The current relationship between sender (policy makers) and receiver
(primary and secondary school teachers involved in the experimental phase)
is one of collaboration, however, this group of teachers is not the real receiver.
The relationship with the real receiver will probably be closer to the RD&D
model, in terms of passivity.

It is therefore possible to exclude the Social Interaction (SI) model at
the starting point of the innovation. It seems to be closer to the RD&D model,
with exceptions such as the fact that, up to the present, it is developing the
communication network rather than preparing packaged solutions. We should,
however, bear in mind that we are dealing with false receivers, because I am
talking about a period in which general diffusion has not yet started.

Reform teachers represent a relatively small cohesive group who share
a common interest in educational change. Participation in the reform is costly
in time and commitment. They are volunteers and are perhaps representative
of the demography and range of educational institutions in Spain, but they are
not representative of the teaching profession. Non-reform teachers, the majority of the profession, appear untouched by the experiment. To this extent, the
reform could be seen as an enclave of activists within the educational system.
What appears to be missing from the innovation strategy is a concern for the
long-term development of in-service training: a strategy for wholesale professional development. Diffusion of innovation is a dominant model for the
transformation of societies, according to which novelty moves out from one
or more points to permeate the society as a whole (Schön 1981).

The effectiveness of a center-periphery system, argues Schön, depends,
among other things, on the level of resources at the center, the number of
points at the periphery, the length of the spokes through which diffusion takes
place, and the energy required to gain a new adoption.

The scope also depends on the system's capacity for generating and
managing feedback. Because the process of diffusion is regulated by the center, its effectiveness depends on the ways in which the information flows back
to the center.

Simple systems of this kind are prone to failure, says Schön, through
resource exhaustion, overload, and mismanagement. Failure takes the form of

simple ineffectiveness in diffusion, distortion of the message, or disintegration of the system as a whole.

Barry MacDonald and Rob Walker (1976a, b) underlined Schön's idea:

> The model of the proliferation of centres makes of the primary centre a trainer of trainers. The central message includes not only the content of the innovation to be diffused, but a pre-established method for its diffusion. The primary centre now specialises in training, deployment, support, monitoring, and management.

Stenhouse maintained that "a central problem in the improvement of education is the gap between accepted policy and practice." Such a formulation would not, however, seem to deal with the main point of Schon's book, that the notion of 'accepted policy' implies a degree of stability that has ceased to be functional in our society.

The identification of the diffusion model has an additional difficulty in this particular case for those considering the analysis of the innovation theory, due to the fact that the experimental phase has not yet been finished, the previous center being the Ministry of Education. The situation could be a variant of the center-periphery model, presumably close to the proliferation of the centers model, but with a higher degree of and therefore a lesser degree of professionality.

The Central Government has created Teacher Centers in its territory, which would be considered secondary centers in Schön's classification. Taking this point of view, the primary center would be the MEC, because it is the engaging organization in the training of trainers and is the same ministerial department to which the Teacher Centers belong. But as a primary center, the MEC has a lack of organization because the relationship with the other departments involved in curriculum innovation is quite weak, due to a lack of personnel resources and facilities.

The Network

The number of centers that establish links between the developer and the periphery and the kind of relationship established between them frame the diffusion. As Barry McDonald pointed out, "Diffusion was not only a model of change; it was also a model for change, a blueprint for the future."

It might be interesting to know how much of the budget has been and will be spent on creating the Teacher Centers and on people and a network devoted to reinforcing the communication between the MEC and the pilot schools. This surely plays an important part in the situation.

We could assume that the Teacher Centers could be the 'secondary centers' engaged in the diffusion of the innovation, because at present they support the administration network of reform. The elections do not guarantee an easy relationship between the Central Government and the Teacher Centers, therefore the role the Teacher Centers will play in what will be the dissemination process will not occur as a result of the initial experimental phase and is uncertain. To a certain extent, the government-funded Teacher Center effort reflects an assumed necessity to build centers where teachers and developers can reach agreements to facilitate the diffusion of the innovation.

This suggests that at the heart of the Reform is the Teacher Center and the coordinator of the Teacher Center. It is the coordinator who is in a position to provide feedback and marshall and distil the experience of the innovation. Looked at in this way, the coordinator is both the facilitator and the evaluator. This suggests that the co-ordinator of the Teacher Center currently plays an intermediary role and in-service courses appear to be used as much to gather intelligence about the Reform as they are to provide support and advice. However, the Teacher Center faces a number of serious problems in providing support for the Reform. First, there is a distinct lack of appropriate curriculum and in-service expertise. Second, there is no tradition and little experience of facilitation and team-based action research from which they can draw. Third, their management committees are too small making them vulnerable to administrative and political attack. Fourth, they are short of resources, particularly given the scale of their tasks and responsibilities. Finally, they are to a large degree dependent on the good will and commitment of teachers using the facility.

There also is a dilemma at the heart of the Reform, and it is the following. On the one hand, the transition from a dictatorship to a democracy is based on political tolerance which, in education, is expressed as a commitment to professional pluralism. On the other hand, for the Reform to be successful it must address directly the authoritarian and hierarchical nature of the education service—it must address the inherited culture of teaching and administrative control.

In fact, the problem of the Reform is to deal with institutional change. The rhetoric is systemic, structural, national, and wholesale; the reality of the Reform is parochial and classroom-focused. The Reform as an experience that is lived appears to have little purchase on the Reform as an expression of national educational purpose. This is more than a problem of linkage or coordination. It is a strategic and political problem, a problem of lack of consensus and purpose, representing tensions between administrative control and teacher control, central specification and local experimentation, the theoretical knowledge of the university and the practical knowledge of the teachers. What is apparently lacking from the innovation strategy is the idea of whole school development, the unit of change being the school rather than the classroom.

Taken at face value, the Reform represents an opportunity for using the experience of innovation to help prepare a new legal and administrative framework for education. As seen by the teachers, the Reform is, however, as much about how they teach as what they teach. Is it a reform of the relationships between teacher and learner? How, then, is this to take root? How does pedagogical change become institutionalized?

The Reform consists of modest school-based initiatives shared with Reform colleagues through the agency of the Teacher Center. This may be sufficient to produce an organic regeneration process of change that slowly spreads and develops a momentum of its own. But it seems that this is not part of the plan. Like the previous administration, the Socialists have their eyes on the central direction of education. The Reform, as it is seen at the Teacher Center, is an intimate process of exchange. The intimacy is part of the character of the innovation and is necessary for its survival. But the intimacy does not seem to extend beyond the boundaries of the Teacher Center or the school, or if it does, it happens because of political ties. As the experience of the Reform teachers is translated into diagnosis and central prescription, the intimacy will no doubt be replaced by more bureaucratic forms of communication, and the impetus for innovation will change from profession and persuasion to administrative compliance.

Action research has in some ways come to play a vital role as the methodology for teacher development and classroom-focused curriculum change. Yet there is no tradition of action research, and at face value only a rudimentary understanding of its theory and practice. This represents a serious problem for the Teacher Center and one that makes it vulnerable, as they are trying to facilitate something which they themselves have yet to grasp.

The new curriculum reflects at least some of the problems of the former curriculum in terms of antiquated content, which are the consequences of the 'closed' and self-sufficient university. At the moment, since the last intake of new lecturers in the university, competence is increasing but the lack of confidence remains.

In the documents published by the MEC (1990, *Libro blanco de la reforma*) it is clear that the curriculum will be centralized and there will be a compulsory minimum content. The curriculum experimented with in pilot schools will only be approved if 85 percent of the pupils achieve good results. This argument is for lowering the 'school failure rate,' described in the document as the percentage of students who do not get the schooling certificate. One of the social consequences of this policy among intellectual social groups is the rejection of the innovation because it does not preserve the 'quality' of education. Such disputes over the curriculum usually indicate disagreement over the mechanism and pace of change and a misunderstanding of the goals and the meaning of compulsory education.

Unlike the United Kingdom and United States, in Spain there are no institutions or private foundations that sponsor curriculum initiatives. Only the MEC and the local authorities promote curriculum development, providing the schools and Teacher Centers with new resources and giving financial support to teams of teachers who are working on programs of a limited scope.

The universities do not participate by advising the policy makers on the design of their programs, nor in developing specific projects in collaboration with primary and secondary schools, as the traditional isolation of the universities would suggest. If we look at the last forty years, the relations between university departments (pedagogic studies, schools of education, and research institutes of education) and schools have never established permanent and effective links. In most cases, the relations are formal, bureaucratic, and of limited relevance in terms of curriculum development.

Creativity, critical reflection, and the development of the students' personality, as well as flexibility, participative pluralism, and democratization are regarded as important goals. All of these are of great relevance in a political time when authoritarianism is still unfortunately present in everyone's attitude. The intention is to promote psychological analysis of the teaching and learning process as a tool for innovation.

The Origin

Up until the beginning of the political democratization period in Spain, pedagogy was hidden away in the universities. Until that moment, the prevailing pedagogy was the 'property' of the academic world, of the faculties of pedagogy who produced studies completely disconnected from practical education, and of no influence on the educative reality of the schools.

On the other hand, the schools of education, who trained the teachers initially, became part of the university due to the Educational Reform of the 1970s. At no time did they have sufficient academic prestige to represent a different pedagogical style to that of the pedagogy faculties, who ignored and even now continue to ignore their existence. These schools of education have worked, since their creation, with experimental plans that have never been definitively approved; this has led to uncertainty and restrictions for those who have wanted to apply their work in a certain direction and has also served as an excuse for many others. At the moment, one can see a varied panorama in the relations that these schools have with the primary and secondary schools, where they send students during their initial training period 'to do practicals.' In this way, in some cases, the disconnection of the teachers with the public schools is total; in other cases, the students do their 'practicals' during their three years of study, and the university teachers not only act as tutors for these practicals but also participate in the teaching within the public schools. This is the main reason why research into educational practices has not been developed fluently, even though it is the place where theory and practice naturally meet.

The research institutes of education, also created by the Educational Reform during the 1970s, did not in fact amount to an 'alternative' pedagogy. This was because, except in some very well-known and honorable exceptions that prove the rule, they worked in such a bureaucratic way that they got no further than being traditional courses given by academics for teachers. They served fundamentally for the obtaining of titles with a view to improving the personal curriculum of the participants. The publications produced by these organisms were of an extremely heterogeneous quality as far as education was concerned; in most cases they could not be considered curriculum materials and, in many cases, had nothing to do with it at all. In this way, in spite of their programatic declaration, they never managed to develop research applied to the classrooms nor research applied to the improvement of the quality of education or have any influence on the educational system.

The creation of teacher centers by the same ministerial department coincided with its first seminar on action research and evaluation, which was given by members of CARE, the Center for Applied Research in Education at the University of East Anglia. The intention was that of helping teachers grouped in permanent seminars to develop projects in which educational problems raised in the classrooms were analyzed. In this way, the teachers were to be implicated in the curricular change and improvement of the quality of education. In fact, several seminars have been developed and have taken place in public schools. These involved previous consultation of the members of the meetings and those who volunteered for the experience, allowing the participants into the classrooms as observers and helpers in their reflective practices, helping them diagnose the problems in their classrooms, thus preparing the way for joint research between helpers (observers) and teachers in this type of project.

Only the practical courses seem to awaken the interest, validity, and utility of the process focusing the problem of the study on concrete subjects in the classroom or center.

If we analyze the questions of the participants in the course, in their task as helpers in the discussions and debates that take place, many of them are directed toward ensuring that their performances in the seminary have a theoretical support, which they find hard to pin down because of the nature of the course itself, which is fundamentally practical, and because of the deductive approach that is used. It is the team who, with their experience, provides in the course the necessary security and confidence to progress to the action stage: this means trying to act without restriction. In fact, an article I wrote with John Elliott, which he gave during the above-mentioned courses, led me to define this process, which was just beginning at that time, in the following way:

> It is the research process based on the teaching practice, by which I mean the teaching that takes place in the schools, where the themes are taken from which in turn are the object of the research, which we hope to contribute to educational theory. We start from a situation in which theory and practice unite. We work on projects in groups where the teacher is a researcher of his own teaching he reflects on it, using criticism as an instrument for the analysis of the action, and he speculates on the development of the process.

However, it is being seriously impeded by a series of tendencies that threaten this way of going about the problems of educational research, in that they characterize the forms of distribution and power relations and give a certain softening idiosyncrasy to the changes and steps that educational reform requires. Apart from the reproductive character of the social stratification through the educational system and the structural inertia with respect to technological changes, cultures, and values, emphasized by numerous social studies, one must add to this a series of traits, still dominant, which are distinctive to the Spanish educational system. They are not, however, exclusive of this, and we can group them under the denomination 'syndromes' because of their persistent and deep-rooted character tending toward the pathological: academicism and aprofessionalism.

The academicist syndrome refers to the theoretical tradition and the formal research of our university institutions that have caused psychology and pedagogy to become impregnated with a cryptic rhetoric, based on theory-bibliographic research and on the dominant scientific presuppositions about the positivist paradigm. If we add this to the rivalry that exists between knowledge and disciplines in the field of research, a consequence in turn of the corporative individualism against the promotion of multidisciplinary and teamwork, we are left with a panorama which, although open to change, impedes as a whole those applied research initiatives focused on social reality that try to have an effect on the practice formulating alternative explanations to the problems posed.

The absence of professionalism, or, what in effect is the same, the lack of professional culture, is fruit of the functionarization of our system, based on the emulation that dominates both the administrative and educational fields. The civil servant as understood as an overpaid heteronome and definitive of the system at the service of the state enters in contradiction with the professional, provides a public service, and is considered autonomous, responsible for his decisions, and open to criticism in his field. The prevailing aprofessionalism causes great imbalance and arbitrariness in terms of professional development, credibility, valuation of acquired experience, neglect of responsibilities, assignation of resources, and so on.

The syndromes mentioned here play a part in slowing down this type of project and in setting the guidelines as to where the initiatives should be directed, which in a field of such a short period of development means they are developed in a risky fashion, not short of tensions. The action-research in our country has created a professional space for itself which can be understood as being applied, but which has to pivot between the political-institutional demand and the demands of the classroom, between its academic credibility and its practical utility, and between its curricular development and its social impact. Ultimately, the tension of the evaluatory function will be between being a committed promoter of change or being part of the prevailing academicism.

ANTEC: An Action Research Project

At the same time as the action research in which it is fundamentally involved, the ANTEC project is based on the hypothesis that curricular development is inseparable from professional development, which is to say that it adopts the position of 'the teacher as the researcher,' which parts from the explication of practical knowledge based on the accumulated experience of the teacher. We understand professional development as the process by which teachers stop acting as a mere career functionary under the orders of the ministerial decisions to become 'autonomous' independent planners in their own right: autocritical judges of their own acts who value their own experiences and those of their colleagues collectively and who think that their professionality is something that is developed during the direct contact they maintain with the practices they carry out, according to the amount they reflect on, plan, and account for their actions, not only to their superiors but also to other interested audiences, such as the parents.

However and in spite of the fact that the rhetoric that is being used is the discourse of action-research, which creates a certain atmosphere, the numeric explosion, the civil servant system, and the homogenization of the political and social situations of the teachers, on top of the approaches in their actualization and recycling, go against this idea of a professional. All of this is reflected in a certain insecurity when going about their profession, above all in moments of innovation, to which is added a devalued social valuation.

In the case we are talking about, professionality is developed in proportion to the extent that the teachers inscribed in the ANTEC assume certain qualities attributed to what, according to the literature, is the wide concept of a professional:

- to consider their work within the most extensive context of the school, the community, and the society
- to participate in an extensive series of professional activities, such as conferences, writing communications, etc.
- to be concerned about linking theory and practice
- to establish some sort of theoretical compromise with the curriculum

The participation in ANTEC during the 1989–1990 course has made the teachers clearly assume the first two qualities, while the following, relative to link practice and theory, are duties that the project plans to develop during its implementation. Without a doubt, the participating teachers possess an at least intuitive and implicit commitment and possibly in the process of change, some kind of theory about teaching and learning. However, what is worth pointing out is the collective effort of the teachers and the rest of the ANTEC team, making the principles and procedures that define the teaching learning strategies that are being implemented emerge, whether through the use of the 'Guide of analysis,' or the new technology resources influence, or through group dynamics, which biology group work follows.

The 'Guides of analysis' provided to help readers have caused a conceptual rejection and have promoted reflection in the attitude and comprehension of the teachers of the project in which they are involved. Its open nature has helped it become accepted as essentially an orientating rather than prescriptive document.

> In this perspective, the point of inflection is the ability that the teachers put into play when gathering personal professional knowledge, as well as their attitude towards choosing which type of action is required in a given case. The ability to discern is largely dependent on an in-depth knowledge of the situation and the knowledge acquired from the experience gathered in similar situations. So, the fundamental tool necessary for achieving practical knowledge is the degree that the teachers reach.

Reflection as a means of achieving change and professional development for the teachers has been characterized in ANTEC's first year by a series of traits that have been inferred from the above-mentioned issues:

- First, it is generally a shared reflection made public (group work, the teachers' documentation, meetings, etc.), which is undoubtedly the fruit of the teamwork which was applied.
- The said reflection is initially stimulated externally, whether because of the 'Guides of analysis,' or because of the presence of a university coordinator and their questions and suggestions, or because the project institutionally requires them to account for their actions.

- When the reflection processes started, they focused fundamentally on the contents of the curriculum, and at the same time they show a concern for the assessment of the learning process and the performance of the students, using the analysis guide and, for the answers of the students, the use of video as a transmitter of knowledge, problems with the selection and sequencing of concepts, and the formulation of the first hypothesis about the work by relating the teaching time with the level of comprehension acquired while using video, etc.).
- The reasoning, however, on which the reflection is founded still has a limited level of inference; by that I mean that the relationship between the evidence and the conclusions drawn are still in an early stage of argumentation, by being based on a more intuitive rather than systematic analysis (statements in the conclusions of the teachers, weak conceptualization of the function of the video, and the curriculum, etc.).
- Last, and in contrast with the above, judgment of a comparative nature is given (between classes, students, teachers, ways of using the video, the importance of memory and comprehension, and so on) which, in the long run, will enable the maturation of the explicative arguments on which these judgments have been founded.
- Ultimately all of this enables the teachers, as I see it, to start reflecting on the teaching strategies they use, and at the same time building up a single curricular culture. It also helps them express the relationships between their teaching practices and theories about education.

In the case that I have talked about, it is more than doubtful that one can make strong claims about the action research, up until now anyway. This is so if a strict criterion of action research is taken. For example, in the sense used by McTaggart (1989), action research is a participative job capable of developing an understanding that changes the teachers' actions in those situations that concern them personally and signify an important landmark in their lives. These teachers can be said to be moving in that direction.

However, the idea of the teacher as a researcher and the idea of action/ research are being introduced in seminars that are given as teacher training courses, organized by the teacher centers and by the Ministry itself, and these, in my opinion, give rise to fundamental problems. First, the problem of explaining 'what both these concepts really are' is posed: this undoubtedly makes it harder to understand the significance in the historical context where they arise and hinder any classroom research. Second, these seminars generate a rejection, which we can see is due to the degree of institutionalization.

This type of program is not, of course, the way to promote work of this kind, at least in the near future, and probably never. It appears to be the logical consequence of the institutionalization, because it does not come from the recognition of the teacher's 'right' but 'the way' that the MEC thinks the anxiously awaited change should come.

Looked at in this way, the example of ANTEC, assuming that we can call it participatory research, has a deep problem from the institutional point of view—its capacity for diffusion. It is a slow process and requires a lot of people for a reduced number of teachers. It will be difficult to ensure stability without establishing a network to back up the diffusers and allow the connection of another nature, which is not permanent personal contact. However, it is also true to say that the network has already been set up, and it would be enough to establish a system of communication and prepare the advisers of the teacher centers for this task, who are in part prepared to undertake the job.

References

Fullan, M. 1982. *The meaning of educational change.* Columbia University, New York: Teachers College Press.

MacDonald, B., and R. Walker. 1976a. *Changing the curriculum.* Milton Keynes, UK: Open Books.

————. 1976b. *The intransigent curriculum and the technocratic error.* Norwich: CARE.

McTaggart, R. 1989. Action research for Aboriginal pedagogy: Beyond 'both ways' education. Invited paper to the Symposium on Action Research in Higher Education, Brisbane, Queensland.

MEC. 1990. *Libro blanco de la reforma.* 6 vols. N.p.: Servicio Publicaciones MEC.

OCDE 1986. *Education in Spain.* N. p.: CIDE. MEC.

Schön, D.A. 1981. A review of the federal role in curriculum development 1950–1980. *Educational evaluation and policy analysis* 3(5):55–61.

CHAPTER 10

Sources of a Theory for Action Research in the United States

William H. Schubert and Ann Lopez-Schubert

Introduction

Our work with teachers for the past fifteen years and our earlier ten years of work as teachers convinces us that many teachers want to reflect seriously and carefully on what they do and why they do it. Extensive interviews with teachers (Schubert et al., 1990; Schubert 1991; Schubert and Ayers 1992) convince us that good teachers entered teaching with at least an implicit desire to engage in inquiry that would help them understand what children and youth could become. Our study of curriculum history in the United States indicates considerable connection between this interest of teachers and a progressive interpretation of action research (with its roots in Dewey 1916b, 1929; Lewin 1948; Corey 1953).

Nevertheless, such inquiry or action research by teachers that raises a host of critical questions by teachers about what children and youth might be and become is often thwarted by larger political constraints. For example, the current educational reform effort characterized by an emphasis on basic skills, higher scores on achievement tests, prespecified guidelines from state departments of education, and state mandated accountability measures is in some ways reminiscent of the post-Sputnik reform movement of the late 1950s and 1960s. While post-Sputnik reform fearfully responded to the perceived need for military, technological, and political competition with the Russians, today's apprehension is triggered by a perceived need for economic competitiveness with Japan and sophisticated technologies from Western Europe. In both cases, the question of what children and youth might be and become is taken from the hands of teachers and controlled by powers ('experts') who hold economic and political capital. Educational researchers, also intent on pursuing sources of funding often are handmaidens to those who promote the economic interests of the day. Such interests diminish teachers' natural desire to reflect on what students might be and become. Teachers' purposes and their experientially derived knowledge are diminished by researchers who delegitimate their capacity to do all but implement prespecified curricula and administer tests.

Our experience as teachers, teacher educators, and curriculum theorists causes us to conclude that teachers in the United States want to keep alive a spirit of theorizing about their work and lives with students. However, external demands on their work make such theorizing (what we feel is the essence of a progressive interpretation of action research) more problematic than when we were teachers. Clearly, there is a great danger of political, economic, and research interests 'killing of the spirit' of education as historian Page Smith (1990) brilliantly warns. We contend that the best hope for revival of teachers' desire to reflect critically on and with students lies in a renewal of a progressive form of action research.

In an attempt to respond defensibly to our hope for renewal of a progressive theory and practice of action research, we turned first to our experience as teachers, second to our work as teacher educators, third to curriculum history, and fourth to the formative role of teachers in what might be called teacher-developed theory.

Sources in Personal Teaching Experience

Introspectively, we asked: During our ten years of public school teaching were we ever engaged in action research? Our initial response was to think about formal involvement in projects labeled *action research*. Our answer to this was *no*. If we thought about the question informally, however, our answer was *yes*, that we were engaged in subtle but nonetheless valuable ways. A prime motivator for our choice to be involved in teaching was to think seriously about the question: What kind of knowledge and experiences should children and youth have if they are to grow well and lead good lives? The vagueness of such terms as *grow well*, *good lives*, and even *knowledge* and *experiences* leads inevitably into the deepest recesses of philosophy. To seek to give such terms meaning in our interaction with the lives of students is one of the most fundamental forms of inquiry we have ever experienced. Clearly, such questioning was a salient part of our lives as teachers; at a deep level it made those lives more worthwhile. If this is not action research, then action research bypasses the essence of inquiry inspired by the act of teaching.

For many teachers, however, this significant depth of inquiry is missed, too often we fear, precisely because teachers are directly and indirectly told by the research community that they are followers, or implementors at best. Researchers thus deskill teachers by delegitimating a quest for purpose and meaning in their work by undermining their confidence. Let us consider the profound character of teacher reflection that can evolve if teachers are not deskilled, that is they are enabled to respond critically to their lives with students. To teach seriously is to continuously ask oneself fundamental questions about what one is doing and why one is doing it. To address the Spencerian question (Spencer 1861) of what knowledge is of the most worth is to invoke philosophical questions that parallel perennial categories of philosophical inquiry. Let us briefly reflect on a sampling of these questions.

Metaphysics. To teach something implies an interpretation of it, a conception of reality that probes natural phenomena and beyond as well. What kind of orientations to the world, what conceptions of it, best serve the students we teach? Should we be content to take for granted the passing on of subject matter distilled for classroom distribution when that knowledge itself is highly problematic and continuously changing?

Ontology. What does it mean to be or to exist in the world? How does one come to grips with the essence of oneself and the world? How should one pursue the quest for fundamental principles? Such questions, it seems to us, are the ground of education, and therefore necessary to the reflection of those who teach.

Epistemology. What is the nature of knowledge and the knowing process? No question seems more central to curriculum and teaching than this. How can one presume to teach if one has not addressed the relative value of alternative epistemological bases, such as experience, authority, science, revelation, intuition, and the like?

Axiology. What is valuable? Nearly every curriculum and teaching decision is couched in the usually taken-for-granted assumption that certain kinds of experience or knowledge are valuable. To what extent is the valuable reflected by desire as contrasted with notions of what ought to be desirable?

Ethics. What is goodness? What does it mean to be good, to treat others with goodness, to lead a good life? How do knowledge and experience deemed worthwhile contribute to a better quality of life? If that is not their purpose, what is the benefit of knowledge and experience advocated through curriculum?

Politics. What sociopolitical arrangements promote a life worth leading? What kind of life is promoted by current sociopolitical arrangements? Given the current arrangements (especially those embedded in schooling), is it possible to provide curricula and teaching that contribute to worthwhile living? In other words, do schools as institutions constitute public spaces where educators and students can ask: What is worthwhile knowledge and experience? What can be done to diminish the structural effects of dominant value systems that prevent the search for meaning by teachers and students alike?

Aesthetics. What kinds of patterns can I perceive in my life as an educator? In the lives of my students? How can I develop the connoisseurship to distinguish beauty in such patterns (i.e. the critical capacity to appreciate educative experience when it occurs and the basis to help it occur)?

Logic. What is defensible reason? What forms of induction, deduction, and dialectic can legitimately be used to justify what I do as a teacher and what I ask my students to do?

These are samples of the kinds of overarching questions that interpenetrated our lives as teachers. It was evident to us that our lives as teachers were interwoven with our lives as human beings, and that reflective teaching went hand-in-hand with reflectiveness about our personal living. To address the kinds of philosophical questions raised earlier requires teachers who thoughtfully study their own work, what they are doing and the environment of the students' lives with which they intertwine; this means sometimes collecting data, setting it aside, or bracketing it for reflective purposes, and theorizing about it—often engaging students in such theorizing.

Thus, the most meaningful image of action research derived from our teaching is a continuous, conscious attempt to seek increased meaning and direction in our lives with students, and in our own personal lives. It is difficult to conceive of a theory for such a broad notion of action research, especially a conventional prescriptive or descriptive theory. A single, positivistic theory represents a superficial notion of action research that would do injustice to the complex calling that is teaching.

Is there any kind of theory that can capture or contribute to the act of teacher reflectivity? To some extent, the perennial philosophical topics noted above might be considered tenets of a theory of action research. However, they would not serve in that capacity primarily as a means to acquire or accept the answers provided by noted philosophers or schools of philosophic thought; instead, they serve as signposts on life's journey that stimulate a broad array of questions to be asked and pondered. They are most useful when seen as heuristic devices. Despite the usefulness of this heuristic, however, our lives as teachers with students brought a kind of theory that runs deeper within us than can be conveyed by a cataloguing of perennial philosophic questions. Teaching, like parenting, is a process of helping others and ourselves become better oriented to the world. Reflection on what is meant by 'better oriented,' we now conclude, was an *organizing center* (to use the curriculum term developed by Virgil Herrick, 1965) that enabled us to have a job (teaching) and simultaneously continue to pursue our self-education. Ultimately, it turned out not to be as self-centered as this; helping others grow and self-development became mutually desirable. Without realizing it at the time, our choice to teach elementary school students enabled us to remain generalists in pursuit of a liberal education instead of specialists who would be required to 'divide the seamless coat of learning'—to use Whitehead's elegant phrase (1929).

Had we been asked as teachers to write or discuss the theory that guided our teaching, we may have tried to explicate it, but we would have believed it to be an impossible task. The theory that guided our reflection as teachers, our theory of action research, is deeply embedded within the repertoire of thoughts, feelings, experiences, images, dreams, hopes, fears, collective unconscious, and whatever else makes up the mind, body, and/or spirit that we are. What is more, this repertoire is always changing. It is as if our organism (or person) itself is a theory of living educationally. Thus, it becomes too unwieldy to manage with descriptive or prescriptive theory. Both are pale and brittle imitations of the organic images needed to guide action research. If there is to be a theory of action research, it resides within the personal constructs of each teacher. Thus, those who want to inspire action research must try to exemplify the process of reflecting on sources of meaning and direction in their own lives as they encourage others to do likewise. Moreover, this is not merely individual work; it requires that the teacher be reflective as a political being, that is, one who engages with other teachers and students to create and continuously recreate an authentic public space. Such a space inspires dialogue that could be initiated in teacher education. Teacher educators should, therefore, be exemplars of reflective action research if they expect teachers to engage in action research.

Sources From Teacher Education

As teacher educators, we find that many teachers attempt to engage in the kind of action research that we discovered as teachers, but they are very reluctant to consider it research or even education because of the aforementioned delegitimation of their work. To counter this, we find ourselves encouraging teachers to ask why they do what they do with students. We encourage them to think about what they might do to improve the quality of educational life with their students.

In our Masters Degree Program in Instructional Leadership, students pursue an internship instead of a formal thesis. The internship involves students in proposing and carrying out a change in their own teaching situation. An option exists for those preparing to be supervisors; these students design projects to enhance supervisory situations. For current purposes, however, let us focus on examples of curriculum improvement projects by teachers. These practical projects, over the past fifteen years, have dealt with a variety of subject areas and types of learning situations. One junior high school teacher observed the discipline problems caused by a number of alienated students and developed a program to regenerate their interest in education by meeting regularly with them at lunch hour, during free periods, and by taking them on weekend excursions. An industrial arts teacher who had significant expertise in stained glass techniques wondered if teachers would treat slow learners in his school differently if the teachers could feel similar difficulty in a learning situation; therefore, he developed a class in which he taught stained glass work to teachers, slow learners, and problem students. The project resulted in more empathic treatment of students by these teachers. A teacher in a school for high-risk, delinquency-prone students saw teachers mired in traditional subject matter and instituted discussion groups in which they could address fundamental questions about the knowledge and experiences most worthwhile to these students. An instructor for a Chicago-based student teaching program for a consortium of colleges from rural areas in neighboring states perceived an emptiness in student experience with urban and global problems. She developed such experiences and designed a conference to generate awareness in these areas. A band director hypothesized that a lack of interest among some of his students might be the result of not knowing much about their lives. He visited the homes of these students and wrote educational criticism (derived from Eisner 1985) about the informal curriculum of their home life; the students' interest generally improved in both band and school. An experienced substitute teacher who had learned the ropes of substituting in a host of very challenging Chicago inner-city schools prepared a book to facilitate the entry and adjustment of less-experienced substitute teachers. Each of these teachers, and others who completed the program, not only developed technical solutions, but engaged in both fundamental reflection about what teachers and students needed and the imaginative consideration of the possibilities and consequences of acting to overcome those needs. Moreover, their inquiries provided evidence, empirical in the broad sense, that was compelling to colleagues, which often led to productive policy changes. Their documented improvements provided more than mere private reflection; they resulted in altered public space. This, we assert, is a form of action research that needs to be more fully recognized.

The conduct of these internship projects strives toward practical inquiry as characterized by Schwab (1970, 1971, 1973, 1983). Teachers focus on a problem or need in their educational situation. They engage in deliberation with an advisor from the university, an adjunct advisor from their school (department chairperson, supervisor, principal, etc.), and fellow graduate students who are pursuing their own internships for three consecutive academic quarters. In contrast to the formal thesis that usually fits Schwab's characterization of *theoretic* inquiry, the internship illustrates *practical* inquiry. The problem source of practical inquiry resides in an actual state of affairs, rather than in an abstract agglomeration in the researcher's mind derived from an array of noncomparable situations. The method of practical inquiry is interaction with problematic phenomena rather than detached induction; and the subject matter derived from practical inquiry is situational insight rather than highly generalized laws of educational behavior. Since searching for the latter is to seek the will-o'-the-wisp, the end of practical inquiry is decision and action rather than knowledge *qua* knowledge, somewhat cynically, *qua* publication (see Schubert 1980b). The teachers draw eclectically upon knowledge acquired in courses and readings; they attempt to apply such knowledge to their problems and needs by matching theories to fit situations, by tailoring theories to fit the needs of situations and by inventing novel solutions to aspects of problems that are unique. To do so they strive to analyze the consequences of classroom commonplaces (teachers, learners, subject matter, and milieu) upon one another.

A reasonable criticism to raise to this position applied as a theory of action research is, what differentiates practical inquiry from mere technical problem solving and infuses within it a sense of meaning and direction? As Connelly (1983) reminds us, one should not read Schwab's practical without realizing that he accepts *eros*, the driving force of life that aspires to goodness, as always associated with truly educative inquiry (Schwab 1954). Schwab's work might well be expanded by integrating critical perspectives with the practice of action research as Carr and Kemmis (1986) set forth, as Kemmis and McTaggart (1988a, b) built upon, and as McTaggart (1991) reconstructed historically.

Unfortunately, a great many who clearly exhibit practical inquiry in their lives with students have learned not to regard that inquiry as an acceptable form of educational research. Research, they have been taught, involves problems abstracted from realities that they encounter, and proceeds by detached pseudoobjective induction must result in highly generalized claims and should be rendered public in a form that resembles research papers. All too often, teachers learn when they return to graduate school that the kind of research (personal reflection and practical problem solving) that gives meaning and direction to their own lives is a lower order of inquiry, unworthy to tread the halls of academe. Why should this be so? Need it be so? Are there alternatives? We suggest that a precedent exists in progressive education literature that recognizes as research the inquiry teachers do as they seek meaning and direction in their lives with students.

Precedent in Progressive Curriculum History

The history of curriculum in the twentieth century (Schubert 1980a, 1982, 1986) can be read as a debate over the character of inquiry that guides education. No one spoke more poignantly to this issue than John Dewey, from both his position as an educational theorist and as an eminent philosopher. It was a Dewey in his thirties who saw the classical curriculum of the turn of the century (supported by William Torrey Harris) and its semiclassical variations (supported by the National Education Association Committees of Ten and Fifteen in the late 1890s) face unrelenting challenges by developmentalists such as G. Stanley Hall, who favored child study, by social meliorists whose goal was exemplified by Lester Frank Ward, who advocated social improvement through education in contrast to Spencer's social Darwinism, and by the application of the empirical survey and business efficiency methods of Joseph Mayer Rice, who called for a carefully monitored and controlled curriculum (Kliebard 1986).

Twenty years later, when emulators of Rice combined with descendants of Wilhelm Wundt (such as E. L. Thorndike, C. H. Judd, and Franklin Bobbit) touted a curriculum built on an interpretation of science that they thought reflected inquiry in natural sciences, it was Dewey who brought a different interpretation of science that spawned the progressive education movement in the United States. These two divergent orientations to curriculum research, and especially the many varieties of each, were archetypical of the *theoretic* vis-à-vis *practical* distinction drawn by Schwab in the 1970s. Practical inquiry heralded by Dewey as instrumental in experiential settings sharply contrasts with the formalized experimental, quasi-experimental, and survey studies promoted by Thorndike, Cattell, Judd, Bobbitt, Charters, and a flock of zealots mesmerized by measurement techniques.

Despite these vast differences, Dewey was mysteriously adopted as a father of both groups. Perhaps some of this mystery can be explained by the need for unity in the still-embryonic curriculum field, which seemed on the brink of disintegration impelled by an overabundance of variety. Concrete realization of this possibility is revealed in the response provided by the Twenty-Sixth Yearbook of the National Society for the Study of Education (Rugg 1927), the result of nearly three years of deliberation. Under the leadership of Harold Rugg, twelve of the most noted and differently oriented curriculum scholars in the United States met to determine if some kind of consensus could be reached. The result was eighteen questions, a composite statement of seventeen pages, a good deal of compromise, and supplementary (minority opinion) statements by each of the participants, comprising 116 pages. Noteworthy, however, is the fact that all of this was followed by twenty-four pages of quotations selected from John Dewey's written statements about curriculum. Despite intense disagreements among one another, the likes of William C. Bagley, Franklin Bobbitt, Frederick Bonser, W. W. Charters, George S. Counts, Stuart Courtis, Ernest Horn, Charles H. Judd, Frederick Kelly, William H. Kilpatrick, Harold Rugg, and George A. Works all contributed to a book that regarded Dewey as an exemplar of curricular thought.

Dewey continued as a recognized paragon of curriculum thought over the years, although the character of theory, practice, and research of those who expressed high esteem for his contributions often blatantly contradicted one another and Dewey. This is in few places more obvious than in Dewey's *Sources of a science of education* (1929), which for over five decades was used as a source of justification for almost any variety of educational research. Despite the claims of formalistic, rule-bound, technical, social behaviorist researchers in education, Dewey clearly sees the essence of educational research in the practical inquiry of teachers. He asserts that "if . . . teachers are mainly channels of reception and transmission, the conclusions of science will be badly deflected and distorted before they get into the minds of pupils . . . this state of affairs is a chief cause for the tendency . . . to convert scientific findings into recipes to be followed" (Dewey 1929, 47). Dewey's general conclusion to the same book is:

> . . . that the sources of educational science are any portions of ascertained knowledge that enter into the heart, head, and hands of educators, and which, by entering in, render the performance of the educational function more enlightened, more humane, more truly educational than it was before. But there is no way to discover what *is* 'more truly educational' except by the continuation of the educational act itself. The discovery is never made; it is always making.' (Dewey 1929, 47)

Here is unmistakably a vision of the teacher continuously pursuing self-education in the course of the act of teaching. We submit that this is a necessary and neglected form of action research, and that the lack of researcher advocacy of these Deweyan ideals of research in practice was due to what Dewey called, "the human desire to be an 'authority' and to control the activities of others" (1929, 47). To understand Dewey as the central force in action research, we must move more broadly to his philosophy of inquiry, wherein lies the link between education and democracy, the individual and the collective.

The appearance of his classic *Logic, the theory of inquiry* in 1938 spurred much criticism as well as praise in philosophical circles, unlike the educational community's response to *The sources of a science of education* nine years earlier. Idealists, realists, and formal logicians looked askance at

Dewey's position that logic is inquiry itself rendered available in theoretic form. In other words, logic is theory about the ways in which people solve problems. It is from this orientation to the meaning of *logic* that Dewey refined and elaborated the five stages in the process of inquiry or problem solving:

1. The experience of an indeterminate situation, that is, disrupted equilibrium between organism and environment;
2. The conversion of the indeterminate situation from a mere dilemma to a problem capable of articulation;
3. The establishment of hypotheses along with broadly anticipated consequences of action upon them;
4. The elaboration and testing of the hypotheses; and
5. The reestablishment of a determinate situation. (Dewey 1910, 1938)

While Dewey's treatment of logic as inquiry embedded in human action is most fully developed in *Logic, the theory of inquiry*, his thought on the matter traces back with remarkable consistency thirty-five years to *Studies in logical theory* (Dewey et al., 1903) and in 1916 to *Essays in experimental logic* (Dewey 1916a). It was in his 1910 book *How we think* that he provided a less technical account of these notions that reached educators. Great enough was the influence of this book on curriculum thought that in a poll of the professors of curriculum, *How we think* was among five of Dewey's works listed as one of the twenty-nine most important curriculum classics (Fraley 1981, 223–5).

Dewey's other major writings on education also point to the inseparable link between democratic action and the method of inquiry. In the *School and society* (1900), Dewey drew upon his laboratory school experience at the University of Chicago to argue that the school must be an embryonic community meaningfully connected with both the lives of individuals who make up the school and the larger society surrounding the school. In *The child and the curriculum* (1902) Dewey set forth his notion of the experimental nature of teaching, which consists of a process of enabling children to engage in dialogue about their interests, probe to deeper and broader human interests that lie below daily caprice, and, finally, perceive the relevance of disciplinary knowledge accumulated by the human race to their own concerns. Dewey often referred to this process as moving from the psychological to the logical.

The connections between society, the individual, and knowledge as bases for the evolution of education and democracy were built more solidly in Dewey's *Democracy and education* (1916b). Here, education is treated as individual inquiry or problem solving enhanced by attention to an interaction with the social milieu in which one is embedded. Educative inquiry attends to the multiplicity of overt and covert consequences of one's decision and action on the context it influences. Since it is impossible for any one person to attend to a full range of consequences, the value of democratic interaction is invoked to illuminate the mutual impact that proposed action might have and actual action has.

This is a job of teachers whose action research is not to establish objectives, control their implementation, and measure the results, but to engage their students in the process of reconstructing meaning and direction. Such teachers see their work as continuous inquiry or research that asks, "What is most worthwhile to do?" But they alone do not ask the question and attempt to answer it, nor do they primarily turn to outside experts. Instead, this question becomes the heart of the curriculum. The curriculum becomes a process of students and teachers engaged together in the continuous refinement of aims, not dry and brittle aims to be written in filed-away curriculum guides, but aims that inform living together and meaning experienced. Of aims or objectives Dewey reminds us that

> education is autonomous and should be free to determine its own ends. Until educators get the independence and courage to insist that educational aims are to be formed as well as executed within the educative process, they will not come to consciousness of their own function. Others will then have no great respect for educators because educators do not respect their own social place and work . . . For education is itself a process of discovering what values are worthwhile and are to be pursued as objectives. To see what is going on and to observe the results of what goes on so as to see their further consequences in the process of growth . . . is the only way in which the value of what takes place can be judged. (Dewey 1929, 74–5)

Here, then, we return to action research as a building of philosophical assumptions or principles that guide one's life. This process occurs in the midst of other lives (those of students) especially for teachers, and therefore must be pursued with others in a democratization of inquiry. Dewey continues:

> Each day of teaching ought to enable a teacher to revise and better in some respect the objectives aimed at in previous work . . . Education is a mode of life, of action. [It] renders those who engage in the act more intelligent, more thoughtful, more aware of what they are about. (Dewey, 1929, p. 75–76)

There is a history of action research that followed Dewey and serves as important footnotes on the characterization he expressed; yet, there are gross misinterpretations in which his proposals were mechanized and debilitated. The well-known Eight-Year Study (Aikin 1942), from 1932–1940, was an attempt by the Progressive Education Association to study and demonstrate the value of progressive education over traditional education. Traditionalists and social behaviorists to this day are reluctant to accept the findings that students from the thirty experimental school systems equaled or exceeded students from traditional high schools on a variety of measures of success in college. Such measures dealt not only with academic performance but social adjustment, self-concept, attitude, leadership, extracurricular activities, self-direction, and the like. Critics, who exemplify a non-Deweyan conception of action research, criticize the lack of uniform prespecified treatment. An operational definition of progressive education would, however, be its own anathema; it would prevent continuous reconstruction of purpose and meaning to meet situational needs. Critics object also to the matched pairs research design, as compared with random sampling techniques that would be used today, on the grounds that it is quite impossible to match students on all influential characteristics. The point that is missed by many critics, however, is that they look for research in the design for comparison of experimental and control groups, while experientialists or progressives see research in the reflective action of teachers who thoughtfully questioned and revised the content of their educative interaction with students. In reflecting on his experience as evaluation director for the Eight-Year Study, Ralph Tyler (1989) recognized teacher reflection during workshops as a fundamental form of curriculum inquiry or research.

Published in 1953, Stephen M. Corey's book *Action research to improve school practices* was influenced by the Eight-Year Study and soon became something of a bible of the action research movement in the United States. It is clear that Corey drew heavily upon Dewey (1910, 1916b, 1929, 1938) and integrated this with the sociopsychological field theory of Kurt Lewin (1948) on the resolution of social conflicts. Interestingly, the first two chapters of Corey's book read like a practitioner-oriented rendition of Schwab's work on practical research twenty years later, but example studies included by Corey move quickly to the technical. They often tend to leave behind the reflectiveness of teachers as a legitimate form of action research. L. Thomas Hopkins (1954) vigorously points out such neglect, calls for a form of research that is one and the same as inquiry that brings growth of self and others, and warns prophetically against mechanizing it.

Action research subsequently made its way into synoptic curriculum books used to orient curriculum workers to the curriculum field in the late 1950s and 1960s, and lost much of its spontaneity and vitality. Those who taught action research in teachers colleges and universities began to encourage teachers to do research projects in their classrooms. They had them do mini-studies using statistical research, sometimes even using sampling techniques that were designed for much larger populations. These professors soon lamented the fact that teachers lacked interest in conducting such research and did not have the methodological sophistication to do sound action research studies. What they failed to realize was that good teachers did research on their students, but it was practical inquiry and did not wear the garb of social behaviorist research papers. With the influx of neo-positivist social science researchers in post-Sputnik curriculum reform of the late 1950s and the 1960s, the idea of thoughtful problem solvers as researchers (i.e. practical inquirers) was dumped on the scrap heap of inert people in education along with 'armchair philosophers.' And it was kept there quite securely during the 1960s and early 1970s, when researchers had to submit quantitative evidence of accountability during the golden age of educational findings. Even educational philosophers and historians often complied with social behaviorist dictates as entire departments of educational foundations metamorphosed into departments of educational policy analysis in efforts to compete for grants in funding initiatives of the 'great society.'

In the past fifteen to twenty years, the spirit of a Deweyan interpretation of action research has been rekindled. The teacher-as-researcher movement in England initiated by Lawrence Stenhouse and others (Stenhouse 1975; May 1982, and Skilbeck 1983) acknowledges serious teacher reflection on their own work as a viable form of research. Other examples are found among the variety of forms of qualitative research and evaluation, such as work patterned after artistic and literary criticism as in cases presented by Eisner (1985) and Willis (1978), as well as forms of responsive evaluation originated by Stake and explicated by Guba and Lincoln (1983).

Autobiographical research by Pinar (1980) and Grumet (1980) illustrates a kind of self-analysis that educators might use for personal growth. A more politically oriented form of action research is emancipatory pedagogy, such as that which transpired in Freire's (1970) dialogic encounters with Brazilian peasants and, more recently, the search for forms of resistance to domination by teachers and students by Giroux (1983), Apple (1986), and Apple and Weis (1983). The essence of this work points beyond the contradiction of acknowledging teachers as knowing subjects but simultaneously treating them as objects of research. Carr and Kemmis (1986) and Kemmis and McTaggart (1988a, b) have helped move action research well along the path of pressing teachers and learners to develop ways to research themselves and their situations.

In such a diverse literature as this, we can still see a central thread: the teacher who becomes more reflective, wide-awake, and interested in questioning the taken-for-granted. We see this too in the work of Max van Manen (1986) and in the journal *Phenomenology and pedagogy* for which he is founding editor. We see it as well in various attempts at collaborative research when collaboration is not just between researchers and school administrators for the purpose of rubber stamping programs, but when it involves researchers, administrators, and teachers in dialogue about the situation of teachers and learners with the assumption that teachers, administrators, students, and researchers can learn.

Toward Teacher-developed Theory

Our work with teachers in pre-service and in-service settings, as well as our review of historical literature of curriculum, reveals a conception of action research that pushes in the direction of educational theory developed in educational settings. While action research, as portrayed in preceding sections of this chapter, points to the goal of teachers who inquire about themselves and one another, so does recent literature about supervision and school improvement. Although space does not permit extensive review of the relevant literature here, we want to note several dimensions of contemporary literature that illustrate the movement toward teacher-developed theory from quite different perspectives.

Stemming from the perspective of Lawrence Stenhouse (Stenhouse 1975; 1980; Rudduck and Hopkins 1985) and others who emphasized 'the teacher as researcher,' a movement started at the University of East Anglia in England in the late 1960s, we stress how Stenhouse and colleagues experimented with a process of putting university colleagues in classrooms to observe and interact with teachers. His hope was to encourage dialogue that made explicit reasons for the activities of teaching and curriculum reconstruction in the course of planning and action. Both teachers and university researchers gained insight from dialogue about assumptions and from the anticipation of consequences intended for and experienced in teaching situations. Teachers became less isolated and more reflective through this process. Moreover, they developed projects such as the Humanities Curriculum Project (Rudduck 1983), a longitudinal study recently compared to the renowned Eight-Year Study (Willis 1988). The major spin-off of the teacher-as-researcher movement for the idea of teacher-developed theory, however, is the rather large-scale organization of teachers who began to engage in peer supervision in emulation of engagement between teachers and university scholars that occurred at the outset of the project. In fact, many such teachers developed a nationwide curriculum study network and initiated a journal called *Curriculum* in 1980. Their conferences and articles reflected a practice-oriented language for the discussion of ideas about school improvement.

A second example of literature intended to foster teacher-developed theory is derived from Joseph Schwab's notions of practical inquiry and eclectic arts (Schwab 1970, 1971). He holds that inquiring practitioners attempt throughout their work lives to develop broadly based repertoires of theories and research studies. Such practitioners-scholars should engage in practical inquiry about specific states of affairs in which they interact, in an attempt to generate situational insights that inform decision and action. As noted earlier, Schwab's practical inquiry proceeds by developing the art of eclectically matching knowledge from theory and research with situations encountered, by tailoring and adapting such knowledge to situations, and by imaginatively inventing responses to practical needs as they arise. Responses to practical needs of school improvement reside in a restoration of balance among the curricular commonplaces: teachers, learner, subject matter, and milieu (Schwab 1973). The context for deliberation about practical problems is what Schwab (1983) calls the curriculum group, that is, representatives of teachers, parents, other community members, and students. Connelly and Clandinin (1990) recently reviewed a wide range of literature that has focused on the 'personal' practical knowledge of teachers.

Closely aligned with Schwab's proposal for intraschool deliberation is the tradition of interinstitutional collaboration that emerged in staff development and school improvement literature under the earlier title of interactive action research (see Griffin 1983 and Lieberman 1986). Models derived from this tradition are based on unique configurations of practitioners and academics who share roles of expertise in the effort to resolve practical problems. The benefits of such efforts are mutual, however, focus on practitioners shows that they become better equipped to reflectively pursue problems on their own.

Although not heavily cited in the above tradition, these practitioners may be said to become reflective in the sense referred to by Schön's use of the term *reflective practitioner* (Schön 1983). Noting the precedent for teaching practitioners in many professions to become more reflective, Schön (1987) further argues that situations can be created to enable practitioners to exercise greater reflectiveness in both planning and in the course of action. Such reflectiveness may be considered an internally directed manifestation of teachers as theorists of their own situations.

This leads to different roles for those whose job description reads 'supervisor.' Recent developments in the work of foremost supervision theorists (e.g., Smyth 1987, 1989; Garman 1987; Sergiovani 1988; Glickman 1988) embody arguments that call for supervisors to decentralize the supervisor role, that is, to make it an ordinary function of being practitioners engaged in monitoring the purposes and consequences of their professional work. This requires that teachers be regarded as intellectuals who, according to Giroux (1983), can critically question such matters as who benefits from knowledge derived from schooling and how it contributes to personal growth and public justice. Such questioning is a necessary and neglected interpretation of action research that democratizes the process of teacher inquiry. It engages teachers and supervisors in what Greene (1988) calls 'the dialectic of freedom,' by making schools public spaces where fundamental curriculum questions are asked about what is worthwhile to know and experience.

Conclusion

The ideals of a Deweyan interpretation of action research are alive in the United States today, but they are not very well. Although we are quite aware of this state of affairs, its power came home to us recently at the conclusion of a doctoral course on curriculum foundations. The students, all mature and seasoned teachers and administrators, were asked to reflect in small groups about their central questions and observations about curriculum as they completed studies for this course. Their central observation dealt with the heavy hand of economic and political forces on their work. They further observed that the pressure to compete in the international market drives the curriculum today more than ever before in their experience. Some could remember living through post-Sputnik curriculum reform as well. They felt they had entered the teaching profession because they wanted to be able to seriously inquire about what it means to introduce next generations of human beings to the world. A sense of purpose drove their desire to be a teacher. Further, they wanted to figure out how to design a means to move toward purposes and to evaluate them. Sadly, they reported a sense of incredible pressure to be deskilled. Purposes were now being given to them by unknown policy makers who barely knew the situation for which the policy was being made, and evaluation was done by testing corporations who provided a test score the equivalent of the dollar, which is the bottom line in the business world.

Admittedly, this is a far cry from the Deweyan emphasis on democratic dialogue among those most deeply embedded in a problem; it is foreign indeed to the ideal of starting with the concerns of learners, viewing those concerns as symbolic of deeper and common human interests and learning to develop knowledge and theoretical perspectives that help to address those interests. Keeping alive the spirit of action research symbolized by Dewey and furthered by others mentioned in this chapter is thus a great challenge. However, hope seems to persist among teachers with whom we work. The drive to 'compose a life,' as Mary Catherine Bateson puts it so well in her recent book (Bateson 1990), is deeply embodied in the process of being human. The essence of action research and curriculum inquiry, in our view, engage the same fundamental human concern: to grow as a person and contribute to the world and to fellow human beings. To contribute evidence for the power of this concern in fashioning a life through education is the great task of action research. The question is how best to call together the strength to demonstrate that something more profound exists in the human spirit than the competitive edge of one nation over another.

References

Aikin, W. 1942. *The story of the Eight-Year Study*. New York: Harper & Bros.

Apple, M. W. 1986. *Education and power*. Boston: Routledge & Kegan Paul.

Apple, M. W., and L. Weis (eds.). 1983. *Ideology and practice in schooling*. Philadelphia: Temple University Press.

Bateson, M. C. 1990. *Composing a life*. New York: Penguin.

Carr, W., and Kemmis, S. 1986. *Becoming critical: Education, knowledge, and action research*. London: Falmer Press.

Connelly, F. M. 1983. Editorial. *Curriculum inquiry* 13(3) Fall:235–8.

Connelly, F. M., and D. J. Clandinin. 1990. Stories of experience and narrative inquiry. *Educational researcher* 19(4):2–14.

Corey, S. M. 1953. *Action research to improve school practices*. New York: Teachers College Press.

Dewey, J. 1900. *The school and society*. Chicago: University of Chicago Press.

———. 1902. *The child and the curriculum*. Chicago: University of Chicago Press.

———. 1910. *How we think*. New York: D. C. Heath.

———. 1916a. *Essays in experimental logic*. Chicago: University of Chicago Press.

———. 1916b. *Democracy and education*. New York: Macmillan.

———. 1929. *Sources of a science of education*. New York: Liveright.

———. 1938. *Logic, the theory of inquiry*. New York: Henry Holt & Co.

Dewey, J. et al. 1903. *Studies in logical theory*. Chicago: University of Chicago Press.

Eisner, E. W. 1985. *The educational imagination*. New York: Macmillan.

Fraley, A. E. 1981. *Schooling and innovation: The rhetoric and the reality*. New York: Tyler Gibson Publishers.

Freire, P. 1970. *Pedagogy of the oppressed*. New York: Herder & Herder.

Garman, N. 1987. The teacher's sacred space. A presentation at the Bergamo Curriculum Conference, October 28, Dayton, Ohio.

Giroux, H. A. 1983. *Theory and resistance in education: A pedagogy for the opposition*. South Hadley, MA: Bergin & Garvey.

Glickman, C. 1988. Supervision as the domain of all: Do we want the revolution? Presentation at the Annual Conference of the Association for Supervision and Curriculum Development, March 12, Boston.

Greene, M. 1988. *The dialectic of freedom*. New York: Teachers College Press.

Griffin, G. A. 1983. *Staff development*. Eighty-second Yearbook of the National Society for the Study of Education. Chicago: University of Chicago Press.

Grumet, M. R. 1980. Autobiography and reconceptualization. *Journal of curriculum theorizing* 2(2):155–8.

Guba, E. G., and Y. S. Lincoln. 1983. *Effective evaluation: Improving the usefulness of evaluation results through responsive and naturalistic approaches*. San Francisco: Jossey-Bass.

Herrick, V. E. 1965. *Strategies of curriculum development*, eds. D. W. Anderson, J. B. Macdonald, and F. B. May. Columbus: Charles E. Merrill.

Hopkins, L. T. 1954. *The emerging self in school and home*. New York: Harper & Bros.

Kemmis, S., and R. McTaggart (eds). 1988a. *The action research planner*. 3rd ed. Geelong, Vic.: Deakin University Press.

———. 1988b. *The action research reader*. 3rd ed. Geelong, Vic.: Deakin University Press.

Kliebard, H. M. 1986. *The struggle for the American curriculum, 1893–1958*. London: Routledge & Kegan Paul.

Lewin, K. 1948. *Resolving social conflicts*. New York: Harper & Bros.

Lieberman, A. (ed.). 1986. *Rethinking school improvement*. New York: Teachers College Press.

May, N. 1982. The teachers-as-research movement in Britain. In *Conceptions of curriculum knowledge: Focus on students and teachers*, W. H. Schubert and A. L. Schubert, 23–30. University Park, PA: College of Education, Pennsylvania State University.

McTaggart, R. 1991. *Action research: A short modern history*. Geelong, Vic.: Deakin University Press.

Pinar, W. F. 1980. Life history and educational experience, *Journal of curriculum theorizing* 2(2):159–212.

Rudduck, J. 1983. *The Humanities Curriculum Project*. London: Heinemann.

Rudduck, J., and D. Hopkins (eds.). 1985. *Research as a basis for teaching: Readings from the work of Lawrence Stenhouse*. London: Falmer Press.

Rugg, H. O. et al. 1927. *The foundations of curriculum-making*. Twenty-sixth year-book of the National Society for the Study of Education (Part 11). Bloomington, Ill.: Public School Publishing Co.

Schön, D. A. 1983. *The reflective practitioner*. New York: Basic Books.

――――. 1987. *Educating the reflective practitioner*. San Francisco: Jossey-Bass.

Schubert, W. H. 1980a. *Curriculum books: The first eighty years*. Lanham, Maryland: University Press of America.

――――. 1980b. Recalibrating educational research: Toward a focus on practice. *Educational researcher* 9(1), January:17–24, 31.

――――. 1982. The return of curriculum inquiry from schooling to education, *Curriculum inquiry* 12(2):221–32.

――――. 1986. Curriculum: Perspective paradigm.and possibility. New York: Macmillan.

――――. 1991. Teacher lore: A basis for understanding praxis. In *The stories lives tell: Narrative and dialogue in educational research and practice*, eds. C. Witherell and N. Noddings. New York: Teachers College Press.

Schubert, W. H., and W. Ayers (eds.). 1992. *Teacher lore: Learning from our own experience*. New York: Longman.

Schubert, W. H., P. L. Hulsebosch, V. M. Jaqla, M. Koerner, C. R. Melnick, and P. S. Millies. 1990. Teacher lore. (Theme issue ed. G. Ponder). *Kappa delta pi record* 26(4):98.

Schwab, J. J. 1954. Eros and education. *Journal of general education* 8:54–71.

――――. 1970. *The practical: A language for curriculum*. Washington, DC: National Education Association.

――――. 1971. The practical: Arts of eclectic, *School Review* 79:493–542.

――――. 1973. The practical 3: Translation into curriculum, *School review* 8:501–22.

――――. 1983. The practical 4: Something for curriculum professors to do. *Curriculum inquiry* 13(3):239–65.

Sergiovani, T. 1988. Empowering teachers through instructional supervision: Reflective supervision—reflective teaching, keys to empowerment. Presentation at the Annual Conference of the Association for Supervision and Curriculum Development, March 13. Boston.

Skilbeck, M. 1983. Lawrence Stenhouse: Research methodology, *British educational research journal* 9(1):1 1–20.

Smith, P. 1990. *Killing the spirit: Higher education in America*. New York: Viking.

Smyth, J. 1987. Towards a critical pedagogy of classroom practice: Some anecdotal evidence from teachers who have transcended their practice. A presentation at the Bergamo Curriculum Conference, October 28. Dayton, Ohio.

———— (ed.). 1989. *Critical perspectives on educational leadership*. London: Falmer Press.

Spencer, H. 1861. What knowledge is of most worth? *Education*. New York: Apple-Century Crofts.

Stenhouse, L. 1975. *Introduction to curriculum research and development*. London: Heinemann.

———— (ed.). 1980. *Curriculum research and development in action*. London: Heinemann.

Tyler, R. W. 1949. *Basic principles of curriculum and instruction*. Chicago: University of Chicago Press.

————. 1989. Reflecting on the Eight-Year Study. In *Curriculum history: Conference proceedings from the Society for the Study of Curriculum History*, ed. C. Kridel, 193–203. Lanham, MD: University Press of America.

van Manen, M. 1982. Edifying theory: Serving the good. *Theory into practice,* guest editor G. McCutcheon, 21(1):44–9.

————. 1986. *The tone of teaching*. London: Heinemann.

Whitehead, A. N. 1929. *The aims of education and other essays*. New York: Macmillan.

Willis, G. 1988. *What the Eight-Year Study and the Humanities Curriculum Project do and do not have in common*. Paper presented at the Annual Meeting of the American Educational Research Association, April 7. New Orleans.

———— (ed.). 1978. *Qualitative evaluation: Concepts and cases in curriculum criticism*. Berkeley: McCutchan.

CHAPTER 11

Integrating Participatory Action Research Tools
in New Caledonia

Jean Delion

Introduction

I worked in the South Pacific from 1974 to 1984. Although I was mainly engaged in agricultural development, my main concern and personal objectives were more in the field of participation and action research. After my first attempt at participatory planning in Vanuatu, I worked in the South Pacific for nine years, mainly in New Caledonia. My interest in participatory action research was strengthened by a few colleagues who were working in the same direction. I also received important support from some political leaders in communities who anticipated some empowerment for their people from their participation in a participatory action research process.

Throughout those nine years in New Caledonia, I felt I had placed myself in a position of conflict. I was supported by my former experiences, training, some practical results at the community level, and reactions when I was training local staff. Still, I felt it was a very uncomfortable position: I could see that our participatory action research efforts were quite isolated, and I had the feeling we would not really influence rural community life in a sustainable, long-term way.

This experience was gained in a small South Pacific country, and I believe there are some useful lessons there about conducting action research on a larger scale. The extremely small size of countries in this region (e.g., there are 150,000 inhabitants in New Caledonia) allows the exploration of a combination of different participatory action research tools, up to the national level, with relatively few people involved. Such experiences would not be possible without huge support in larger countries, and the struggle in New Caledonia shows how difficulties might be amplified in larger populations.

In New Caledonia, participatory action research was used in different fields: agricultural extension, rural credit, agricultural training, regular

223

exchanges on the mass media, and training for field workers in various areas. We had a few links with universities. Like many people fully engaged in action programs for community development, I had no precise strategy to begin with, no blueprint in activating those different levels. More than ten years later, as I am now invited to write about this experience, I realize I was very close to what other people have been trying to do in a much more systematic way, through establishing participatory action research networks.

Our experience might be used to think about developing and improving a participatory action research network in New Caledonia and to give indications about what seem to be major constraints on the creation of appropriate strategies. This brief paper is itself a reflection on past participatory action research efforts and provides a research base for lessons about participatory action research. On the basis of this experience, it can be argued that participatory action research developments are quite easy to establish at the community level in most small countries such as New Caledonia. Even there, national action research efforts are not so easy to put into place. Of course, extrapolations to bigger countries would be delicate.

The entire experience during those years in New Caledonia also places subtle nuances on a common theme: participatory action research can work from small changes and grow through cycles of small improvements. My experience is that this might be a nice lure for people who do not dare to face the political challenges. It *is* true that, under favorable conditions, small efforts can possibly grow upward and outward. But it seems to me that in nearly all developing countries, those favorable conditions are not met. Resistance to participatory action research in communities can be strong, both within the local context and from outside it especially. Under those conditions, we should not advise people that just setting up small changes which will grow will be enough. Larger-scale changes must be thought about from the beginning. If I had been more aware of that, I would have acted differently in New Caledonia, and my ten years of local fights might have been more useful in the long run. I hope the experiences I describe later will prevent dedicated participatory action researchers from being as naive as I was. If they ignore these lessons, in most cases their isolated efforts, like mine, will just bring small results, compared with the rich yield they could have brought if they had worked for deep political support and an institutional participatory action research foundation.

Those foundations rely a lot on links with universities. If I had to start again in the same conditions, I think I would concentrate on establishing permanent links between university and field workers engaged in participatory action research efforts. The wisdom of this general strategy has been confirmed by my later experiences in rural development in Southeast Asia and Central Africa, where I am now working. In most cases, I found there was no reliable link between the necessary dedicated intellectuals in universities and the few field workers who were trying their best in a technocratic environment that did not comprehend the interest of participatory action research.

Contact with universities is not an absolute guarantee of the support necessary for what I consider participatory action research. Even in some supposedly 'action-oriented' participatory action research papers, I have found that research is dominant over action: somebody engaged in participatory action research might be accepted as a 'participant interpreter' (Johnson and Morse 1988, 3). In the experiences described later, I did my best to stay at this level, but I often had to act on participants' requests to influence action. I was a participatory actor in the events of the communities concerned. This is a key feature of participatory action research: you become deeply engaged in the lives of people. That is a very different perspective on the role of a researcher. It is also a very complex role. When participating in community activities, I was engaged in conflicts, and despite my efforts to bring people together, I found I was perceived to be acting *for* some people and against others. From that point of view, I think the experiences described below are quite 'participatory,' but more 'action' than 'research.' Yet I still prefer the same approach I developed fourteen years ago: If I myself am participating in a participatory action research process, I think I really have to act rather than remain an outsider and simply help people prepare their strategies, collect information, and study what is happening to them.

This degree of active engagement is not yet accepted in many universities or even in some writings about participatory action research. I had the opportunity to be invited to the East-West Center in Hawaii in 1987, and I developed some arguments against this 'pure research point of view (Delion 1988). Luckily, I found encouraging support in Hawaii, as my hosts wrote papers insisting on the deep interest of 'the constant oscillation between real world practice and abstract conceptualization to provide meaningful power to any theory that results' (Johnson and Morse 1988, 4).

Context and Objectives

Education and Experience

I worked in the South Pacific from 1974 to 1984: first in Vanuatu as an Assistant Senior Agricultural Extension Officer (1974–1975), then escaping briefly to Africa and returning to work in New Caledonia in 1976 until 1984. In New Caledonia, I was chief of the Cooperatives Division in the Agriculture Service for two years, chief of the Training Division in the same service for one year, then Senior Agriculture Extension Officer in the Loyalty Islands for

one year. After that, I worked for two years as a consultant in close relation
with the local 'development agency,' called ODIL. I finally joined this agency
as chief in its training division, a position that lasted nearly three years.

My educational background was mainly in the discipline of sociology
(Ph.D. from France in the sociology of rural development), but I also had
qualifications in agriculture (especially tropical agricultural engineering) and
postgraduate studies in economics (planning rural development). My studies
in France, mainly in sociology, were influenced by the French experiences of
'Animation Rurale' (IRAM-IRFED),[1] labeled since 1960 as 'participatory
action' (Colin 1978). This approach was quite typical of one major trend of
French sociology, which was highly critical of traditional sociological studies
typically conducted by outside researchers, a trend that emphasized the need
for clear positioning of sociologists as agents of sociopolitical change. In this
new tradition, the 'researchers' should be expected to clarify their own social
objectives and values before interfering with local communities through conducting 'sociological studies'; and those studies should be conducted in a very
participatory way with full results discussed and negotiated with the populations concerned before publication (Meister 1977).

In line with this trend, Animation Rurale put a strong emphasis on the
basic learning process that must happen inside each community. Each community was to study its own circumstances carefully. This became a preliminary step before the community could decide any position regarding rural
development projects. After this step, communities would have a better understanding of their socioeconomic environment, and they could direct and manage the ongoing implementation of decisions they had made for their development.

Practically speaking, Animation Rurale developed a careful participatory action learning methodology with a long sensitization period at the community level. This was systematically used in some rural development projects, literacy projects, and rural education projects. Attention was paid to
training local *animateurs* in each community. Those animateurs then had to
act as 'catalysts of conscientization' prior to any action in rural projects. The
methodology demonstrated a real efficiency in setting up responsible local
organizations in many development projects. Then it developed a lot of precautions for institutional development. Animation Rurale was highly criticized as being too close to politics inside the communities and in their relation with the outside world.

On first acquaintance, Animation Rurale might be viewed as quite close
to the approaches of Paulo Freire. In fact, it was more of an applied methodology of participation and action for people involved in development projects.
It was mainly applied in the field for organizing small farmers' groups, training farmers, cadres, and women's groups, and for designing participatory

action learning processes in rural development projects. It was used in various projects in West and North Africa and in South America. Animation Rurale brought some good results, but it quickly met with strong political resistance and, in a few cases, led to violent clashes. Then, after 1970, it was criticized by many 'technicians' as an 'intellectual and political' approach in agriculture development. Still, the methodology has been growing under various names, joining other trends on 'participatory organization of rural people' (Oakley and Marsden 1984) with an emphasis on institutionalization (Colin 1979). The rationale for Animation Rurale was subsequently reinforced by attention on participatory action research in other parts of the world. In the last ten years, IRAM moved to a more pragmatic approach, as presented in recent publications (Beaudoux and Nieuwkerk 1985 and Gentil 1986).

Objectives

Part of my thesis in sociology was on the Animation Rurale approach in designing a rural education project after two years of sensitization in one division in Senegal. This made me quite conscious of possible political constraints when applying participatory action methodologies. Upon arrival in the South Pacific, my main objective was to then try and introduce participatory action research approaches through my actions as a rural development actor. This objective was quite clear, but I had no blueprint for application in the new context. Before working in New Caledonia, I had worked in Thailand (for a study on rural education), had been an extension officer for two years in the New Hebrides (shortly before it became Vanuatu), and had worked for six months in a World Bank project for rural education in Upper Volta (shortly before it became Burkina Faso). In the New Hebrides, I had tried participatory planning mechanisms. All of these in turn influenced my approach in New Caledonia.

Political and Cultural Context

New Caledonia is a French Territory, ruled by a local parliament under the control of a French High Commissioner for the Territory. During the period I worked there, from 1976 to 1984, there had been growing pressure from the indigenous population (Melanesians, who call themselves Kanaks) for their independence from France. In most cases, the Kanaks live in rural areas or work as unskilled labor in the towns. France refused to allow independence to this Territory, because a majority of the New Caledonian inhabitants voted against it on various occasions. This was because the voters included many 'immigrants,' non-Melanesians who were afraid of a possible control of the Territory by the Kanaks. Those immigrants included around two-thirds of the people who had been there for more than two generations and one-third who were recent immigrants or workers who had been there for just a few years. As long as they were French citizens, they were allowed to settle in the Territory and take part in the local votes. A very active group were the so-called 'White Caledonians,' descendants of French migrants who fought fiercely to remain French citizens.

This was, in my understanding, the core of the political problems. Up until 1981, the centrist and right-wing coalitions in the French Government supported more directly the right-wing party in New Caledonia, with a great majority of recent immigrants, non-Kanaks, against independence. During this phase, working too closely to Kanak people was viewed by all of the non-Kanaks as a very strong political commitment for independence. The 'white people,' suspected of being political activists for independence, were regarded as 'traitors' acting against French interests in the region. On the other hand, many young Kanaks were fighting those 'white people' working in the Kanak villages: many thought the Kanaks had to reject any collaboration with the French public services (including the agricultural services with whom I had affiliation). The Kanaks were quite wary of risks of 'contamination' if Kanak farmers were dragged into the field of loans, technical services, and marketing services.

In this context, my position as a white man trying to help Kanak people was always extremely uncomfortable, and I have always been attacked from both sides. However, major support came from the fact that a preliminary participatory action research process had introduced 'participatory action' in the first development agency (FADIL). This is why I shall speak of 'our efforts.' Many people should be mentioned; behind this collective some have been supporting participatory action research efforts just occasionally, while others have been fighting daily for its development. It would need very detailed research to analyze all of the forces that acted more or less for or against our efforts. Among the people who were directly involved was a trainer from FADIL, a key leader of the major Kanak political party, and a few other Kanak leaders in FADIL and ODIL. Those institutions were mainly concerned with financial supports to rural development projects, primarily toward the Kanak people, but both developed important training and animation components. Other active supporters took part in our participatory action research efforts, coming from the Directorate of Catholic Education (DEC) and Kanak political parties. A few even came from the right-wing party, as they were deeply concerned with bringing responsibility and real control into the Kanaks' hands in their farmers' groups and cooperatives. It would be simplistic to assume the forces for and against participatory action research resided in the traditional left and right political differences. In fact, the political pressures against our efforts mainly came from the local administration, Agricultural Chiefs of Services, and isolated people. As a 'technician,' I was usually rejected violently by the Director of Agriculture of that time, because he was against all "those talks, too close to politics, in a period when technicians should just concentrate on technical matters."

It is important to point out that our efforts took place in the period of a growing pressure from the Kanaks, but before the violence erupted. During this period, in 1981, the political context changed with the election of a French socialist president, bringing a first socialist government. As many Kanaks had voted for the socialists, they were expecting independence would come soon. Important changes came in the Territory, but not independence, because the Socialists were embarrassed by all of the votes against independence.

This was the time when a new Rural Development Agency (ODIL) was launched, together with another agency for land tenure reform in favor of the Kanak people. I then joined ODIL, with a team of motivated Kanak trainers. Some of our efforts are described later. Unfortunately, the conflicts grew and signs of social explosion were clear in 1984. At this time, as the French government came back to the right-wing party, many Kanaks decided that the only way to achieve independence was through armed struggle. I was allowed to interrupt my contract to work for one year with the United Nations (FAO) in Asia. The violence began in New Caledonia just one month after my departure. The French right-wing government followed the local right-wing party that aimed to "clean up the socialist agencies." ODIL, like other agencies, was put under other people's control. When I asked to come back, after one year, I was refused. Since then, many fights have occurred, but a pause has been negotiated for ten years. Meanwhile, most of our participatory action research efforts were abandoned, as will be explained later.

From a cultural point of view, many pages would be needed to describe the compatibilities and incompatibilities of participatory action research in Kanak societies. Basically, I found that Kanak social life is very mindful about tactics of alliances and separations with other people and groups. All Kanak clans are still connected by sophisticated links, coming from ancient times, disjoined and repaired after centuries of disagreements and fights. The cohesiveness of Kanak society is a dazzling puzzle, always changing, and differently interpreted by the Kanaks themselves, according to their positions, strategies, and ambitions. This feature gives a specific advantage to the Kanaks when they are involved inside a participatory action research process. I think they are acutely aware of some empowerment mechanisms made possible through participatory action research. I often regarded myself as part of a chess game: my participatory action research approach, like any other move in Kanak social life, was used by some people to strengthen their positions and was fought by others because it was threatening their positions. It was difficult to tell whether democratic aims were being fulfilled.

Within each community, I formed the impression that the traditional hierarchies and institutional sharing of power had been partly overthrown by new cultural patterns of power. Those patterns came through Christian churches, French democratic ideology, and images from Western ways of life (with individualistic ideology, through films, television, books, and direct cultural contact). Any general appraisal is impossible because the conditions are quite different in the various regions, depending upon former traditional forms of organization and exposure to different outside influences. In those fluctuating contexts, participatory action research approaches were generally welcomed as they fit well with some Christian and democratic values, present in most situations. Still, it was usually hard to have all of the people take part in community meetings. Women and young people were often rejected.

Setting Up An Action Research Association

After a year of fights inside big and bureaucratic cooperatives, I found myself so isolated that I decided, with friends, to try to establish some kind of foundation to support the participatory action research process. A few people involved in agriculture, education, and health were interested in exchanging views about their problems and in conducting research about their experiences. As I was member of a French-Canadian 'open university' (Université Co-operative Internationale, UCI),[2] we founded, mainly with Philippe Missotte, a local Association de Recherche-Action en Sciences Sociales (AREA Sciences Sociales). With around twenty members in the beginning, we began to meet nearly every week. After a few basic explanations of the process, we helped members identify their own research fields in relation to their own professional experience; then we tried to bring our own sociological knowledge to help them formulate and explore their first questions. We exchanged advice about books to read. After a few months, all members had started their own research projects. Each week, we exchanged reports about each member's progress and discussed the many questions each member faced. I started to conduct my research on the ongoing process of establishing such an association with all of the kinds of problems we were meeting and were likely to meet. We were linked with UCI, with 'resource advisers,' in the network, mainly in France and Canada.

A major problem was to obtain some kind of credit for the research work conducted by the members. It would take too long to give all of the details of the dozens of attempts made with Australian, U.S. and French universities to have our research efforts recognized in some way. This is, of course, a common problem in participatory action research experiences, but it is especially difficult in an isolated South Pacific country. On many occasions, we found dedicated support from isolated people. But we never received formal recognition from their institutions. I must mention here that UCI (mainly the chairman, Professor Henri Desroches) tried its best and prepared many requests for us. We were quite stimulated by some University of South Pacific (USP) support. Professor Ron Crocombe tried his best to provide some kind of recognition for our action research projects. But USP bylaws did not allow for the kind of researches we were conducting. We met with strong resistance locally: we prepared detailed documents proving the trainers' qualifications were in agreement with the usual university requirements. We introduced official requests for university credit for trainees who would follow two years of theoretical training and produce a substantial research report. We asked for credit at the bachelor, master, and doctorate levels (according to the initial level of the researchers). We never received any recognition. Because we could not receive a formal credit for the researches conducted, most of our members abandoned the process after two or three years.

Then we found a partial answer: we invited members to look for some recognition of their work within their own professions, and some teachers received credits in the Catholic Education service, some nurses received credits in the local nursing school, and some members became involved in establishing a new rural education network (Maisons Familiales Rurales); this network designed the training for its trainers with a participatory action research phase. After the initial three years, I moved, as did most members, inside those established institutions. AREA finally strengthened participatory action research approaches inside those institutions.

Considering the level of the members of the initial association, the results were quite good. More than half of the members were able to complete their research and receive some credit for it: one, a Ph.D. credit from UCI in Paris, others at the master's level, locally. As the Territory is quite small, some members who improved their qualifications were attracted to higher positions. Then, they influenced their own institutions in including participatory action research approaches for training their staff in their institutions.

Looking at the Territory level, I found it was far too small and felt that my efforts had failed. Up until now, there is still no foundation for most field workers who would like to think acutely about the work they are doing and to have meaningful exchanges with people engaged in the same activities. During the last three years, I tried again to establish a link of this kind, working from inside my own professional situation: I was in charge of training five Kanak colleagues in ODIL. Again, I called on my friend Ron Crocombe in the University of South Pacific in Suva. In this particular case, considering the level of the five trainees, he proposed to arrange a credit for researches conducted in the field of land tenure problems. This work was falling within the requirements of a land tenure course he was running in USP. He assisted us through radio contacts (USP is commonly using satellite communications to link with students all over the Pacific islands). I served as a local tutor, Ron Crocombe provided guidance, and the trainees were able to conduct small research projects on problems of rural development related to land tenure issues. Unfortunately, this experience was interrupted when the ODIL team was dismantled.

Participatory Action Research Efficiency at the Community Level

As chief of the Cooperatives Division in New Caledonia, I was only allowed to work as a traditional technician: all I could do was check the cooperatives accounts, encourage more members to participate, and provide management advice. My few attempts on a deeper level to encourage more participatory approaches met with major obstacles. After a few failures in heavy cooperatives on the East Coast, I understood that I could not directly influence the big cooperatives established by the agriculture department. I then requested permission to go to an isolated community in the extreme north of the mainland, 500 kilometers from Noumea.

In that area, I was challenged by the collapse of a big fishermen's cooperative, Groupement d'Exploitation des Produits de la Mer et de l'Agriculture (GEPMA). In one of the villages concerned, Arama, I found that many fishermen were expressing calls for some kind of continuation of a community activity for marketing their fish. This village is quite isolated in the very far north and is essentially Kanak. I followed the usual Animation Rurale process: over three months, I visited them twice each month and invited them to conduct a deep reflection about the reasons for the GEPMA collapse. I was greatly assisted in all of this work in Arama by my colleague from FADIL, Philippe Missotte. In the beginning, we faced some problems with the local administration: we explained that our intentions were to help in analyzing the situation and potential strategies, but we insisted that we were not fighting for taking over the collapsed GEPMA. We declared we would not mind if they did not want to move into any cooperative action. During those first three months, I spent a lot of time clarifying this position and describing the objectives of the analysis aimed at people working through issues for themselves. Most local leaders were asking questions like, "Could we get grants if we start a new cooperative?"

After three months, the women had been included in our meetings, and we had come up with a basic analysis of the advantages and handicaps of their village from a socioeconomic point of view. The analytical charts had been discussed seriously between my visits, and people were preparing lines of possible actions. Furthermore, I had been accepted as a sincere friend, dedicated to finding some way to clarify their problems. This brought much more genuine discussion. Each meeting was lasting until late at night, and talks were proceeding with the local 'Great Chief' in his house, where I was staying. This leader, André Theinyouen, was a former catechist, dedicated to social development and teaching: he significantly influenced the whole process. We developed an intimate relationship, as the Kanaks know how to do in introducing foreigners into their families, when they so choose. This personal relationship became part of my motivation to proceed in the first hesitant steps. It kept my motivation high when we discovered many difficulties later. Some colleagues told me that the Arama people were manipulating me. I always answered that I loved them, I was happy to drive my old car up there behind the mountains, and I was happy to stay in their old houses near the sea.

After two months, an old man appreciated this personal involvement, and he said:

> We must decide whether we trust him or not. I think we can trust him, because he is the first white man who comes here, stays more than one or two hours, eats our food, and sleeps in our houses.

This was part of the process. I was aware that they had concluded a kind of alliance with me. Of course, I was not at all a neutral catalyst sustaining a pure endogenous role. Nevertheless, I was clearly inside their community life. For example, the mere fact that I was staying in André Theinyouen's home each night when visiting them was heavily influencing the local distribution of leadership. André Theinyouen used our relationship to support his own position, in his own community. Nothing is ever neutral when someone acts from inside a community.

After three months, the discussions started again about how to sell their fish. It took approximately two months before community members agreed on a new strategy: they planned to create a new small cooperative (with their local traditional name) to take over the existing small truck belonging to GEPMA and to go ahead with paying the existing GEPMA loan. But they also asked for two new freezers to produce ice locally for their fishermen. They asked for a big insulated box for carrying their fish to Noumea, the capital, 500 kilometers south, twice a week. Based on those objectives, we started a precise process of planning provisional costs and, accordingly, provisional margins for their small cooperative. This phase looked like the most important one from a participatory action research point of view. We were in the core of researching *Kanak* tools for adequate financial management for the community. My friend Phillippe Missotte and I insisted that all preparatory steps should be written and kept in the cooperative. Most people did not understand French well and some were illiterate. Still, they produced detailed plans of quantities of fish per month, costs of fuel, oil, snacks for drivers, and other needs for each trip. We helped them present those costs in detailed charts, and they established a sophisticated, precise, provisional budget on a big chart.

After a few hesitations, and with the dedicated support from André Theinyouen, everybody finally got involved in the process. Discussions lasted longer than before, and the people really mastered the planning exercise. On this basis, the cooperative decided to run a *kermesse* (a feast, usually on Sunday, where everybody brings something for sale, and the money is used for a special objective) for gathering funds for an initial contribution from the new cooperative. I was requested, as a member, to take part in the feast by bringing my own things for sale. We all went fishing on the eve of the feast. At this time, there was great enthusiasm in the whole community for the new cooperative. The women were especially involved and active in all of the meetings. The feast ran well, and the cooperative was able to gather enough contributions in cash to request the transfer of the former GEPMA truck.

But even then there was another obstacle. Nothing would have happened without the support from FADIL Director Jacques Iekawe. We met with strong resistance from a ruthless financial analyst in FADIL. He was against the ambitious project of taking the truck and advised us to buy a new, much smaller, truck. He increased the amount of the contribution requested for taking over the GEPMA truck. He could not understand our strategy of following the community analysis and plan. I finally decided to counter this outside influence by putting a small amount of my own money in the Arama contribution. Emotionally, it made a big impression on co-op members. It mainly increased their confidence in their ability to perform a detailed plan for the first year:

> If he puts his money in, that means he really believes we can make it!

Again, in a participatory action research approach, action is needed, and action means being fully part of a process. Of course, I was acting as an ally and was far from being a traditional 'catalyst' from outside.

There is not space here for the detailed story of this cooperative, but a summary is possible. After the preliminary work on the planning tools, the research concentrated on developing 'simple' accounting tools. We designed a system that would look quite complex for traditional accountants (many small cash boxes, following the various levels of activities and flows of money). But it was easier to control for members because they had invented it. They could check directly each week if the co-op had lost money on crabs, or whether it had spent too much money on fuel or anything else. The process continued for over two years, with many further improvements brought about by members themselves. At the end, the co-op manager and some members of the coop committee were able to prepare their annual results accounts by themselves and present and explain them to members in the general meetings. The members were able to understand the meaning of the reports and to advise on price adjustments for their fish and crabs.

Like any business, the co-op was faced with many problems. But the local participatory process worked quite well to handle them, and solutions were brought about. Still, the process was not just a problem solving one. The emphasis was kept on learning new tools and mastering new ways to conduct community activities. From this point of view the first annual meeting after one year of work was completed, and it was a great moment. It appeared that the cooperative had been able to achieve around 95 percent of its planned production. I remember it was quite impressive to see on the initial chart, the detailed 'quantities really sold' near the column 'planned quantities.' The total was something like 26.5 tons of fish (against an objective of 27 tons) and 9.2 tons of crabs (against an objective of 9.5 tons). The costs and incomes had been quite close to the provisions and, accordingly, the final balance was close to the initial provision. Modern managers fight hard to achieve such results. In this isolated village, this result amazed most members: "It's incredible, we did it!" This was an essential step in their own confidence in planning and acting in the modern financial world. By the second year, the cooperative knew how to plan and prepared much more quickly precise, yet provisional, budgets. As the people were extremely cautious, they adjusted their provisions around 10 percent down for the second year.

After three years, the cooperative started to break down, mainly because of internal fights. Finally, it proceeded with just a small team of fishermen, mainly from one family. Still, many people had learned from the experience. André Theinyouen bought his own small truck with a loan from a private bank. He developed a small business using his own way of simple accounts, in line with the former co-op tools. He ran annual meetings with his entire family on their business results, and those meetings were open to all of the villagers. In the meetings, he used the same planning charts as in the initial cooperative. He succeeded in demonstrating that local business could be planned and mastered with modern financial tools.

After five years, André Theinyouen resigned as Great Chief, and internal fights went ahead in Arama. Some other community projects started, and failed. Some colleagues accused André Theinyouen of playing his own game against community projects. I got the feeling that the internal disputes were too rough, and that André Theinyouen was slowing down the projects because some basic land tenure problems had not been solved.

For my colleagues who tried to work after me, Arama was just a place like many others, with a lot of disputes. The community had no special motivation, no particular capacities, and did not work much for development. Was it all a failure then? Not really, but it is right to say that the long-term results are quite important.

Setting Up Communication Opportunities for Rural Development Actors

One of my major objectives was to try to link together many rural development actors who could learn from each other's experiences. In Arama, for example, I had the feeling that the local actors had learned something about the way Kanak people could conduct a cooperative project and deal with financial management with all of the members' participating. I found that the results had to be widely spread out, with the actors expressing their own points of view. At this time, the display of some Kanaks' efforts in development was particularly important, as many images about Kanaks in development were negative. That is why I went knocking on the doors of radio and television stations and the press, to find a way to broadcast the results achieved by some people.

Use of Mass Media

A first step was to negotiate running a radio broadcast every week, in the evening. I met supportive people at the local radio station, and I was able to run this broadcast for three years. Later, it was taken over by technicians from the agriculture service, with a more technical point of view. This changed the way I had been presenting it, which had involved interviewing farmers and community leaders about their experiences and about action research findings that could be useful to other village groups. The main local newspaper (*Les Nouvelles Caledoniennes*), although linked with the right-wing political party, followed the radio: it published articles on the people interviewed, with pictures. During the three years, more than 100 people were interviewed. In most cases, we interviewed them in their villages. Most of them were Kanaks, but quite a few were white Caledonians or other recent immigrants. This broadcast became quite popular in the rural areas but also in towns where many people were amazed by the great number and variety of small research efforts being conducted in the villages.

After one year of radio broadcasts, I received support from the local television network. We were able to produce broadcasts once a month, for nearly a year. The local network invested in field trips to bring detailed images of the community processes concerned. Those broadcasts created a big impression all around the small Territory. They were occasions for long discussions in the villages: "Our brothers, down there, can make it, so why are we sleeping here in our village?"

The broadcasts were followed by discussions with the animateurs, described later, and in the Maisons Familiales Rurales, training young people in agriculture. Those good results created more problems with my technical supervisor in the Agriculture Service, as they were embarrassed by all of those spots on the mass media with somebody who was not a 'traditional technician.' They also created sharp reactions among some political extremists. As I was taking part in the interviews on television, my face became well-known, and I received a few insults on the street, calling me an 'independence conspirator.' On the other hand, some Kanak extremists started to spread insults and threats against me, as they thought I was putting the Kanaks in danger of 'contamination' through development projects. Those kinds of problems are quite common in small countries like those in the South Pacific: because there are so few people, anyone who begins to be seen regularly in the mass media is likely to receive negative reactions.

In spite of those problems, I think the use of mass media was extremely positive. André Theinyouen was interviewed on a few occasions on radio and television and in the press. He presented, with his own eagerness and evidence, his deep conviction that the Kanaks could succeed in modern economic activities, working in Kanak ways. He explained in detail how participatory action research and a learning process occurred together with the cooperative experience in Arama. On radio, with a sweet, quiet voice, and on television, with a smiling determination, I think he did a lot to develop new images of positive Kanak development. As André Theinyouen was involved in the traditional hierarchy and as Arama has an important position in the long sequence of the history of Kanak clans, he also acted discretely through traditional channels. He spent many days and nights with small groups in remote villages, or in political Kanak meetings, repeating details about how they had started their cooperative, how they were running it, and how they were evaluating their progress with regular meetings.

The Fair

I also fought for establishing an agricultural fair in the Loyalty Islands. My main aims for this fair were to promote some positive lessons gained by Kanak enterprises. Many groups running development projects were presenting the results of their efforts, and meetings were organized to allow them to exchange and learn from each other. An exhibition of all planned development activities in the Islands also was included, with detailed explanations from the various technical agencies concerned. I confess that, on my last visit to this fair in 1984, I was quite disappointed with the way it had changed. The commercial side had been growing, but the exchanges between groups, the meetings on current development projects in the Islands, and the exhibition of all planned development activities were quite reduced. The lesson was that those participatory action research activities needed support in the long run. If not, they would be easily displaced by other objectives.

Setting Up a Network of Animateurs

In 1982, as I already explained, I joined a new agency for rural development set up with strong support by the French socialist government to try to boost Kanak participation, mainly in rural development. After a few experiences at the community level, like Arama, I thought I had enough arguments from field experience to try to set up an animateurs' network. We discussed the point with many Kanak leaders and with my colleagues in ODIL. The proposal was informally accepted in ODIL. This animateurs' network was part of a global strategy: we established development committees in each municipality (the French 'communes'). Those committees were participatory planning institutions involving technicians and local representatives from the various villages and groups, under the guidance of the mayor of each municipality. The animateurs were supposed to help the village people establish a more responsible relationship with all of the outside technical and financial supports for rural development. They also were to help those village people influence the way they wanted to orient rural development in their areas. With my colleagues in the ODIL training unit, we were able to establish this network in the Territory after one year of hesitant agreements by political leaders. As we had many personal connections with mayors, locally elected in each municipality, and with many people from villages involved in some development projects, we used a wide network to inform people about training those animateurs.

In the second year, we trained the animateurs through local workshops and two meetings of all animateurs. Most animateurs were quite young (between twenty and thirty years old); most were Kanaks (but a few others joined); and most had been appointed by their communities after long talks among the villagers. In the beginning, they were not supposed to be paid. But we had prepared a project on a European Development Fund (EDF) line of assistance for rural training. Under this project, EDF was supposed to pay small allowances to the animateurs, to allow them to move around their villages and visit the technicians. We also planned to receive a small amount of financial support to train and recruit those animateurs. This outside assistance never came into effect, as agricultural services were competing for use of this line of assistance for agricultural training and many people openly attacked the animateurs' network as a political force. During that second year, we had a network of nearly 200 animateurs, covering most of the main villages in the Territory. As the adult population in rural areas was estimated at around 40,000 people, our ratio was around one animateur for 200 adults. This was a very dense network, compared with similar experiences in other parts of the world.

After their initial training, the animateurs quickly spoke out with questions about the essential problem of Kanak identity in relation to the existing assistance to rural development and the risks of contamination of Kanak culture with outside financial supports. This was the aim of our participatory action research approach, but most people did not understand it. Many young animateurs expressed their questions in an aggressive manner, and I was often personally insulted about the risks of contamination. On a few occasions, I was directly attacked by young Kanak extremists who accused me of drawing the Kanaks toward corrupting financial assistance. At the same time, as television broadcast images of all of those young Kanaks gathered in annual meetings, many right-wing political leaders developed fears that this was the beginning of a Kanak army, installed in each village of the Territory.

Still, the network worked quite well for two years, and many people agreed that the process was interesting, as most animateurs were sincerely considering their problems and asking questions of each other. At this stage, experiences such as the Arama one were seriously discussed. On those occasions, I learned a lot about many other people who were experimenting with participatory action research approaches, through education, cooperatives, and inside political parties. Although I had trained animateurs before, I was amazed by the rich experiences among the Kanaks in participatory development, cultural analysis, and participatory action research generally. Most of it was kept private, and most people concerned did not realize the importance of their experiences. An entire book could have arisen from each general meeting of the 200 animateurs. We looked for support for publishing the most interesting experiences. We did not receive immediate answers, but were close to receiving them from the Kanak Cultural Institute and from old partners in our participatory action research approach in Maisons Familiales Rurales and Catholic Education services.

The network did not work long, as all of its organizers were sacked, or firmly put into minor positions after 1984. For many animateurs, it was a brief but positive experience, and it strengthened many hesitant efforts in rural development. It also demonstrated to many observers the rich outcomes of such exchanges, based on people's careful analysis of their experiences. For me, this experience with the animateurs' network was among the most disappointing. The animateurs' network and the municipal development committees were quickly stopped. The whole team assisting the network was dismantled: I had been working hard to train five Kanak colleagues with the University of South Pacific and, later, with the International Cooperative University. Shortly after their training, ODIL was turned into a more technical 'Agency for Agricultural Development (ADRAF),' and I was not allowed to come back and work in it. Most of the animateurs were put into minor positions and the network stopped working. As violence started soon after, I heard that many 'animateurs' had been actively involved in leading the Kanak fights. After a few years, I learned that a few of them were now active political leaders at the municipal or regional level.

Lessons for Participatory Action Research in New Caledonia

Writing this paper is itself part of my own experiential learning process. But all of it is action-oriented. I hope the observations made earlier might be useful to other people engaged in participatory action research efforts, and I would advise them to foresee clearly the limitations of any participatory action research efforts, if not endorsed by some existing political institutions. In too many cases, as in my experience in New Caledonia, efforts are just isolated attempts without much sustainability. Participatory action research efforts do not readily fit inside the local political debates: my objectives were not exactly to support Kanak independence; they were much more general, dealing with villagers' empowerment in their cultural and socioeconomical development. I was not fighting for the Kanaks against others, although most people were turning any question into this simple dispute. As I have already said, I really feel I have been too naive when hoping that my efforts, not fully integrated into the local political strategies, could influence some sustainable experiential learning processes in some communities.

If I had to begin the experience in the same conditions, at the same time, I think I would spend much more time trying to explain my objectives to political leaders, to look for much more support. Aside from this, I think I would not change many of the things I did. I think our information shows that it could easily have worked as it was. We were only missing some appropriate political support, and the experience was hindered by political fights with both 'inside' and 'global' elements. When reflecting on my sixteen-year career in rural development, I think I never came so close to an emerging participatory action research process at so many levels of intervention as I did with such a dense network of animateurs. We came close to transforming a lot of things in most villages, with active participation of women, old, and young people.

Although I feel we failed in many ways, I am still advocating trying again. We did change things, and many things have changed in the political situation: Kanaks are being exposed to a phenomenal level of contamination by various financial subsidies. The French socialist government has been able to freeze further immigration for ten years. Emphasis is being put on developing the Territory, and there is a belief that Kanaks should become more active and responsible in the socioeconomic field. But this is being done with such a huge outside financial assistance that Kanaks might be caught by getting used to an easy, heavily subsidized way of life: many observers see increasing social problems as a growing crisis of identity among the young people. I am far away from the South Pacific now, but I feel many Kanak friends might be overwhelmed by too much money acquired too easily. They do their best to manage this outside money for their communities, but big disagreements are occurring about sharing the profit from new facilities. Many social problems are submerged in the process.

The result might be a high level of contamination by outside assistance. After ten years, when the Kanaks will finally be asked to choose between independence or going ahead with France, many might simply vote for the second option, because they would lose too many advantages in the first option. As many young Kanaks are feeling quite uncomfortable in this socio-logical context, a few extremists might again put the fire to the house.

I am not a political specialist, but I think participatory action research might still be useful as Kanaks are experiencing a high level of outside assistance that influences their daily life, their culture, and their control over the essential roots of their situation. This suggests to me that participatory action research approaches should remain in New Caledonia, as elsewhere, as permanent institutions to facilitate a perennial experiential learning process.

Some Possible Futures

Twice again I tried to launch such a process. I worked with the French Centre National des Arts et Metiers (CNAM), a vocational training institution, with a center in Noumea. Just before leaving New Caledonia in 1984, I prepared (with friends and a colleague) a project for setting up a permanent training course in the socioeconomic aspects of rural development. Nothing came out of it. I tried again after two years in Southeast Asia, when I understood that going back to New Caledonia was not possible since all doors had been closed to me. With my friend Ron Crocombe from the University of the South Pacific, I prepared a project called 'Action research on Melanesian group enterprises in relation to land and water development.' This project was to be conducted inside the University of South Pacific, with funds from the Food and Agriculture Organization (FAO) from the United Nations. The idea was to follow a few Melanesian researchers from different South Pacific countries who would conduct action research with group enterprises and community projects. Then the project aimed to link with local institutions in each country, developing a similar learning process. Again, after months of hesitation, the project did not develop, as FAO was at this time in a difficult financial position.

I think that small countries such as New Caledonia in the South Pacific could easily apply national level participatory action research strategies, which I would call 'global participatory action research mechanism' with low costs and important benefits. In New Caledonia, I feel few people seized what I was trying to initiate through all of my efforts with my colleagues. It might be possible, today, to again start thinking about the general participatory action research objectives and the tools that were experienced. Considering their present situation, their objectives, and their political strategies, Kanaks, with or without others, might have some interest in reactivating participatory action research tools in a more cohesive strategy.

If this was the case, I think the 'Kanak Cultural Institute' (ICK), now well-established, could be the kind of institution that could launch and manage the main participatory action research tools. Those kinds of strategies need to be established in strong permanent institutions under local people's control. In my former experience, I had no such anchorage for my participatory action research efforts, and this was one of the main limitations. This is also, from my point of view, one of the major limitations of so many efforts by isolated field workers working with participatory action research tools all over the world.

Giving a new foundation to a new participatory action research process in the ICK would bring another key advantage: this institute is deeply engaged in social and cultural practice and studies and is currently working in the field of communications. I think participatory action research is basically helping people learn about themselves and master possible changes in their lives. Agriculture, education, and other fields where participatory action research is efficient are just application fields. The core of the participatory action research process is a social and cultural analysis, conducted by the people themselves as they change things. That is why, in New Caledonia as in other places, institutions concerned with applied support in social and cultural fields seem the most relevant places from where participatory action research could be activated.

This also means I would strongly advise that 'global participatory action research approaches' should leave universities: participatory action research must develop more action, and universities are not the proper places for this. Universities should be closely involved in the research component, but they are not usually the right institutions for action. One exception would be some 'applied institutes,' which exist in some universities and might be able to engage fully in operations of that kind. I think participatory action research must leave its 'experimental phase' wherever it started in universities to develop in local institutions for massive application.

Practically, for example, a participatory action research 'global mechanism' in New Caledonia could involve ICK, in close connection with a few universities, because I would prefer to keep New Caledonia open in various directions. The University of the South Pacific, the East-West Center of the University of Hawaii (Resource System Institute and Communications Center), an Australian university, and a French university might also be approached. ICK could have a small team in a participatory action research project working with Kanaks in development, for example. This team might initiate a systematic explanation phase in local communities and with all local leaders. Approaches like the one presented earlier could be discussed, with other possibilities. After this phase, some precise strategies could be decided as the work unfolded. In the field of rural development, participatory action research studies could involve:

- identifying some individual, group, or community enterprises that are exploring new ways of mastering rural development and initiating participatory action research analysis inside those enterprises;
- identifying others who would like to explore, with sociological supports, their own experiences in rural development with projects sharing experiences;
- providing regular support to all people involved;
- promoting exchanges between those people and existing technicians involved in assisting rural development, which would allow the people engaged in participatory action research to analyze this assistance and possibly to influence the technicians themselves;
- providing some university or other appropriate credit for the research that meets those requirements;
- activating again a network of animateurs and participatory planning mechanisms;
- providing facilities for communications, like the use of mass media, the publication of books, and the broadcasting of direct interviews by people engaged in development activities, with analysis from local people engaged in the participatory action research process; and
- organizing once or twice a year large meetings for meaningful, direct exchanges between participants.

Those are just suggestions, but all of them could be possible. I want to insist that participatory action research should leave its experimental phase and deeply influence a whole country, for example, in the field of mastering its rural development.

One key limitation that I met in New Caledonia was that so few people had heard about participatory action research. Because people were unfamiliar with the ideas, I was watched like a strange sociologist dropped into the technical field of rural development. More publications like the present book might help explain possible participatory action research applications, to prepare a better understanding about participatory action research and create more cooperation among the few people who are trying to systematically use participatory action research approaches.

Notes

1. IRAM-IRFED: IRAM is the Institut de Recherche et d'Application des Methodes; IRFED is the Institut International de Recherche et de Formation. They are both located in Paris, 49 rue de la Glacire, Paris. They have produced a lot of documentation since 1960 and are still operating as rural development and training agencies.

2. Universitié Co-operative Internationale is an open university with headquarters in Paris and Montreal, which has links with many universities, mainly in Europe, Canada, Africa, and South America. It primarily acts through small groups of field workers, working cooperatively in their researches, largely in the field of participatory development. Present headquarters are in Paris, rue du 11 novembre, 92 120 MONTROUGE.

References

Beaudoux, F., and M. Nieuwkerk. 1985. *Groupements paysans d'Afrique*. Paris: L'Harmattan.

Colin, R. 1978. *Les méthodes et techniques de la participation au développement*. Paris: UNESCO Rapports/Etudes.

———. 1979. *L'institutionalization de la participation au développement*. Report for DAKAR conference on rural participation. Paris: UNESCO.

Delion, J. 1988. *Objectives, pedagogy, and institutions of participation in rural development*. Honolulu, Hawaii: East-West Center Resource Systems Institute.

Gentil, D. 1986. *Les mouvements co-operatifs dans l'Afrique de l'Ouest francophone: Interventions de l'état ou organizations paysannes*. Paris: L'Harmattan.

Johnston, K., and R. Morse 1988. *Interpreting participatory development: Histories and projections.* Honolulu, Hawaii: East-West Center Resource Systems Institute.

Meister, A. 1977. *La participation pour le développement.* Paris: Editions Ouvriéres.

Oakley P., and D. Marsden. 1984. *Approaches to participation in rural development.* Geneva: International Labor Organization.

CHAPTER 12

Action Research: Improving Learning from Experience in Nurse Education in Thailand

Arphorn Chuaprapaisilp

Introduction

Clinical teaching is a major component of the health professions. In nursing education, clinical teaching has been found to be as problematic as it is in other practice-oriented professions. It is often cited in the literature as an area needing further research. It also is a major problem in nursing education in Thailand.

I believe that learning from experience in the clinical setting in Thailand has not been effective. Clinical teaching has been regarded in the same way as teaching in the classroom. Clinical teachers have focused too much on content, and it has been assumed that students are able to apply theory in practice by themselves.

I began with the premise that clinical teaching methods do not encourage students to learn from experience or to turn experience into learning. What support was there for such an argument? Was there a basis for it or was it only my perception? What is the proper view of it? How can it be investigated? If this argument is true, how can learning from experience be improved? In response to these questions, the problem for the study (Chuaprapaisilp, 1989) was formulated as: How can clinical teachers in Thailand assist students to learn more effectively from experience?

My reading of Kolb's work (1984) on experiential learning, Schon's (1983) work on the reflective practitioner, the work of Boud, Keogh, and Walker (1985) on reflection as a way of turning experience into learning, and the work of Carr and Kemmis (1986) on critical theory and knowing through action research highlighted the problem and led to this study.[1]

In selecting an appropriate research methodology for the study, I chose action research to achieve an improvement in teaching practice. However, this approach had been developed in the context of Western culture. The application of this method in a non-Western culture was an issue that required further exploration.

While the major part of this paper will concentrate on the research and inferences that might be made from the findings, there also is a need to discuss experiential learning and learning from experience in nursing education.

Experiential Learning Theory

Experiential learning has long received considerable attention in the literature of education. Experiential learning can be described basically as 'learning by doing.' However, the concept of experiential learning is more involved than this. Experiential learning includes the whole person in the learning process, not only the intelligence but also emotions, feeling, values, and interpersonal aspects (Zuber-Skerritt 1989). The origins of experiential learning can be traced to the work of Dewey, Rogers, and Maslow (Dewey 1938, 1958; Rogers 1961, 1969; Maslow 1968) in the area of humanistic psychology. In their view, experiential learning relates personal involvement and human experience. However, in their work there was a missing link between concrete experience and abstract generalization, between theory and practice, and between cognitive and affective domains. Kolb (1984) provided a theory of experiential learning to close this gap.

Kolb's experiential learning theory suggested that the central idea of learning is the process whereby knowledge is created through the transformation of experience. He proposed that "knowledge results from the combination of grasping experience and transforming it" (Kolb 1984, 41). Kolb explained the process of experiential learning as "a four-stage cycle involving four learning modes: concrete experience, reflective observation, abstract conceptualization, and active experimentation" (Kolb 1984, 40).

Kolb concluded his discussion of lifelong learning by raising the issue of integrity. In illustrating the experience of integrity, Kolb used the Mandala symbol, which refers to a basic teaching of the Buddha-Dhamma (Buddhism) known as the law of cause and effect or *Paticcasamuppada* (Pali language). There are similar links between Buddha-Dhamma and experiential learning through the practice of meditation and the search for enlightenment. Kolb (1984) linked the practice of meditation with lifelong learning in experiential learning. This idea and my own experience stimulated me to develop this method of investigating learning from experience in the Thai culture.

Kolb explained the nature of experiential learning clearly but did not adequately explain how learners transform experience. Another model that aims to help learners learn from experience is the 'FEU' model (Boud, Keogh, and Walker 1985). This model was proposed by the British Further Education

Curriculum and Development Unit (FEU). Experience, reflection, and specific learning are three phases of the model. By reflecting on experience, learners identify skills and knowledge that provide preparation for further experience. However, like the Kolb model, the FEU model does not adequately explain the role of reflection in the learning process to help learners turn experience into learning. The further reflection process, as provided by Boud, Keogh, and Walker (1985) strengthened the experiential learning theory by highlighting the importance of 'returning to experience,' 'attending to feeling,' and 'reevaluating experience.'

The concepts of experiential learning mentioned earlier provide potentially greater opportunity for helping students learn from experience. It appeared that no study had been conducted in nursing education to assess the effectiveness of these strengthened concepts. I explored and highlighted the approach of improving learning from experience in this study through action research.

Learning From Experience in Nursing Education

In the early development of the nursing profession, when nursing education was under control of the hospitals, very little emphasis was put on clinical teaching. Training was haphazard, poorly organized, and concerned primarily with the development of manual skills and strict adherence to rules and regulations. Nursing students had the image of dependent, obedient, and passive learners. They were taught to obey orders and discouraged from much independent thinking (Christy 1969). When nursing education moved to the system of the college and university, clinical teaching became a major component of nursing education because the educational institutions were responsible for clinical education. However, the same teaching strategies were used. That is to say, teaching strategies did not change to allow for clinical education. Even today, such criticisms are applicable to programs in nursing education (Infante 1985).

The nature of clinical teaching in nursing education is that clinical teachers assign students to patients so students can provide nursing care. For example, nursing students are responsible for giving total care to patients while they are learning in clinical teaching, unlike medical students who do not have to take responsibility for patient management. Clinical teachers are still portrayed as being the supervisors or helpers in the hospitals. Although now, the idea of producing independent, creative, decisive, assertive thinkers for the practice of nursing is the aim of nursing education, the educational strategies used in clinical teaching still remain amazingly constant, except for the effort of a few.

In Thailand, the first degree program, the bachelor of science in nursing, was started in 1950. At the present time, most of the programs are basic degree programs, whereas four universities offer masters degrees and many varieties of short-course training. The doctorate program in nursing was implemented in 1990. In spite of the university-based program in nursing, learning in the clinical setting in Thailand is still separated from the concepts of learning from experience in higher education. The traditional concept of 'doing in order to learn' is still very much in evidence. Whereas learning is the process whereby knowledge is created through the transformation of experience (Kolb 1984), learning in clinical nursing in Thailand is usually understood as the process by which students render care to patients. Clinical teachers appear to use clinical teaching strategies in the same way that they are used in the classroom, for example, the use of short lectures in conferences.

Design of the Study

The broad structure of the study was based on the conceptual framework of experiential learning theory, critical theory, and action research. A central approach of these three techniques of knowledge development is reflection. The elements of critical theory (Habermas 1972) by means of highlighting contradictions and developing an awareness of historical and social constraints by exposing power relationships are used to try to meet the aim of improving learning from experience through the conduct of pre- and post-clinical conferences in this study.

This study has been based on the assumption that if teachers provide an opportunity for students to prepare for their nursing interventions by clarifying the nature and purpose of those interventions, and they provide an opportunity for students to reflect on those experiences, then it is believed that students will learn more effectively from experience.

This assumption led to the study of pre- and post- clinical conferences (PPCCs) in nursing education in Thailand. The author conceived of the pre-clinical conference as a 'preparation for experience' and the post-clinical conference as a 'reflection on experience.' The study was divided into three phases. First, there was an ethnographic study of the current conduct of PPCCs, which was conducted in the three nursing schools and aimed to investigate and understand the nature of PPCCs. Second, a participatory workshop was conducted at one school of nursing to plan for an alternative approach that would enhance learning from experience. This step was also the first step of action research in the implementation of an alternative approach. The final phase, action research, aimed to improve learning from experience through the conduct of PPCCs.

The Participants in the Study

The action research phase of the study was conducted in the Department of Medical Nursing in the Faculty of Nursing at Prince of Songkla University and its three practicing wards. The participants included nine lecturers and 110 third-year nursing students in the regular Medical Nursing Practicum of the program of the academic year 1987. All participants volunteered to participate in this study. The students took turns to practice in this department in four groups, and each group stayed together for four weeks.

Action Research

The major reasons I employed action research as an approach were as follows: Action research helps teachers improve the practice of teaching through the development of critical reasoning ability. This ability enables teachers to become more analytical about their practice, thus they can view their practice in a different light and develop ways of improving it. In addition, action research lessens the gap between theory and practice. Finally, action research allowed me to include serious consideration of the cultural context in the study.

The two major aims of action research are improvement and involvement. The aim of improvement focuses on three areas: to improve practice, to improve the understanding of the practice by its practitioners, and to improve the situation in which the practice takes place. The aim of involvement means including all of the participants in the process of planning, acting, observing, and reflecting to achieve the aim of improvement (Grundy and Kemmis 1988).

Using the action research process of planning, acting, observing, and reflecting, the four cycles were implemented. One cycle was four weeks in duration. One group of students, with the clinical teacher, practiced in the three medical wards in each cycle. There were six to eight students in each ward. The cycle started with an orientation phase, followed by four weeks of practice, and ended with a conclusion phase where students demonstrated knowledge developed from their four-week experience. Each week consisted of an intermediate cycle of three clinical days. For a minor cycle of one day, the pre-clinical conference was conducted before providing nursing care and the post-clinical conference was conducted when the day was completed.

Monitoring and Analysis of the Study

In monitoring the events of the study, I employed the techniques of participant observation and interview described by Spradley (1979, 1980). My role involved developing good rapport, writing field notes, keeping reflective diaries to describe, explain, and help draw conclusions from events, and using audio and video recordings. In conducting the participatory workshop, I played the role of 'facilitator.' During the process of implementing the plan through action research, I was the facilitator, consultant, and participant observer, but not the teacher.

Data were collected through document analysis, interviews, participant observation, audiotape and videotape recordings, and reflective diaries. Analysis of a variety of data was based on theme analysis and componential analysis, which were used throughout the study to classify and group data. Description and explanation of data and cross-checking were also used. The underpinning principles in analysis were triangulation techniques (Lofland and Lofland 1984), grounded theory (Glaser and Strauss 1967), and illuminative evaluation (Parlett and Dearden 1977).

Findings

Ethnographic Study

The ethnographic study of three nursing schools indicated that for nursing education in Thailand experience was not the center of learning in clinical teaching, but that content learning and academic excellence were stressed more. The conduct of PPCCs tended to be oriented toward acquiring subject matter rather than benefiting from experience. Teachers tended to be authoritarian and students tended to be passive learners. There was a gap in the relationships between teachers and students, teachers and nurses, and nurses and students, as well as between theory and practice. Thai culture played a major role as both an inhibiting and a facilitating factor in the conduct of PPCCs. The strengths in the conduct of PPCCs included the contributions of teachers, nurses, and students who were strongly committed to their profession and had a strong sense of responsibility. The conduct of PPCCs also was strengthened by the strong background knowledge of the teachers and nurses, which enabled them to apply scientific principles once an appropriate nursing strategy was decided upon in the conference situation.

Participatory Workshop

An alternative approach known as the PPCC Learning Model was a major outcome of the participatory workshop. I also organized the collaborative work between two groups of nurses to implement the alternative approach to PPCCs. One group included nurse educators from the Medical Nursing Department under the School of Nursing and another included nurse practitioners from three medical wards at Songkla Nagarind University Hospital under the School of Medicine. At the same time, associated projects (writing Nursing Care Plans and Nurse's Notes by using nursing diagnosis), aimed at improving the quality of nursing care, were implemented in these three wards through the collaborative work of these two groups.

Action research. The implementation of an alternative approach through four cycles of action research resulted in both an improvement in learning from experience and an improvement in nursing care. The significant knowledge development is the Critical Experiential Learning Model. *Kid-pen tum-pen kid-pai tum-pai roum-mue roum-jai* (know how to think, know how to perform, and know how to perform better by thinking while we perform in an atmosphere of collaborative working) was developed as the Thai slogan for the process involving critical reflection within an atmosphere of collaborative work in this study. My work was becoming an important catalyst in moving toward the unity of theory and practice. The teachers (as participant researchers) and nurses (as supportive participants) enhanced the success of the study.

One of the theoretical contributions of this study is a model of 'Action research spiral based on Buddhist culture.' Action research with the enhancement of Buddhist teaching was the method of approach employed in putting all of the elements of the model into practice. This model of action research strengthened the general form of the action research spiral developed by Kemmis and McTaggart (1988) by highlighting the importance of Buddhist culture. The central theme of this model is *Satipatthana* (Pali language, Satipattan in Thai). Satipatthana is a Buddhist technical term that means the 'foundation of mindfulness' (Khantipalo 1981). Mindfulness is the state of mind with respect to full awareness of both actions and feelings. Satipatthana is similar to what Fay (1987) called 'consciousness raising' in his theory of critical social science. Mindfulness can be developed through Samatha and Vipassana meditations, which include the processes of contemplation of the body, the feelings, the state of the mind, and the concomitant of the mind. The result is that the mind becomes calm and clear. When the mind is calm, concentration develops. According to Buddhist teaching from Samyutta Nikaya 2, 29, Ajahn Brahmavamso explains:

Concentration is the supporting condition for the knowledge and vision of things as they really are,

The knowledge and vision of things as they really are is the supporting condition for disenchantment,

Disenchantment is the supporting condition for dispassion,

Dispassion is the supporting condition for emancipation,

Emancipation is the supporting condition for the knowledge of the destruction of the asavas (the most deeply rooted obstructive habits) (Ajahn Brahmavamso, 1991, 29)

The above formulation of linking factors shows how one can develop
(purify) the mind to gain freedom from confusion and bias, to attain wisdom
and enlightenment. This state of mindfulness helps one overcome false consciousness and see things as they are. Thus, mindfulness is the way in which
one gains insight and enlightenment, since it enhances understanding and elim-
inates confusion through the attainment of penetrating wisdom. However, it is
the personal knowledge and knowing that one must practice to gain the results.

There have been criticisms of the effectiveness of action research, arguing that it depends more on personal and interpersonal factors than on
methodological factors (Reason and Rowan 1981). The approach outlined
here helps individuals overcome such personal limitations by developing
mindfulness through Satipatthana. Since mindfulness helps free the mind
from confusion and bias, the individual can focus more on the method than on
the personal factors.

Kemmis and McTaggart (1988) used a downward spiral to portray
action research, but I prefer to use an upward spiral representing an increase
in the development of knowledge and improving practice. The attainment of
knowledge and the improvement of practice is directed to Satipatthana and the
effectiveness of the action research process.

One important outcome that highlighted this improvement was a change
in attitude and learning behavior by teachers, nurses, and students toward their
practice. These changes included the movement from the traditional approach
(where observing, remembering, and copying provided a basis for learning) to
a critical approach, where reflection on experience was the center of learning.
The teachers had moved from being authoritarian instructors to being facilitators in preparing students for experience in the Pre-Clinical Conferences and
in helping them to reflect upon experience in the Post-Clinical Conferences.
Students had moved from being passive learners to self-directed learners, thus
creating autonomous learning among students. However, the level of achievement depended on the individual teachers and students. The main difficulty
was the development of understanding between the two groups of nurse educators and nurse practitioners and among the members in each group.

In improving the quality of nursing care, as the result of the projects mentioned earlier, incorporated with the influence of the Critical Experiential Learning Model, nurses in three wards were able to put each step of the nursing
process into their practice. This led to the movement away from the traditional
approach of routine work toward a more critical approach. However, like the
improvement of learning, the level of achievement varied from ward to ward.

The Critical Experiential Learning Model developed from this study has three significant advantages.

1. It provides a framework for learning from experience. This framework has three phases, which may be outlined as follows:
   - *Preparation for experience*: This phase provides an orientation for students before entering the practicum course and guides them through the preparatory process of the Pre-Clinical Conference.
   - *Managing the experiential learning process:* This phase involves the art of facilitating experiential learning. It provides a link between the preparatory, practice, and reflection phases. This managing phase consists of five strategies that provide an organizational structure for the whole process. These strategies include structuring, organizing, controlling, facilitating, and emancipating.
     - *Structuring*: This is where teachers assess the environment that includes patients' conditions and students' ability, objectives, and experience. They then construct the activities within a set time frame, identify the process to supervise students, and develop a systematic way to share ideas and experience in the post-clinical conferences.
     - *Organizing:* Here teachers prioritize the activities, identify which students or objectives require the most supervision, and allocate them appropriately. They decide what experiences should be shared in the post-clinical conferences.
     - *Facilitating*: Using this strategy, teachers assist students in processing their plans and help them achieve their objectives. They explore ways to achieve a successful experience and provide ongoing individual consultation.
     - *Controlling*: Here teachers maintain the activities within the set time frame and control their own teaching, for example, by asking what they need to do or what additional information they need, what knowledge students 'must know' and 'should know,' and what knowledge should be reserved for further study, as described by Abbatt (1980).
     - *Emancipating*: This is where teachers stimulate students to challenge existing approaches and decide on the adoption of a better approach.
   - *Reflection on experience:* This phase is conducted through the reflective process that draws upon the work of Boud, Keogh, and Walker (1985), but also involves elements developed during the course of this study. The main elements drawn from the former were the emphasis on 'returning to experience' and 'reevaluating experience.' The main additions to the process that were developed through the current study are outlined further in the second and third phases that follow, but primarily teachers and students clarify reflection and the process of gaining emancipation through experience.

2. It provides the process of preparation for experience in experiential learning in nursing education. This process increases the effectiveness of pre-
clinical conferences by preparing students for practical experiences in the
hospital situation.
3. It introduces critical theory to experiential learning theory.

As mentioned earlier, experiential learning in nursing education in Thailand seemed to be too simplistic when technical and practical approaches
(Carr and Kemmis 1986) were employed. The approach I developed
expanded on the foregoing reflection process by adding a step called 'clarifying reflection,' which sought to enhance the understanding of the teachers and
students before they became involved in the reflection process. Teachers created a 'free learning environment,' set a 'democratic atmosphere,' and clarified together with students the objectives, structures, processes, roles, and
assumptions in the conduct of the post-clinical conference.

The model included a process of gaining emancipation through experience, which was added to the reflection process developed by Boud, Keogh, and
Walker (1985). Teachers and students gained emancipation by challenging
structures, identifying contradictions (historical context, power relationship),
establishing clear communication (ideal speech), and adopting new approaches.

Through the implementation of action research in this study, and by adapting and reinterpreting the process, it was possible to contribute new aspects to the
epistemology and methodology of action research. This study revised the action
research spiral developed by Kemmis and McTaggart (1988). The central theme
of this revised model is Satipatthana (including Buddhist teaching, which is a key
to overcoming inhibitions). Also, the spiral moves upward, representing an
increase in the development of knowledge and improving practice. The attainment of knowledge and the improvement of practice is directly connected to
Satipatthana and the effectiveness of the action research process.

According to Khantipalo (1981), Satipatthana is a Buddhist technical
term that means 'the foundation of mindfulness.' Mindfulness is a state of
mind with respect to full awareness of both actions and feelings. As mentioned earlier, Satipatthana is similar to what Fay (1987) called 'consciousness raising.' This state of the growth of mindfulness can be promoted through
the contemplation of the body (the body in Buddhism has a wide meaning; it
includes the person and the environment), feelings, mental states, and mental
events (Phra-Thepvatee 1980, Khantipalo Bhikku 1989).

Inferences From the Findings

The results indicate that the Critical Experiential Learning Model developed from this study provides an opportunity for clinical teachers to assist students in learning from experience in the following manner:

1. Clinical teachers can employ the model as a framework for learning from experience through the process of preparation for experience and reflection upon experience. Teachers can provide an opportunity for students to set their objectives, express their feelings freely, and understand themselves, their environment, interaction, and factors that inhibit them from being active learners, for example, passive memorization of 'textbook' knowledge before entering the practice setting. Students are then encouraged to reflect upon their experiences and identify their learning before leaving the practicum field.

2. Clinical teachers can perform a role as facilitators, not lecturers or demonstrators, who initiate critical thinking with students and empower them to reach out in their thinking beyond the confines of their regulated day-to-day professional activities to enhance learning from experience.

3. By employing strategies in managing the experiential learning process, teachers help students learn more effectively from experience, since a time frame is important for learning in the 'natural' setting, such as a hospital.

4. Clear understanding of efforts to develop the symmetry and reciprocity of the 'ideal speech' and improved communication generally help create a supportive and creative atmosphere that enhances learning from experience and clarifies the mutual support role of the nurse teachers and nurse practitioners.

5. Critical reflection and collaborative work of nurse teachers and nurse practitioners are the keys for learning from experience, since critical reflection allows them to monitor their effectiveness together.

6. A condition of 'social harmony,' that is, understanding of the self (full awareness of actions and feelings) and understanding the situation and performing accordingly, is important in locating learning within the normal context of the natural learning environment, such as hospitals. This includes the art of managing equality and balance and reciprocity of technical, practical, and critical modes of approaches. In Buddhism, this condition of 'social harmony' is known as the 'midway' of approaches.

7. There is a need for training teachers in investigating, interpreting, and improving their own practice, for example, writing a reflective diary and developing reflection skills.

Other health professional educators can benefit from the Critical Experiential Learning Model developed in this study, since the model offers a process of preparing students for learning and practice and encourages students to reflect upon their clinical practice. For example, medical teachers can facilitate clinical teaching in ward rounds and encourage students to reflect upon their daily activities by using the suggestions previously listed.

Personal Reflection

I started with a technical question: 'How can I improve the product of nursing education?' This thinking stimulated me to focus on setting a quality assurance program for clinical teaching. I then realized, after spending half a year in study, that this way of innovating change did not allow teachers to control and improve their own practice, since it was controlled by a system (program). I then moved to a practical mode of approach, 'How can nurse educators improve their practice of clinical teaching?' When I discovered more about action research (in my literature search and from critical friends), I intended to use a critical approach but was not sure how it would work in Thailand. When I was in the field implementing the alternative approach, it was the emancipatory approach of 'How can we (nurse educators and nurse practitioners) improve our practice?' By reflecting on these approaches and the nature of clinical teaching in nursing education, I concluded that no one single method can be applied to improve practice. It requires a multidimensional approach. This depends on the persons, environment, and interaction between the persons and environment. Culture plays a major role in both inhibiting and facilitating innovation. Not only is the emancipatory approach the powerful approach, but we need to adjust to the situation and move along the three modes of approaches.

Conclusion

This study produced evidence, within the context of nursing education and nursing practice in Thailand, about how clinical teachers assist students in learning from experience by applying experiential learning theory, critical theory, and action research. The major outcome is the development of the Critical Experiential Learning Model. Through action research, the participants in this study were able to use an action research approach (developed in a Western culture) to cultivate a deeper knowledge of their own 'nursing culture,' without simply transferring or copying Western technologies and becoming 'dependent practitioners' in their own setting. However, the study explored a theoretical framework of experiential learning, which provided specific implications for teachers of an experience-based profession. Earlier in this paper, it was pointed out that it appeared that no study had been conducted in nursing education to assess the effectiveness of experiential learning theory. Hence, it is possible for this study to widen its implications to nursing education in general. Furthermore, knowledge developed from this study might be applied in other health professions.

Afterword

This study is just the beginning of a journey forward into the realm of lifelong learning. It is influenced by events of the past and, in itself, provides a focus for future events. By fully gaining insights from the past, contemplating the present (using emancipatory wisdom), and taking responsibility for the future we gain the force to drive forward by drawing fully upon our experiences. This is illustrated by the Buddhist Mandala that links a related cause and leads to continuous change (*Paticcasamuppada*, The Dependent Origination). The result is not permanent, but will be transformed to another form. Knowledge and technological changes are related through the interaction between person (mind and body) and the environment. To borrow from Buddhist terminology, productive Contemplation, supported by Virtue, will ultimately lead to Wisdom. To the participants, the researcher, and the readers of this study, the Mandala Wheel, which is based on changes in cause and effect, allows us to move forward in seeking ways to learn from experience.

Note

1. The author wishes to thank Dr. Ruth White and Associate Professor David Boud at the University of New South Wales, Australia, for their support and critical suggestions. Grateful acknowledgment is extended to IDP (International Development Programs of Australian Universities and Colleges) for financial support of this study. Sincere appreciation is also extended to Professor Stephen Kemmis, formerly of Deakin University, Australia, for providing constructive suggestions.

References

Abbatt, F. R. 1980. Teaching for better learning: A guide for teachers of primary health care staff. Geneva: WHO.

Ajahn Brahmavamso. 1991. Samatha meditation. *Forest Sangha Newsletter*, October 4–6. England: Amaravati Buddhist Center.

Boud, D. J., R. Keogh, and D. Walker (eds.). 1985. *Reflection: Turning experience into learning*. London: Kogan Page.

Carr, W., and S. Kemmis. 1986. *Becoming critical: Knowing through action research*. 3rd ed. Geelong,Vic.: Deakin University Press.

Christy, T. E. 1969. *Cornerstone for nursing education*. New York: Teachers College Press, Columbia University.

Chuaprapaisilp, A. 1989. Improving learning from experience through the conduct of pre- and post-clinical conferences: Action research in nursing education in Thailand. Ph.D. thesis. University of New South Wales.

Dewey, J. 1938. *Experience and education*. Kappa Delta Pi.

————— . 1958. *Experience and nature*. New York: Dover Publications.

Fay, B. 1987. *Critical social science: Liberation and its limits*. Cambridge: Polity Press.

Glaser, B. G., and A. L. Strauss. 1967. *The discovery of grounded theory: Strategies for qualitative research*. Chicago: Aldine.

Grundy, S., and S. Kemmis. 1988. Educational action research in Australia: The state of the art (an overview). In *The action research reader*, eds. S. Kemmis and R. McTaggart. 3rd. ed. Geelong, Vic.: Deakin University Press.

Habermas, J. 1972. *Knowledge and human interests*. trans. J. J. Shapiro. London: Heinemann.

Infante, M. S. 1985. The clinical laboratory in nursing education. 2nd ed. New York: John Wiley & Sons.

Kemmis, S., and R. McTaggart. 1988. *The action research planner*. 3rd ed. Geelong, Vic.: Deakin University Press.

Khantipalo Bhikku. 1981. *Calm and insight: A Buddhist manual for meditators*. London: Curzon Press.

————— . 1989. Satipatthana. Personal interview, 13 July.

Kolb, D. A. 1984. *Experiential learning: Experience as the source of learning and development*. New Jersey: Prentice-Hall, Inc.

Lofland, J., and L. Lofland. 1984. Analyzing social settings: A guide to qualitative observation and analysis. 2nd ed. University of California.

Maslow, A. 1968. Towards a psychology of being. 2nd ed. New York: Van Nostrand Reinhold.

Parlett, M., and G. Dearden. 1977. Introduction to illuminative evaluation: Studies in higher education. California: Pacific Sounding Press.

Phra-Thepvatee (Prayudh Payutto). 1980. *Buddha-Dhamma*. 7th printing. Bangkok: Komol Keem Tong Press.

Reason, P., and J. Rowan. 1981. *Human inquiry: A source of new paradigm research*. London: Wiley.

Rogers, C. 1961. *On becoming a person: a therapist's view of psychotherapy*. Boston: Houghton Mifflin.

————— . 1969. *Freedom to learn: A view of what education might become*. Ohio: Charles E. Merril.

Schon, D. A. 1983. *The reflective practitioner: How professionals think in action*. New York: Basic Books.

Spradley, J. P. 1979. *The ethnographic interview*. New York: Holt Rinehart & Winston.

————. 1980. *Participant observation*. Sydney: Holt, Rinehart & Winston.

Zuber-Skerritt, O. 1989. Action research as a model of professional development at the tertiary level. Paper presented to the Action Research in Higher Education, Government and Industry Conference, 19–23 March. Griffith University, Queensland.

CHAPTER 13

A Census as Participatory Research

Srilatha Batliwala and Sheela Patel

Introduction

The Society for Promotion of Area Resource Centres (SPARC) was founded in December 1984, with the express purpose of working with the poorest women in Bombay City. Each of the founding members of SPARC had, through their diverse experiences, come to believe that traditional welfare services resulted in dependency rather than development. We discovered that awareness-building, through nonformal education or 'conscientization,' was a far more potent means of empowering people—especially women—to realize their own goals. We had also found that participatory research is one of the most powerful instruments of conscientization.

In our work, however, we do not view participatory research as a time-bound, issue-specific activity, but as the fundamental principle of our strategy, infusing every action with the need to join people in learning about their own environment and locating solutions to problems.

In this paper,[1] we attempt to show how this commitment led to an unusual—if not unique—effort in the annals of participatory research: a census of 27,000 pavement dwellers in Bombay City, completed in the short span of four weeks in September 1985.

The Background: What Led to the Census?

A brief review of SPARC's objectives and work from January to August 1985 is a necessary prelude in understanding how the pavement dweller census came about. SPARC was conceived from the idea of working with the poorest of poor urban women, which, in Bombay's context, meant the pavement dwellers. We chose to begin our work within the confines of 'E' Ward (the administrative unit of the City Council), an area with a high density of pavement slums—or 'clusters,' as we call them.

Our first task was to locate all of the clusters in the ward, that is, to systematically 'map' them. Using an official street map of the areas, we walked every street and lane in concentric circles, marking every group of pavement huts on the map until the center point was reached. The mapping exercise also was meant to acquaint ourselves with the people—especially women—and vice versa. The most common questions asked were, 'Who are you? What are you going to do? If you are social workers, why don't you give us something?'

It was from this very early stage of fielding these questions that we introduced our concept of participation: we were a group of people interested in the problems of pavement women. We did not know what we would do. We had nothing to give. We wanted to sit and talk with women and see if we could understand their problems and work together to find solutions.

During the visits to each of the identified clusters that followed mapping, we soon realized that women knew very little about their clusters as a whole. For example, they did not know how many families lived in their clusters, where they were from, or how long that particular settlement had been there. Indeed, there had really been no need for them to know these things. But if SPARC's objective was to first build bridges between the women within each cluster, and later between clusters, then generating an awareness of a common cause was important.

To do this, we again utilized an informal participatory research approach: a 'cluster profile' comprising some twenty basic items of information about the community was devised. This profile included the place of origin of the different families in the cluster, their duration of residence in the current location and in Bombay City, the major occupations of the men, women, and children, how many possessed ration cards (an important identification and legal document in India), how many were registered voters, and the water sources, toilets, and health facilities used. The cluster profile achieved several ends:

1. It provided useful data about the community to the people and to us.
2. It enabled women to learn about and become aware of their own clusters while sharing information with us.
3. Since the cluster profile required women to consult each other before providing answers acceptable to all, it initiated the process of collective reflection and the viewing of their environment and daily life objectively.
4. It established the process of collecting, sharing, and analyzing information together, as the hallmark of SPARC's approach.

One example will serve to prove the point. Women in one cluster wanted to obtain ration cards and explained the failure of their past attempts to do so through the usual middle man. Would we get them cards? No, but we could all go together to the ration office and find out how to get them. In this exercise, even finding out the location of the ration office was done together, along with going there, meeting the ration officer, learning the procedure, and so on. Thereafter, we only played the role of scribe to fill out the application forms, although each woman had to independently get her family details, which were required on the form. In these ways, SPARC had combined participatory research and action from the inception of its work.

For us, the value of the participatory approach does not lie so much in the achievement of the objective or goal, but in the process. In the above illustration, for example, women did not merely learn how to obtain ration cards, but they gained experience and confidence in dealing with the system, a confidence that could be carried over to tackling a whole range of problems in their lives. For SPARC, the process of obtaining ration cards led to insights about many other aspects of people's lives, such as food economy and food storage problems (a pavement house cannot be locked), as well as an opportunity to talk about legal rights and public resources.

Feedback of cluster profile information across clusters and regular meetings with women from the various clusters formed the bulk of our work until the onset of the monsoon in June, when the fury of the rains caused serious disruption to our work. We were just beginning to resume our normal routine when a historic event occurred, which eventually led to the massive census that is the subject of this paper.

The Supreme Court Judgment

On July 11, 1985, the Supreme Court of India delivered judgment on what had come to be called 'The Pavement Dweller Case' (Olga Tellis & Others vs Bombay Municipal Corporation). This was the outcome of a four-year legal battle that began in July 1981, when, overnight, thousands of pavement hutments were demolished by Municipal Authorities and their hapless dwellers deported from Bombay City. A Bombay journalist, among others, sought and obtained a stay order from the Bombay High Court, contending that both the demolitions and the deportation of Indian citizens from a city of their Union was completely illegal. The case soon moved to the Supreme Court, which delivered the now-historic judgment granting that the Bombay Municipal Corporation (hereafter BMC) Act of 1888 was both legal and constitutional. This act authorizes the BMC to demolish all illegal encroachments on public lands, including homes, *without providing any alternative shelter or sites to the affected.* By upholding the BMC Act, the Supreme Court dealt yet another blow to the poor, even while paying prodigious lip service to the socioeconomic realities that forced them to migrate to the cities for survival and create for themselves the only form of housing they could afford: on the pavement or on vacant land.

The impact of the Supreme Court judgment on both SPARC and the nearly 3,000 pavement families with whom we were working was devastating. While we had anticipated this eventuality to some extent when choosing to work with pavement dwellers, we had hoped that the highest court in the land would consider the plight of the marginalized and dishoused in their judgment and provide them with a just and human alternative.

As many families came to us for advice, information, help, and reassurance, we determined that SPARC should play five major roles in the impeding crisis:

1. As a resource center, read and understand the judgment and all of its legal implications and disseminate this information to women and their families.
2. Seek out all authorities who may be involved in the implementation of the judgment, determine what they propose to do, and provide feedback to people.
3. Interact with other agencies, groups, lawyers, and concerned citizens who may be involved in the issue and participate in and provide feedback about their strategies to people.
4. Identify and collect all available information about the number of pavement dwellers in the city, the public housing policy, urban development plans, and any other programs that people could utilize to their benefit in the situation.
5. Assist people in planning how they would face the impending crisis and devise alternatives for themselves.

It was in the course of taking the aforementioned steps that the need for a people's census was born, as we shall see.

While relating the facts and implications of the judgment, it became clear that the vast majority of people had no idea whatsoever that what had been obtained in 1981 was a *stay* and not a judgment in favor of pavement dwellers. Apparently, several legal and other activists who had been mobilizing people at the time of the 1981 demolitions had never returned to provide any feedback to people about the status of the case once the stay had been obtained. Most people, therefore, felt that some sort of terrible *volte face* had occurred. This highlighted some of the serious drawbacks of issue-based activism and the lack of sustained commitment to keep people informed and involved when one presumes to represent them or fight their cause.

In the several meetings SPARC had with the BMC and state government officials, two things became clear. First, it was understood that no mass demolitions would be undertaken, but rather clearing of pavements would be done in a 'phased' manner, starting only with certain key areas where pavement slums were obstructing traffic on major arterial roads and where certain public works projects (laying water supply pipes and enlarging sewers and storm drains) had been held up due to the presence of pavement dwellings. All officials expressed their desire to find a 'humanitarian' solution to the problems, offering serious consideration to any 'feasible' alternative organizations such as SPARC might care to work out. Second, none of the concerned officials had any idea about the numbers involved, even if, hypothetically, every pavement slum in the city was to be cleared. The oft-quoted 1976 Government Slum Census had not, by their own admission, included pavement dwellers. Thus, the questions uppermost in our minds—How many people would be affected if all pavements are to be cleared? and What was the actual magnitude of the problem we were all talking about?—went begging. The authorities had no more precise answers than did we. Meanwhile, all possible information gleaned from these meetings was given back to people.

 ˙Initially, we had concentrated on keeping women informed of all developments, but the menfolk soon protested that they would be equally affected by demolitions, so why were we only meeting the women? We had been waiting for this query and soon began our Sunday meetings where as many as 200 people attended at one time. However, sensing that men would now once again monopolize information and take over leadership roles, we insisted that there must be a heavy representation of women from each cluster at the meetings. Our rationale for this—that more often than not it was the women who were at home when the demolition squads arrived, hence they needed to know their rights and what steps to take—convinced most of the men.

 Simultaneously, SPARC participated in several meetings called by a host of joint action committees, concerned citizens forums, and housing action groups, which sprang into being after the judgment. These groups comprised lawyers, social workers and social work faculty and students, architects, activists, and others. In these meetings, certain commonalities as well as differences in approach emerged. For instance, many elements were vehement about what pavement dwellers should be told to do. SPARC felt no one should dictate any one course of action except the affected people themselves. We also questioned the right of these intellectuals and radicals to pontificate when the vast majority of them had no sustained mass contact with pavement dwellers, yet they were busy outlining strategies for them. We felt our role was only to facilitate people identifying their own alternatives and achieving consensus within their own areas, so each community was not fragmented among themselves.

 As of mid-August, however, no concrete course of action had been agreed upon at a city-wide level. Feedback about these meetings also was given to people.

Meanwhile, SPARC's own data search on pavement dwellers revealed a blatant lack of facts and figures. No one—whether research or demographic institutes, government and municipal authorities, or action groups—seemed to know how many pavement dwellers lived in the city. Moreover, our literature scan on low-income housing, slum upgrading, and general urban development policies showed that pavement dwellers had never specifically figured in any of these. Clearly, in the urban development totem pole, even slum dwellers were well above those who sought shelter on the pavements. In personal meetings with some of the aforementioned bodies, moreover, we discovered a number of myths and misconceptions about the difficulty of enumerating the pavement population. The chief one was that pavement dwellers are a floating population, drifting from one footpath to another at frequent intervals, thus making an accurate census impossible. But from our years of contact with pavement women (several members of our group had been working with pavement dwellers long before the formation of SPARC), we knew this belief to be quite incorrect. In fact, most families we know had been living on the same footpath since their arrival in the city, as much as four decades ago. As a rule, they moved only when they were forced to by the municipal authorities.

Last, the three major studies of pavement dwellers that we came across were all sample surveys, covering at best a few hundred families (Mahtani 1982; Ramachandran 1972) Since the sampling methods used here had been rather rough and ready (in a cluster of fifty huts, canvass five, if more, canvass ten), skewed results could not be ruled out. The fact is that scientific sampling could not be done when no one knew the size of the universe! Most important, these exercises had been one-sided: pavement dwellers were surveyed and analyzed, but the results were never shared with or given back to them. Reports had been given to the powers-that-be, but not to the people from whom the information had been taken. As such, these surveys had been of no use to the people they purported to represent.

All of these discoveries convinced us that effective advocacy by the people, whether for alternative accommodation prior to demolition or any other relief, had to be based on solid, sound enumeration of their numbers. This was even more vital since the state government and BMC announced that only those covered in the 1976 slum census would be given alternate accommodations and notices prior to demolition. It therefore seemed evident that pavement dwellers must enumerate *themselves* and demand alternatives in the language of the bureaucracy, specifically the language of numbers and statistics.

Most important of all, they had to eradicate their invisibility in the eyes of the policy makers, planners, civic and government administrators, political parties, and the powerful city elites who benefited most from their labor; they had to demonstrate their vital role in the urban economy and the factors that led to their settling on pavements with hard facts, *not* by appealing to the nonexistent humanitarianism or sense of justice of a society based on inequality and exploitation. At that point, the most effective and feasible way of doing this seemed to be census of pavement dwellers.

The Census

We have, in the preceding pages, described both the events and trends that led to SPARC's undertaking of the census of pavement dwellers. Before we elaborate on the census itself, two milestones that preceded it must be mentioned.

First, even before the idea of doing a large-scale census arose, a 'people's census' had already begun. When feedback from SPARC's three main endeavors (interaction with officials, action groups, and the data search) was given to people at the Sunday meetings, the issue of their invisibility was defined by the people themselves. The more articulate among them immediately perceived the need to make their communities 'stand and be counted.' We suggested that even though their leaders were busy making demands and representations to the BMC and to local officials, without a list of families in each cluster, their major occupations, length of residence, and other basic facts, they could not even begin to negotiate with the BMC for alternatives. From this emerged the plan that in each cluster one or two literate people would be nominated to prepare such lists for each community. Even if the authorities ignored these efforts, such data would help them put their plight before the public and mobilize opinion.

The people's census was already underway in three or four clusters, and we began exploring the possibility of computer processing the results. When talking to friends, well-wishers, and select officials about it, we found that the data thus collected by people was fine as a means of mobilization, but that it had no credibility whatsoever in the eyes of anyone else. The data would be dismissed since it was collected by the affected, and not by an 'objective,' independent body.

This caveat did not, in our view, negate the people's census, since we saw it not purely as data collection but as a means of people's mobilization and empowerment by providing a basis for them to plan their own alternatives. However, we *did* realize that in the prevailing political climate, a mass census by an objective 'respected' organization could turn the tide; it could force everyone to face the reality that a problem of such magnitude and complexity could not be solved by demolishing hutments and evicting people. It was a gamble, but one that might pay off.

Accordingly, we approached the College of Social Work which had undertaken the last major sample survey of pavement dwellers in 1981. This was in mid-August, with two and one-half months to go before demolitions were scheduled to begin on November 1. At that juncture, unfortunately, the response was negative. It was felt by the College that there was not enough time to carry out a city-wide census, or even a census of a few wards, and that the financial, human, and other resources required could not be found to undertake the task.

These were perfectly reasonable if somewhat discouraging constraints. Little did the college realize that their response triggered SPARC into taking a step which, for its sheer audacity if not insanity, continues to amaze our associates and us. We simply decided to conduct a census of our own.

The process and results of the census and a brief history of pavement dwellers is available in *We the invisible (SPARC, n.d.)*,[2] therefore, we concentrate here on the nature of people's participation in the census and then on raising certain questions about both this exercise and participatory research as a whole.

The idea of doing our own census took shape on August 18, 1985. Within a week, cluster meetings were held throughout 'E' Ward to discuss the idea with people, who ratified it with few reservations. The objectives and a list of tentative questions were defined during these discussions. We sought the assistance of sympathetic research professionals who helped us design the questionnaire that we ourselves pretested and then had printed. The scope of the census was expanded from only 'E' Ward to the major arterial roads of the 'island city' (or southern third of Bombay City), since these areas were to be prime targets for clearing operations.

Pavement clusters on the arterial roads were charted on city maps by volunteers over one weekend. According to their hut counts and SPARC's 'E' ward cluster profile data, approximately 6,000 households would have to be covered.

By the third week of August, fifteen investigators and eight coders were hired from a market research agency and were trained. A field supervisor was appointed and all six members of SPARC's staff undertook an on-the-spot supervision of the investigators. The census began on August 30 in 'E' Ward and concluded on the last arterial road on September 29. One in every ten questionnaires was cross-checked by a SPARC staff member. Coding was commenced almost as soon as investigators began their work, so all questionnaires were coded (under the continuous supervision of one of our staff) and dispatched for data entry on October 2, 1985.

Ironically, electronic data processing posed more difficulties than any other aspect of the census. Our data was stuck at this stage for over a week, and our final tables were delivered only on October 11. Working around the clock, the results were analyzed, written up simultaneously in English and

Hindi, and the final report printed overnight to be released at a press conference on October 14. The report was also given, on the same day, to every BMC and state government minister and official concerned directly or indirectly with the issue. Copies also were dispatched the same day to key decision makers in New Delhi. Meanwhile, vernacular copies were distributed among those who took part in the census.

Let us now examine the census as a participatory research exercise. What were the main elements of people's participation in this census?

The Census As Participatory Action Research

First, the idea for the census was not a brilliant brainwave of our own. It may never have occurred to us without the catalyst of the people's own desire to represent their economic contribution to the city and the reasons for their dwelling on pavements. During the numerous discussions and meetings that followed the Supreme Court judgment, people voiced their feelings of despair, injustice, and anger in terms that triggered our own thoughts. "They want to throw us out," said many women, "but who will sweep and swab their floors and wash their dirty clothes and vessels for pittance?" "Break our houses and drive us away," said the men, "and who will ply the handcarts? Who will unload vegetables at the wholesale market? Who will come to your door and sell you your daily needs at a cheap price?" "Do they think we like living on the pavement? Let them give us houses and we will live like them."

It was the feelings of the pavement dwellers themselves that made us realize that indeed, their contribution to the urban economy was totally unrecognized—invisible. They were seen only as eyesores, noticed only for the apparent squalor and filth in which they lived. The need to represent them differently, truthfully, arose from people. The census was merely the shape and form that we used to express that need.

This brings us to the second participatory element. Having conceptualized the census, we sought the people's ratification for it. It must be stressed that at the time we had established sufficient credibility and rapport with people to ask for and to get their cooperation for any endeavor we might undertake. There was no need, strictly speaking, to put the idea before people, discuss its pros and cons, and elicit their reactions. We did this because we believed we should have. We believed people had a right to decide *how* their lives and causes were represented and also to decide upon the methodology by which this was done. We also believed that until people gained a firsthand exposure to research techniques, they could never take control of the outcome of such research and use it to their own advantage.

When the broad framework of the census was discussed, many expressed doubts and reservations. "So many surveys have been done before," they said, "and where have they got us? People keep coming to us and filling up forms and we never see them again." This was the level of cynicism about the role of research. Still others thought it may do no good, but also no harm. The majority, however, liked the idea of a census as a means of community mobilization and of presenting one's case to the policy makers in a concrete, factual manner.

Two particularly successful allegories were developed and used. The first was that of bread (*rotis*): In a household, unless your presence is recognized and accounted for, you are not likely to get your share of bread. The second allegory compared the role of pavement dwellers in the city to that of the women in the family: it is she who works from morning till night, doing all of the tasks that ensure her family's comfort, yet the family barely sees or acknowledges her vital contribution to their welfare. These are some of the ways in which the census was made meaningful to people.

As for the cynics, they were somewhat mollified by our pledge that the census report would be distributed in the local languages throughout the thirty-nine clusters and that all findings would be explained to people in detail. We agreed that the census would not affect the impending demolitions much—such a change of heart was most unlikely—but it could be used to strengthen *people themselves* by helping them see the value of their role in the urban economy and by bringing out the common history of rural poverty, which could help them unite across barriers of district, state, language, and religion.

It would be foolish in the extreme to pretend that all of the 3,000-odd families SPARC worked with knew about, understood, and ratified the census. Anyone with experience in community work knows (even if they will not admit it) that even if one-tenth of a given group becomes actively involved in an issue that is an optimum level of participation. Nor was it different with us. What was important however was that those who actively participated in discussing and ratifying the census idea were the most articulate, aware, strong, and concerned in their communities. They were the decision makers, which included both 'leaders' as well as many others who provided the checks and balances to the potential oppression or autocracy of such leaders. Notwithstanding this, every family in every cluster was informed about the census, its objectives and importance. This was done by holding on-the-spot cluster meetings on each street the day before the investigators were due to arrive there. More frequent meetings were held on the arterial roads where SPARC had never previously worked, once again explaining the whys and wherefores of the census to this population that had no previous contact with SPARC.

In these meetings, which concentrated mainly on women, emphasis was placed on explaining the questionnaire (why and how each question would be asked) to people, discussing how much time it would take, relating the fact that the results would be given back to them as well as to BMC and state government authorities, and determining the best time for the investigators to come to each cluster.

The level of participation created by this process was immense: not a single household was suspicious of or refused to cooperate with the investigators. Most important of all, thanks to people's support, data collection proceeded at a speed that most people found difficult to credit. Surely there can be no more convincing evidence of people's participation than the fact that over 6,000 families were canvassed by fifteen investigators in a matter of thirty-one days.

In fact, Indian journalist Ashok Row Kavi was so convinced about the impossibility of this feat that he implied in an article that the SPARC census was a fake. Needless to say, he neither visited SPARC's office nor any of the families who took part in the census to verify his impression. Finally, people's identification with the importance of the census was so great that anyone who was not at home when their area was canvassed came to SPARC's office and demanded that their household be covered there and then, rather than wait for the 'mopping up' stage of the last few days of the exercise.

An interesting feature of the data collection process was its mobilizing effect. Inevitably, no investigator nor householder was isolated during the interview. An interested crowd, which grew in size as the investigator moved down the line, always attended each interview. This was a unique and unanticipated bonus of the census: people listened for the first time to each other's responses to the same set of questions, indeed to their life stories. The similarity of these had a mantra effect and created a palpable sense of shared history. Often, when a woman described her family's poverty in the village and the family's migration to the city, there would be cries of "It was the same with us," or "It is true!" from the crowd of listeners. It would not be an overstatement to say that the act of answering the same set of questions created for the first time a *conscious* sense of a common plight in a group of people who were hitherto isolated and fragmented by the narrow bonds of caste, district, or language. Listening to each other's stories made people realize the similarity of their stories, whether Bihari or Bengali, Hindu or Muslim, hawker or laborer.

After the four hectic weeks of data collection, we were at last ready to send in the questionnaires for computer processing. It was at this stage that we learned another valuable lesson: here, *we* were the ones who could not participate in our own research. We learned firsthand what it felt like to have data taken from you and to not know what is happening to it. Since none of us had any training in computers, we were totally mystified by the 'computerese' spoken by our EDP friends, as they no doubt were by our 'activese.' We were told that the sheet size of our data—6,000 households and almost 27,000 individuals—was creating a host of problems for a program normally designed to handle a much smaller volume of data. By the time the program was debugged, there was no time for anything but simple frequency tables.

Being pressured for time was the cause of our haste. The Supreme Court had recommended that no demolitions be carried out until October 31 (the official end of the monsoon). Therefore, if demolitions could theoretically begin November 1, a report of the census had to be released at least a fortnight earlier if it was to have even a slight chance of influencing public opinion and the authorities. Accordingly, we had called a press conference on October 14 to release the census results to the print media. However, we received our final tables only on October 12 and through a herculean effort we analyzed them, drafted, typed, and printed and delivered 100 copies of the report by the afternoon of October 14, a mere hour before the press conference.

The press conference itself produced an interesting debate about participation. Some friends and members of the group felt that if SPARC really believed in the participatory approach, then some pavement dwellers should be present. Was it right for us to speak to the press on their behalf? This was met with a rebuttal: having pavement dwellers attend the press conference would smack of tokenism, and it would not be participation but a patronizing gimmick to bring them into an alien milieu that was neither familiar to them nor under their control. When ratifying the census idea and how it could be used, they had entrusted us with the task of doing so at levels at which they felt uncomfortable.

Finally, *we* had called the press conference, not the people. If they wished for one of their own, we would have helped them organize it in their own environment and on their own terms. Having handfuls of intimidated pavement dwellers facing fifty journalists as if they were specimens under a microscope was hardly a sign of how deeply we believed in participation.

The doubts and questions raised by this debate were soon resolved when, the day after the press conference, the whole team was absorbed in the task of preparing sets of charts through which the census results would be relayed back to people. The design of the charts demanded both creativity and the effective use of our knowledge of what people would (and would not) relate to. Statistics per se would be meaningless to people who had no need for them in their daily lives; who thought of percentages and proportions in terms of 'four annas in the Rupee,' 'three-fourths,' 'one-half,' or indeed in total numbers. Thus it was a challenge to put the results into terms intelligible to people and to develop corresponding graphics and visuals.

When the data charts were exhibited and discussed at cluster meetings, a number of desperate and interesting responses were received. Without exception, the one single item of data that stirred everyone was the total number of people surveyed. The fact that in just one segment of the city there were 27,000 others like themselves moved and visibly strengthened people. "There are so many of us! Thousands and thousands! Now government must do something for us! They can't just sweep us away like dust." The impact of just this one fact was so great that it alone justified the entire census. Until then, most pavement dwellers imagined that at most there were a few hundred others who would be affected by demolitions. We also witnessed the empowering effect of this statistic when hundreds of people from our clusters attended the protest rallies and marches that were organized toward the end of October.

They invariably exchanged their newfound information with co-marchers from other areas. Other pieces of data, though less galvanizing, created their own effect: the large number of people from the same districts and states (Ratnagiri, Sholapur, and Ratnagiri in Maharashtra, Gonds and Basti in U. P., Madhubani and Darbhanga in Bihar, Salem in Tamilnau, and Culbarga in Karnataka) impressed listeners who thought they were the only ones from those areas. The large number of people in the same occupations and the importance of these to the city's economy excited comment. Finally, the fact that hundreds of families shared similar reasons for leaving their rural homes—unemployment, low wages, droughts, floods and other calamities, communal riots and desertion, widowhood and family conflicts—moved and stirred people, especially the women.

However, we found that on the whole people responded to the census data much more meaningfully when it was linked to other issues. One must bear in mind though that at that time people were much too frightened and insecure about their fate after November 1 to care much about anything else. Consequently, it was in the context of demolitions and the demand for possible alternatives that the census results really became useful to people. For example, people were unanimous in demanding alternative sites if evicted from pavements. But the census had shown that the majority lived within walking distance of their work, so people had to think about how relocation and the need to use public transportation would affect both their current occupations and budgets. Again, women realized that it would be harder for them to find work in distant city peripheries when at present most of them relied on domestic work to earn a living.

Another manner in which the census data was made meaningful to people was to use it to talk and think about the future in a totally new way. For instance, the census showed that 11,000 of the total population included children below the age of sixteen. Would these 11,000 children grow up and live on pavements too? How could parents plan for change?

The latter half of October saw a marked change in the entire attitude toward the pavement dweller 'problem.' This was largely due to the fact that various political parties realized that joining issues with this hitherto ignored population could bring many future gains. Consequently, parties with various leanings—from center liberal to progressive—organized marches and rallies galore. People were exhorted through handbills, loudspeakers, and street meetings to participate in large numbers. This they did and the sense of their strength due to numbers—first generated by the census results—was further reinforced. We also distributed abridged vernacular copies of *We the invisible* during the marches so pavement dwellers from all over the city could use the census information.

When Does Research Become Participatory?

Having described the census and the elements of participation within it, let us raise some questions: When does research become participatory? And are there or should there be limits to the 'participatoriness' in any piece of research? In the case of *We the invisible*, it was SPARC and not the people who decided to conduct a census. Does that then mean that it was not truly participatory, but an idea conceived by others and imposed on people? Does the impact of the census on people (not to mention on the authorities and on public opinion) become negated by the fact that the census per se was not the people's idea but SPARC's? Does the participatoriness of the census become diminished by the fact that we did not have the time to involve people in designing the questionnaire and administering it to each other? Did our excluding pavement dwellers from the press conference indicate a serious lapse, a lack of real commitment to participation?

We have attempted to answer these questions from our present perspective and hope you will examine them from yours. But if this census helps to further the debate on participatory research, provide new insights, and answer some questions while raising others, we believe it has contributed more than its share.

For us at SPARC, the census was an unforgettable milestone because it brought us close to people, a closeness that normally takes years to achieve. The census also has provided to both people and SPARC a foundation of understanding upon which countless initiatives have been built in the fields of employment, education, housing, and many others. And in all, participatory research and action is the hallmark of our strategy, the hallmark that people have come to recognize and expect.

In the ultimate analysis, this is the most vital ingredient of any participatory research exercise: it must form part of a continuum of many other such exercises that people undertake over a period of time. Only in this way can the true spirit of participatory research emerge, since people gain more and more confidence and control over research tools, and the quality of communication gets increasingly enriched. If the main objective of participatory research is to place information and knowledge in the hands of people, then it can only be achieved through an ongoing process, not a single attempt.

Afterword

The fact that *no* mass demolitions took place on or after November 1 is now history. The powerful combination of people's awareness, their mobilization by activists and political parties, and the growing tide of public opinion demanding alternative sites before eviction radically altered the government's stance on the whole issue. From the 'ostrich' attitude of three months earlier, they were now talking of relocating people as much as possible to vacant lands in the city. We hope the census contributed to this significant change in a small but meaningful way. Even if it did not, we live with the conviction that it contributed much to people's awareness.

Notes

1. Editor's note: This paper was suggested to me by Suneeta Dhar of the Society for Participatory Research in Asia (PRIA) as an example of the participatory research endorsed by the Society. See also Anil Chaudhary's contribution to this collection. Anil is the joint coordinator of the PRIA, with Dr. Rajesh Tandon.

2. *We the invisible* is available from both SPARC and PRIA (The Society for Participatory Research in Asia, 45, Sainik Farm, Khanpur, New Delhi, 110 062).

References

Mahtani, R. 1982. *A profile of pavement dwellers in Bombay*. Bombay: Research Unit, College of Social Work.

Ramachandran, P. 1972. *Pavement dwellers in Bombay City*. Series No. 26. Bombay: Tata Institute of Social Sciences.

SPARC. (n. d.) *We the invisible*. Bombay: Society for Promotion of Area Resource Centres.

Index